VAN ARNEM
TECHNOLOGY PIONEER

VAN ARNEM
TECHNOLOGY PIONEER

Harold Van Arnem

VAN ARNEM: TECHNOLOGY PIONEER

Copyright © 2024 by Harold Van Arnem

All rights reserved.

No part of this book may be reproduced or transmitted in any form or by any means, electronic or mechanical, including photocopying, recording, or by any information storage and retrieval system, without permission in writing from the copyright owner.

Published by GoPublish, a division of Visual Adjectives.
Delray Beach, Florida.
www.visualadjectives.com
info@visadj.com

ISBN-13: - 978-1-941901-51-9 (trade paperback)
ISBN-10: - 1-941901-51-4 (trade paperback)
ISBN-13: - 978-1-941901-52-6 (Ebook)
ISBN-10: - 1-941901-52-2 (Ebook)

First American Paperback Edition: January 2024

CONTENTS

PREFACE | 9

INTRODUCTION | 13

CHAPTER ONE | 17
GROWING UP IN CINCINNATI

CHAPTER TWO | 31
SHATTERED GLASS, SHATTERED DREAMS

CHAPTER THREE | 45
GENERAL ELECTRIC
AND THE BEGINNING OF THE COMPUTER INDUSTRY

CHAPTER FOUR | 61
ME AND 24 PHD
THE BEGINNING OF THE INTERNET AND THE CLOUD

CHAPTER FIVE | 67
FORD AND ACTS JOINT VENTURE

CHAPTER SIX | 73
FORD ENGINEERING TO ELIMINATE SLIDE RULES

CHAPTER SEVEN | 83
FUN AND GAMES IN DETROIT
YPO - BUSINESS TYCOONS TRANS AM CHAMPIONSHIP

CHAPTER EIGHT | 91
BIRTH OF SILICON VALLEY,
INNOVATION OF CLOUD COMPUTING,
FOUNDING OF BERKLEY COMPUTER CORPORATION

CHAPTER NINE | 107
FDIC MICHIGAN BANKING BAILOUT

CHAPTER TEN | 113
RACETRACKS - NASCAR

CHAPTER ELEVEN | 119
HELLO HOLLYWOOD

CHAPTER TWELVE | 125
BONITA SPRINGS DISCOVERED
AND THE FOUNDING OF COMPUTER LEASING
WITH MERRILL LYNCH GM
AND WESTERN SOUTHERN INSURANCE CO.

CHAPTER THIRTEEN | 135
LOVE AT FIRST BITE
GEORGE HAMILTON

CHAPTER FOURTEEN | 149
SILVERDOME, NORTH AMERICAN SOCCER LEAGUE,
DETROIT AMERICAN SOCCER LEAGUE NATIONAL CHAMPIONS

CONTENTS

CHAPTER FIFTEEN | 161
AMERICANIZATION OF THE US SOCCER ASL CHAMPIONSHIP

CHAPTER SIXTEEN | 169
AFL - NFL - STRIKE GAMES

CHAPTER SEVENTEEN | 175
AMERICAN SOCCER LEAGUE NATIONAL CHAMPIONS

CHAPTER EIGHTEEN | 181
HEIDI
INTERNETS WOMAN OF THE CENTURY

CHAPTER NINETEEN | 185
JOCKEY CLUB, DETROIT RED WINGS, ABBA

CHAPTER TWENTY | 189
HEIDI SHOT AND QUADRIPLEGIC
ADA FOUNDING - ENTREPRENEUR

CHAPTER TWENTY-ONE | 201
DETROIT GRAND PRIX
CHRISTIE BRINKLEY - OLIVIER CHANDON

CHAPTER TWENTY-TWO | 207
WORLD'S LARGEST TECHNOLOGY LEASING COMPANY
FINALCO ACQUISITION OF PUBLIC COMPANY
WESTERN SAVINGS & LOAN

CHAPTER TWENTY-THREE | 217
EXODUS TO BOCA RATON

CHAPTER TWENTY-FOUR | 223
MEMORY TELEX-CIS

CHAPTER TWENTY-FIVE | 227
ENTRY INTO EUROPEAN UNION
AMERICAN EXPRESS, CREDIT LYONNAIS, ZURICH REINSURANCE

CHAPTER TWENTY-SIX | 233
TELECOM DEREGULATION IN EU,
EUROPE'S LARGEST NETWORK INTEGRATOR

CHAPTER TWENTY-SEVEN | 247
DISCOVERING DELRAY

CHAPTER TWENTY-EIGHT | 259
MOTHER THERESA AND DOMINIQUE LAPIERRE

EPILOGUE | 263

PHOTO GALLERY | 269

AUTHOR'S BIO | 345

Where there's a will, there's a way.

PREFACE

Growing up in the Midwest in the middle of the twentieth century provided limited vision and ambition to a young college graduate, from a family secure with a weekly paycheck and health benefits. Sports gave me a new perspective and a realization that you can achieve anything, beyond your own expectations, simply by self-determination, discipline and hard work.

After graduation from UC, I was selected by GE and sent to Phoenix Arizona, where they had just completed the construction of GE's computer manufacturing plant. It was the beginning of the computer global industry, at the time dominated by IBM. I learned quickly that operating a computer console was far too complex and inhibiting. GE had developed a user-friendly interactive computer.

I left GE and co-founded one of the 1st Doctoral Programs in Computer Engineering at the University of Detroit, in collaboration with the University of California, Berkeley and University of Carnegie Tech (now Carnegie Mellon). Concurrently, I founded ACTS Computing, in partnership with the University of Detroit school of Engineering. Jointly, we acquired a state-of-the-art multi-processor timesharing computer system which provided a user-friendly interactive CLOUD, accessible remote Computing by dial up from anywhere in the world.

ACTS was subsequently hired by ARPA Department of Defense Director, Dr. Larry Roberts, principal developer of the INTERNET Data Packet Transmission, in partnership with Dr. Mel Pirtle, EE Department head at the University of California, Berkeley, to administer the integration and top security national defense applications through the Institute for advanced computation, which were located in Palo Alto during the late 60's. IAC/ACTS was the first software company in Silicon Valley. ACTS oversaw the design and hardware development for the ILLIAC IV, then the world's largest and fastest computer, located at Ames Research Center, after being transferred from the University of Illinois to ultra secure Ames Research Center in Moffet Field (Vietnam War), California. The ILLIAC IV would serve as the primary ARPANET Central Processor/Server to manage the massive seismic data files, to detect atomic and nuclear activity around the globe during the Vietnam war, also accessible through what we currently refer to as the CLOUD.

In the mid to late sixties, core memory was extremely limited and the then, 'world's largest computer', the ILLIAC 64 parallel CPUs with only 64k for each central processing unit (CPU). Limited memory for software logic was mitigated by a process that created the overlaying of programs that would was constantly being ported to a secondary storage device to allow for unlimited Virtual Memory. VM permitted massive amounts of software and data to be processed with limited memory before the unlimited memory that existed 55 years ago.

Further, we provided global or CLOUD access to all our software and data which could be accessed remotely around the globe through network and telephone dial-up access to the CLOUD. These were first the pioneering network communications connectivity and applications provided through the utilization of the INTERNET.

We hear forecasts of artificial intelligence today sixty years after AI was first applied in the sixties at Ames Research Center scientific and academic software applications utilizing the INTERNET on CPU of the ILLIAC IV.

ACTS and The Institute for Advanced Computation were employed by ARPA Department of Defense to create one of the first and critically important AI application. The detection of seismic global testing activity and seismic data analysis to monitor atomic and nuclear testing on earth.

AI has existed since the invention of both calculators International Business Machines (IBM). Each computer was an AI enabler with program logic (software) and data.

Artificial Intelligence is simply program logic utilizing Data. It is not magic and there is unlimited functionality created by the intelligence of the programmer.

Back to Michigan, owner of the Detroit Express Professional Soccer team of the North America Soccer League (NASL). The Detroit Express was headquartered and played in the Pontiac Silverdome as co-tenants the Detroit Lions and Detroit Pistons.

As board member of the NASL, I was introduced to Stephen Ross, CEO of Warner Communications and owner of the New York Cosmos.

VAN ARNEM
TECHNOLOGY PIONEER

We then agreed to create WARNERAMEX VAN ARNEM Cable, Inc. and became one of the first cable developers in the Midwest. I then focused on programing for cable channels.

I then made offers to purchase the Silverdome in collaboration with Warner Communications and the Pritzkers of the Hyatt Corp, at the urging of then Michigan Governor Milliken and Michigan Senator Griffin.

I hired award winning writer Bob Kaufman to write the script of the blockbuster movie 'Love at First Bite' in partnership with George Hamilton and Kaufman. Additionally, I co-produced with Columbia pictures the spectacular Formula One movie called 'The Quick and the Dead", witnessing multiple driver deaths, and starring Stacey Keach and Jackie Stewart. This was the last 70 MM film produced in Hollywood, following Star Wars.

Back to making money. After tax reform, I acquired controlling interest in Finalco, a public company and the world's largest technology financing and leasing company at the time, with a multi-billion-dollar portfolio.

Shortly thereafter, I co-founded CYBERGATE, the very 1st Internet Service Provider in South East USA. I then Introduced one of the 1st WEB hosting sites in the world "TARGET NET" and "VALUE WEB".

After selling Cybergate, and unable to compete in the US, due to a non-compete sale clause, I focused on telecommunications deregulation in Europe and founded TOTALe, based in Paris which acquired Thomainfor, France's largest network integrator, owned by Thompson CSF, a French Government owned company. At the same time, we acquired Olivetti's Decision Systems, Italy's largest network integration company. We also purchased a dozen application consultancies. The combined companies had over 1,500 network engineers, 2,300 systems and software engineers, and 22,000 computer and network customers in 16 countries. We became IBM and Telecom Italia's largest EU partners and Europe's largest Network integrator after deregulation.

Robertson Stephens, a leading technology banker, organized an IPO for TOTALe which was fully subscribed at a market capitalization of 2 billion.

"You're fired!"
"No, you're fired!"

INTRODUCTION

Everything I thought I knew about business was tossed out the window one day in January 1988 when I discovered that both the CEO and COO of a company in which I owned almost sixty percent of the shares, had sold its corporate income funds in direct contravention of my instructions.

The company was Finalco, one of the world's largest computer leasing firms. The CEO was a man named Jim Boris, with whom I had clashed on various occasions. Boris wanted to dump the funds to the brokerage firm Raymond James. I agreed their offer looked good, but we had not obtained a firm appraisal of the funds before agreeing to the deal. "Don't sell them," I told Boris. A few days later I arrived at the office one morning to find a note on my desk indicating Boris had sold the funds.

My first reaction was disbelief. My second reaction was anger. Trailing smoke from my ears, I exploded out of my cubbyhole office and raced down the hall to Boris' office.

"I told you not to sell those funds!" I bellowed as I came through his door. Boris shrugged.

"Too bad," he said. "It's a done deal."

"It better not be," I replied, "because I'm going to stop the sale right now."

"The hell you are!" Boris yelled back at me, and when I repeated my words, he pointed a finger in my direction as though it were a loaded weapon and shouted, "You know what? You're fired!"

I could not believe it. I owned over half the company and my own CEO was firing me? I was so shocked I left Boris's office, went back to my desk and called my lawyer. "Fred," I said to him, "Boris just fired me!"

"He can't fire you," Fred said, "You control the company!"

"So, what do I do?"

"Go back and fire him!"

Fire Jim Boris? I did not like the guy much, but I needed him around to keep my partners happy. I retraced my steps to Boris's office.

"We have to work something out," I said, keeping my emotions in check, "because if we don't, we could wind up hating each other. We will also destroy the value of this company, which just happens to represent a substantial part of my net worth. And by the way, my lawyer says you can't fire me."

"You're right," Boris said. "So, I quit."

Looking back at it from a perspective of twenty years later, I must smile at the memory – two heavyweight businesspeople trying to fire each other. On a more serious note, I see it now as one more lesson in a career that has been full of lessons, accomplishments, disappointment and tragedy. But then, that is what life is all about, isn't it? Thank goodness I learned so much about life from sports. My lessons about business came later.

Playing sports taught me a good deal. It taught me the sacrifices you need to make if you want to win, it taught me how to learn from your mistakes, and most of all it taught me how to build and work with a team.

In sports, of course, a clear winner always emerges. In business, you can never be certain. Like my experience with Finalco. There I was with most of the shares of a company in my pocket, so to speak, and the guy I had hired to run the company tried to fire me.

Sports prepared me for business. Business prepared me for life.

Sometimes the preparation was comic, and sometimes it was tragic. But the lessons were always there for the learning. My achievements in sport, in business and in life have ranged far and wide. They have been painful, fulfilling, disturbing, rewarding and illuminating.

But they have never been dull. Not one moment of them.

VAN ARNEM
TECHNOLOGY PIONEER

CHAPTER ONE

GROWING UP IN CINCINNATI

Every successful person has ambition, but the source of that ambition can sometimes be surprising.

My father's work experience shaped me as much as any aspect of his personality. From an early age I understood the importance of retaining as much control as possible over the decisions I made by being aware of the way my father dreams of self-sufficiency were crushed at the hands of others.

As a youth, Dad worked as a lifeguard and a high diver in an amusement park and acquired skills in several trades including carpentry and tile-setting. Settled down with a wife and family to support, he sought prosperity as a house builder, and he might have succeeded. He built a few houses, sold them at a profit, and invested the money into new projects, eventually moving up from small houses to apartment buildings.

Things went well until Dad assigned his properties to a partner who needed security to obtain a mortgage. His trust was misplaced. In a classic case of betrayal, his partner disappeared with the mortgage funds, and Dad found his assets gone and his dreams shattered. No longer his own boss, my father swallowed his pride and went to work as a laborer for General Electric where he worked long hours and eventually rose to a supervisory position. But I knew he wanted to be his own boss, and that his dream had been wrested away from him. I'm not sure that Dad's string of promotions at GE was attributed to pure ambition. I suspect that he worked those long hours at least partly to avoid the wrath of my mother, who demanded perfection from everyone including herself. To me, Mom seemed always angry about something, except on Saturday nights when the drinks were poured, and music started to play. That's when the laughs began and the gossip, often in Gaelic, started to flow.

Those were different times, of course. The years following World War II may have been filled with hope and promise, but working-class people struggled from paycheck to paycheck, scrimping wherever necessary. While I was growing up, we lived in various suburbs of Cincinnati, all of them blue-collar communities where people never wasted things because they couldn't afford to. My children may think recycling is a product of today's culture, but almost nothing in the 1940's and 1950's, including leftover meals, clothing and cars, was tossed away by our family and the families around us. My mother, like the mothers of my friends, knew various ways to keep us well-fed on the least amount of money. Fish and steak may be the preferred meals for our kids today, but how would they react to eating fried chicken livers, stewed kidneys, grilled liver, and home-made soup that was stretched over three or four suppers? It's not exactly lip-smacking cuisine, but those were the things my mother built our meals around, stretching every penny as far as she could.

We used to joke that everyone died in our house. Not everyone who lived there, just everyone in our family who my mother believed had reached the end of their days on earth. My mother insisted on setting a small wing of our little suburban house aside for this purpose. When their time came, my grandfather, grandmother, aunts, uncles and others were placed in this darkened room by my mother, who assumed the role of supervising their deaths just as she supervised the lives of her husband and children. No one dared question the process. No one dared question my mother about anything. Her strict Catholic upbringing determined what must be done on any given day at any given time, and her Irish heritage kept emotions close to the surface. Mom always seemed ready to explode in anger or erupt in laughter, drinking and dancing. I've been rebelling most of my life against the strict rules set by my mother, who insisted that everything must be perfect according to the rules she set. If so, I have her to thank for my successes.

Everything was valued and almost nothing discarded. When my parents purchased new furniture for the living room, my mother insisted on wrapping the sofa and chairs in clear plastic to keep them looking new forever. The fancy brocade upholstery was isolated from the rest of the world like a work of art in a museum display case. We might look, but we were not permitted to touch. Not that we could anyway – children were banished from the living room except when company was present. Adults, I suppose, were less likely to generate wear and tear on the family possessions, so they were permitted to be seated on the furniture. Any unapproved venture into the living room by us kids launched shouts from my mother to vacate the area immediately, accompanied at times by a sharp swat across the backside or whatever part of the body was within reach with whatever she had in her hand – usually a broom.

As her eldest child, I should have been her favorite, but she had no favorites. Her favorite description of me was "stupid." I knew I wasn't, of course, but in those circumstances it's always easier to go along with things than to challenge an adult's opinion. If my mother figured I was stupid I decided I might as well prove her correct. In grade five, I put so little effort into school that I was held back for a year, a humiliating experience that I never permitted myself to repeat. Nobody was going to hold me back again.

There was a good side to Mom, just as there is to anyone. When her family gathered at our house and the beer began to flow and the music began to play, Mom could relax and enjoy herself as much as anyone. A woman with little material wealth, she made up for it by emphasizing her Irish-Catholic faith and her family ties. And while I hated our diet built around cheap organ meats and potatoes, we never left the house hungry or without clean clothing, and in winter we were always kept warm and dry.

We were constantly reminded of the darker side of life, but my siblings and I failed to avoid it as adults. I was told that three of my ancestors, all named Harold, had been killed by trains. Few details about their deaths were provided; for all I know, they might have been tramps riding the rails. In any case, three Harold's, 1 including my grandfather Van Arnem, had died on the railroad. So, when I was six years old and almost met the same fate, it was no surprise to fatalists like my mother.

It happened one day when my sister Nancy and I were riding in the back seat of my grandfather Smith's 1940 Ford. Grandpa Smith had enjoyed a pint or two of some alcoholic beverages before setting off with us in the back seat, so he probably did not see the warning sign for the railroad level crossing. And he certainly did not see the train, because he crashed right into the side of it.

Fortunately, the train was moving slowly, but I have a clear memory of the train dragging the Ford, my dazed grandfather, my sister, and me along the railroad right of way accompanied by loud grinding and crashing noises. My instinct was to get out of the car, and I managed to open a door, grab my sister's hand, and bail out on to the ground, where we stood watching the remains of Grandpa's treasured Ford sliding away, joined at the nose with the side of the freight train. All of us, except the Ford, survived and I was congratulated later for breaking the railroad jinx attributed to males named Harold in our family. As the youngest of a series of Harold's, including my father, I was named Sonny from an early age, and it has managed to stick with me all these years.

My sisters were not so lucky.

Nancy, who was in the car with me that day, grew up, married, and had three beautiful daughters. Her eldest girl Kristin was diagnosed with Wilson's Disease and endured liver transplants before dying tragically at age thirty-three.

My sister Patty, twelve years younger than me, fell into heroin addiction, which led to her murder in 1990 when she was also thirty-three. She left two young children and an ache in my heart.

And then there was Heidi. Her life story may deserve a book, as you will see. She was also gone at age thirty-three. If I were more superstitious, I would make some frightening connections there.

With luck and determination, you can open a door and leap

away from heartaches and tragedies, but you can never avoid them entirely. That has been a powerful lesson in my life.

I inherited my father's athletic skills, which enabled me to use sports as a means of escaping my turbulent home life. Sports for children during the years I was growing up were nothing like today's organized mini-industry. Any kid with a bat, a ball and a glove were considered privileged. The only athletic gear most of the kids in my neighborhood owned was their Converse All-Star basketball shoes. No kid with Nikes today was any prouder than my buddies and me of our high-cut canvas-and-rubber Converse shoes back in the 1940's.

Community baseball teams played in "Knot Hole" leagues, which were managed by community organizations and sponsored by local businesses. Making the team earned you a t-shirt bearing a sponsor's name printed on the back – Joe's Dry Cleaning, Smitty's Plumbing, Marty's Meats. The shirts were all you received; everything else depended on your own initiative. If you wanted to play baseball, you found your own way to practices and games. Mothers and fathers were too busy to drive you, if they had a car, and they were too distracted by their own concerns to attend games and cheer from the sidelines. You worked for your own fun and satisfaction. I support the organized sports that kids enjoy today, but I wonder if kids like me, who depended on our own discipline to attend practice and work hard, didn't learn more from the experience.

Baseball and basketball were my favorite sports through grade school because you didn't need much equipment to play them. High school was different, however. Football dominated the high school sports scene, and football in Ohio and Pennsylvania high schools was considered serious, and conducted with the same complex strategy, as fighting a war. In Cincinnati, football games involving my high school, Purcell, drew 15,000 fans at Friday night and Sunday afternoon matches. At Purcell High, football players earned respect from kids and grown-ups alike and scoring the winning touchdown in a game brought a kid more adulation and celebrity status than scoring straight A's in any academic subject.

By the time I entered Purcell, I had matured with the height, weight and determination to become a football player, but I faced several obstacles. The first obstacle was basic: I had never played the game. Cincinnati grade schools had no football in their sports curriculum, so I arrived at high school knowing nothing about the game's positions, skills, techniques or even all the rules. This didn't deter me as much as the sight of other kids with the same ambition who showed up for practice on the first day. Over two hundred boys my age wanted to be chosen as a Purcell football player. Purcell, an all-boys Catholic school operated by the Marianist Brothers, drew students from about one-quarter of the city's grade schools. Every Catholic schoolboy in Cincinnati wanted to join this legacy of champions, and they all appeared as determined as me.

I tried not to let the competition bother me when I gathered with other grade nine students looking for a place on the freshman squad. But when I discovered that the school uniforms would be distributed alphabetically, my heart sank. With a name like Van Arnem and two hundred kids ahead of me, I knew I wouldn't be going home with a uniform that day. And I didn't. But I left more determined than ever, and determination is worth more than any stitched and tattered football gear, as I discovered at the practice.

Purcell was twenty miles from my home, and the practice field was a half-mile from school. Kids who had been issued football equipment walked from the school to the field wearing full gear. I walked with them, willing to practice as long and as hard as it took to be awarded a uniform and equipment of my own.

The practice field was called the Owl's Nest, although "field" isn't quite the word to describe the place. It was basically a depression in the ground, covered with more dust than grass. Our first practice had nothing to do with the skill and finesse, and everything to do with toughness when it came to hitting other kids and absorbing their hits in return. The drill never varied: Two boys were sent into in the dusty pit. One was given a ball and ordered to run past the other boy who, of course, was ordered to stop him. Nobody was told how to break tackles or prevent the ball carrier from advancing, and neither boy wore a face mask. The coaches were looking for strength, power, speed and determination, but the two qualities that counted most were toughness and a total lack of fear.

I watched some kids ahead of me lose their enthusiasm for the idea of playing football, especially at the sight of a broken and bloody nose. I could hardly wait to enter the pit. Nobody was going to stop me when the coach handed me the ball. And nobody was going to get past me when I was assigned to tackle them.

Inevitably, some did, but they were always bigger and stronger than me. I couldn't overcome their physical advantages on strength alone, but I learned to create my own with willpower and a need to prove that nobody was mentally tougher than me. After two weeks of showing the coaches how aggressive I could be in the pit, I was outfitted with a jersey, pants, helmet, shoes and shoulder pads. Every time I put the uniform on, I felt a rush of joy because I finally belonged somewhere. I was a member of the team.

I quickly learned how to "fire out" from the three-point stance on the line of scrimmage. Firing out was the coaches' term for exploding into action, going forward with total determination to succeed. If getting past the other team meant breaking their faces – or mine – I never gave it a second thought. On offense or defense, the technique was the same: stay low, keep your balance, and fire out. I had several qualities that impressed the coaches back then, but perhaps the one they valued most was this ability to explode move forward and keep my balance all through the play. Firing Out. It became a basic approach to playing the game and one that has stayed with me throughout my business career. When it came to making a pitch or closing a deal, I always recalled the concept of firing out, of holding nothing back to reach my goal.

Achieving recognition as a football player at Purcell was a real challenge, even to kids who showed up with their raw talent they needed to succeed. No matter how hard you worked, nothing happened until you impressed the coaches. Purcell's head coach was

Jim McCarthy, who developed a unique football program that made Purcell a powerhouse and has probably been copied, in one way or another, by high schools across America. Tall and slim, McCarthy became known as The Silver Fox as much for his intelligence as for his head of thick white hair.

Each freshman year, McCarthy and his staff of ten coaches would evaluate the boys seeking glory by playing football at Purcell. While the usual athletic skills were being assessed, the coaches were assessing their desire, discipline, toughness and determination. The hundred or so boys with the best combination wore black practice jerseys on the freshman team. By sophomore year, the team would be shaved to about 50 boys and the weeding-out process continued. Sophomore practices were more demanding, special skills were sharpened, and players began to be selected for positions that exploited certain abilities.

The ultimate achievement for a Purcell football player was to be awarded a green jersey in his junior and senior years. Winning the right to wear a green practice jersey during your sophomore year was almost unheard of. No matter how talented you might be, if you were not a junior or senior you did not wear a green jersey with one exception: If an injury occurred to a player in one position that no other junior or senior could fill adequately, and if a sophomore was assessed as good enough to do the job, he might be handed a green jersey. But it was a rare event.

I made the freshman team as an end. I was a starter on the fourth game, and by the end of the season I was selected by the coaches to be team captain. I wasn't the biggest player on the team, but I believe I was more committed and determined than the others. I had also learned how to hit the other guy with full force, and I appreciated the advantage that the hitter has over the "hittee." For one thing, the hittee was more likely to suffer more pain than the hitter.

My peripheral vision grew sharper, and I controlled my body in the manner that athletes acquire and that non-athletes cannot fully understand. More than all those qualities, however, I had the intensity to succeed, powered perhaps by a compulsion to make the team and share in its success.

When the almost impossible happened – when injuries to guys playing end on the green-jersey varsity team meant no one was left to fill that position – I was elevated to that level in my sophomore year. This was a major achievement; even Roger Staubach didn't make the varsity team until his junior year. Playing on the varsity team as a sophomore created more pride and personal satisfaction than I have ever felt before and have rarely felt since. The confidence it generated in me carried over to other parts of my life. My class marks improved, and my home life settled down.

The risk of being injured never occurred to me, which is amazing because the equipment we wore was so primitive. We wore pads but no one wore a facemask, and the helmets were basically leather hats with a strap that fit under your chin. Yet we all blocked, tackled and hit with one hundred percent effort, convinced that we were invincible. We watched other players being carried off the field with broken arms and concussions in almost every game, but none of us worried about being injured ourselves. Injuries happened to other guys because they were not paying attention or not playing up to their ability. We believed that playing 100 percent all the time, especially if we were the ones doing the hitting, made us immune to injury. If anyone were going to get hurt, it would be somebody on the opposing team.

Almost every boy who made the first three teams at Purcell displayed broken noses and missing teeth. The best of us didn't care about the change in our appearance. In fact, we wore the scars on our faces and the casts on our arms with pride.

Many qualities separate good players from outstanding athletes, and I suspect the most important one is the ability to divide the personality they reveal to family and friends from the one that emerges on the football field. Off the field, athletes may demonstrate the same personality they have displayed all their lives, ranging from loud, flamboyant characters like Joe Namath to quiet, unassuming types like Roger Staubach. Once the whistle blows, however, every good athlete changes into a win-or-else personality. The legendary Vince Lombardi really didn't have to say, "Winning isn't the most important thing, it's the only thing." The best athletes already have this attitude.

Roger Staubach was a Purcell kid but a year behind me. He went on, of course, to become one of the greatest quarterbacks in NFL history. He started playing football at the end position, but the coaches moved him to quarterback in his sophomore year. Roger was a good athlete, but he didn't stand out among all the other guys around him because there was so much competition at the school. It was as if God created a bunch of 15- and 16-year-old boys with all the qualities of football players, making them six feet tall, 175 to 190 pounds, with great speed and a competitive nature, and dropped them into one high school over a two- or three-year period. You may recognize only Staubach's name, but the group included guys like Stan Budd, Alan Shroeder, Ron Kunkel, Hugh Cahill, Vince Eysatt and others. Depending on the season, you'd find us all on the football field, the running track, the baseball diamond, the basketball court, and in the swimming pool, each of us battling to prove we were faster, stronger and tougher than the other guys. In terms of athletic abilities and determination we were an elite group, and everybody we competed against knew it.

In my junior year, I was made first team defensive end. Later the coaches moved me to offensive end, which meant catching passes, blocking for runners, evading tacklers, and generally performing all the actions demanded of the game. My play improved with experience and I added height and muscle on my body. We finished the season by winning the league championship. Along the way we set records that have remained unbroken to this day, averaging more than 60 points a game while holding our opponents to less than 5 points. In those years, the college football powerhouse was Oklahoma; in the state of Ohio, Purcell was known as the Oklahoma of high school football.

Success at sports affected my social status in and out of school. It enabled me to break through the barriers that exist in every high school, and at that time these were based on the neighborhood you lived in and occupation of your father.

My circle of friends grew wider to include many of my teammates in football, basketball and baseball. I felt comfortable with them, not only at school but at parties held in their families' homes, which were usually much larger and more luxurious than my own. In those days, Cincinnati and its neighboring cities celebrated two social seasons: Christmas and summer, and the seasons were celebrated with debutante "coming out" parties, where lovely young girls were introduced to the world as lovely young women. The girls needed escorts, of course, and the escorts had to be every bit as socially acceptable as the girls. Thanks to my new status as a high school football star, I was frequently invited to serve as an escort.

The debutante network extended well beyond the Cincinnati area, and I eventually received invitations to parties in Lexington, Philadelphia, Grosse Pointe and even Palm Beach. I was probably not the best-dressed guy at these events. In fact, while all the other guys had real tuxedos, I managed to get by with Madras plaid jacket and black trousers. Attending parties, meeting girls, acting like grown-ups, I loved it all. Almost as much as I loved sports.

I couldn't get enough of sports, of any kind. When I wasn't playing football, baseball or basketball, I went swimming. This was good exercise, and it earned me a job as manager of a swimming club. Later, I was promoted to managing the entire pool facility, which led to a new series of adventures. One of them involved returning late from a debutante party. Extremely late. In fact, it was early the next morning, and several people were already in the pool when I arrived in my Madras plaid jacket and black trousers, slipping first into the office and then into my bathing suit, trying to look cool all the while.

Next to competing in sports, my biggest ambition was to make money, and the summer I turned 18 years old, I was hired to run the swimming pool at the Carousel, an upscale local motel.

The Carousel was a local gathering place for men, some married and some not, who got together for weekend parties. The parties had three requirements: Rooms, alcohol, and girls. The girl supply took care of itself. I provided the other necessary ingredients, reserving the rooms and arranging for alcohol, while adding a tidy profit to both. Weekends at The Carousel were quite an experience for a good Catholic boy like me. The men had deep tans, greasy hair and lots of money, but the girls were there for one reason only, and when the men turned their attention to gambling or watching television, the girls were ignored. With no men paying attention to them they would wander over to sit and talk with me. Naturally, I loved the attention. Few things can get a young man excited faster than a sexy older woman – "older" in this case meaning between twenty and thirty – paying attention to him. I ran errands for the girls and drove them on their shopping sprees or just took them for rides in the country when they wanted to get away for a while. In return, the girls tipped me in cash.

It was my first lesson in marketing and economics. The wealthy older men bought pleasure from younger women who, in turn, bought the attention and assistance they needed from an even younger man. It was all about supply and demand, not to mention the fulfillment of needs and wants. Of course, I didn't see it in those terms at the time. I just knew I was lucky to be earning money while having fun. I never developed a taste for alcohol, however, so on Sunday morning I had nothing to tell the Father in confession. Honest.

In my junior year at high school, everything began coming together for me. As a varsity starter on the football team, I continued to receive recognition and respect from students and teachers, and this encouraged me to work even harder at my studies. Even my parents changed their attitude towards me. Suddenly I was a source of pride to them. My mother calmed down and ceased worrying about my future, leaving her free to worry about everybody else's future, I suppose. My father found time to attend my football games. He especially enjoyed taking me with him to the GE plant where he worked. I would be introduced to his working buddies, who knew all about my exploits on the playing field. It may have been high school football, but in the Cincinnati area, games were more closely followed than college football, and Dad overflowed with pride during those visits.

Changes swirled around me during that year, all of them related to my involvement in sports. We dressed over 100 players for every game, all of us in crimson jerseys over pants trimmed in gold, our helmets the same model and style as those worn by Notre Dame. The sight intimidated our opponents even before we stepped onto the field, and when play started the intimidation turned to annihilation. We scored as many as 83 points, often preventing the other team from getting on the scoreboard at all.

Being part of that team was unforgettable, made even more memorable when, at the end of the season, I was voted Most Valuable Junior and selected as co-captain of next year's senior team. The other captain was our quarterback, Al Schroeder; his back-up, just for the record, was Roger Staubach. To top everything off, the awards were presented by Birdie Tibbit, manager of the Cincinnati Reds major league baseball team, and the legendary Woody Hayes, head coach at Ohio State. During the ceremony, Woody Hayes talked to me about joining the Buckeyes. Ohio State was a national powerhouse, as dominant in college football as Purcell was in the high school leagues; if you could play for Woody Hayes, you could achieve almost anything.

I could not imagine anything in my life being more important or more personally satisfying than meeting Woody Hayes and hearing him talk about playing at Ohio State. The experience raised my confidence level to new heights. If I could beat out hundreds of boys bigger than me, be selected captain of a football team that was already a legend, and impress the great Woody Hayes, I could achieve any goal I set for myself. Nothing could stop me!

I was wrong. Something could and did.

CHAPTER TWO

SHATTERED GLASS, SHATTERED DREAMS

With football season over for that year, I turned my attention to basketball. One day, barely a week after my encounter with Woody Hayes, I was outside the locker room hanging out with some other guys. Someone began tossing a ball around and I ran down the hallway preparing to catch a pass, pursued by Bob Clarke, a senior. Just as I was about to pull in the ball, Bob pushed me from behind and directly through a glass exit door.

In those times, everybody was responsible for his or her own safety. No laws mandated the use of seat belts in cars, smoking was permitted everywhere, and glass doors were made of the same easily shattered material installed in windows. When a six-foot kid encountered it while running at full speed, as I did with my arms extended ahead of me, the glass shattered, and every shard pierced through me.

I recall nothing about crashing through the door, but I will never forget the sight of my arm and hand when I opened my eyes. The muscles of my left arm had been peeled away from the bone, and my left thumb dangled from a tendon. My right hand was almost severed at the wrist. I remember no pain, and amazingly almost no blood flowed, yet I could see the bone of my right wrist shining white through the wound. The artery had been severed so cleanly and powerfully that it remained closed, in the way that you can close a garden hose by stepping on it.

Not yet in shock, I knew I had to find help, or I would bleed to death there in the hallway. I ran out of the school and into the street, my arm and hand flapping uselessly, leaving a trail of blood behind me. A man in a passing car saw me, opened his door, and motioned for me to get in. I did, and just as he pulled away from the curb, the pressure within the severed artery erupted in a crimson explosion. Instantly, it appeared as though someone had thrown a bucket of blood onto the windshield of the car.

The horrified driver sped around the corner and somehow, with my lifeblood literally pouring from my body, he got me into a doctor's office. The doctor's response was immediate: he cauterized the arteries to stop the bleeding, bandaged the wounds as effectively as he could, shot me full of penicillin, and rushed me to the hospital.

In my memory all these scenes are to me like images from a movie watched long ago, the kind of movie where you remember little about the plot line and everything about three or four critical, unforgettable images.

On the way to the hospital, I began telling myself that the worst was over, that I was on my way to being repaired and healed. Of course, it wasn't. No one, including me, knew I was allergic to penicillin. With the chance of hemorrhaging to death less likely, I now risked dying from anaphylactic shock. I began having difficulty breathing and felt myself slipping into unconsciousness. By the time we reached the hospital my head had swelled to the size of a basketball. My blood pressure dropped, I lost consciousness, and over the next few days I lay in a coma while the hospital battled my allergic reaction.

Finally, I regained consciousness, which was a relief to my family of course and, so I was told, a surprise to some of the hospital staff. Through it all, no one chose to treat three ribs I had broken in my collision with the door. Considering all my other problems, broken ribs were a minor concern.

Over the next several months I underwent at least a dozen operations to restore movement to my left and right hands. My left thumb, I was told, would become essentially a dead appendage, with no feeling or function. The wound to my right hand was even more severe. All the tendons had been sliced through, leaving my fingers immobile. Repairing this kind of injury involves microsurgery, which at the time was in its early stages of experimentation. No one had the skills, instruments and knowledge to perform microsurgery with the degree of success it is used today, but I was lucky enough to attract the attention of a young surgeon named Dr. Holmes, who was willing to experiment at correcting my injury.

Dr. Holmes was brilliant and dedicated, but he was literally feeling his way through the complexity of the human hand and its mechanism. After undergoing surgery to attach the tendons, I would return to Dr. Holmes' office where he would remove the bandages and instruct me to move my middle finger. And I would. Or at least I would try. But instead of my middle finger wagging, it would be my index finger that went into motion. "Wrong tendon," Dr. Holmes would say, and it would take another operation to sever the repaired connection and attach a new one to the correct finger. It was like wiring a house without a schematic – you wouldn't know which outlet had power until you plugged something into it.

Eventually, all the tendons in my right hand were reattached correctly, but I had lost 90 percent of mobility in the hand. The frustration was enormous. I eventually learned to write with my left hand, but playing basketball and baseball were out of the question. The first time I tried to swing a baseball bat it flew out of my hand because I was unable to grip it with sufficient strength. I gave up on that sport, and I never played either baseball or basketball again.

Not being able to compete in basketball and baseball began to take a toll on my personality. I grew angry at my disability and more than a little sorry for myself. How could this happen to me, when everything good had seemed so inevitable just a few weeks earlier? Even the smallest chores, like going to the toilet, taking a shower and getting dressed were difficult. I was losing control over my life, and I resented being a disabled person in a normal world.

I was determined to continue playing football, however. I could still hit the other guy, even with disabled hands. At least that's what I told my coaches before summer practice began. They were doubtful, especially when Dr. Holmes said I needed more surgery to complete the repairs. I didn't want more surgery; I wanted to play football, and

I was so insistent that both the coaches and the doctor gave in. Dr. Holmes fitted me with casts on both hands, and I quickly realized they were more than casts – they were also weapons.

Thanks to the casts and fueled by the anger and frustration I was feeling, I began hitting harder than ever during practices and games. My speeds had improved, along with my blocking skill. I even learned to catch passes almost as well as before the accident, knocking the ball down with my right hand and cradling it in my left arm. Amazingly, I caught more passes that season than the previous year when I had full control over both of my hands. I felt that I had even more to prove than before. Woody Hayes had praised me, and not even the near amputation of my hands would prevent me from proving he was correct. Success remained a goal, both in football and in my studies. My school marks improved, and the team had another great season, with me as co-captain of one of America's best high school football teams.

At the end of the season, the guy who had been told to forget about football after his accident, was chosen a member of the first-string All-Star team for southern Ohio.

Through hard work and determination, I had overcome tremendous odds. If I could do that, I believed, nobody would stop me from achieving the goals I had set for myself before the run in with the glass door. Well, almost nobody. I hadn't counted on the influence of my girlfriend. Later, my daughter Heidi taught me what it really means to be disabled, and how it can be overcome with courage and determination.

All through my junior and senior years of high school, my girlfriend represented part of an adolescent dream coming true. I was totally smitten with her in a way that boys can become over their first steady girlfriend. But at the end of my senior year in high school, with two dozen scholarships awaiting me from some of the best schools in the country, the unthinkable happened: she dumped me.

I couldn't believe it. She and I had been the ideal couple in school, the football hero and the gorgeous co-ed. We were destined to lead an ideal life together, earning a college education leading to a rewarding career, a suburban house, perfect children, and all the perks of the American dream. She couldn't possibly destroy the dream before we even had a chance to make it reality. But she did. Instead of becoming a wife and mother, her ambition was to become a top model in New York and Hollywood. She had both the beauty and the ambition to achieve it, which everyone knew. The only thing she didn't need was me.

I spent that summer after my senior year vainly trying to change her mind. After everything I had achieved in sports and academics, plus overcoming the injuries to my arm and hands, I refused to admit failure in my romantic life. I spent so much time chasing her and wallowing in my heartache that I missed the opportunity for admittance to the Merchant Marine Academy at King's Point, the school I had favored above all the others. It took more than academic and athletic excellence to be accepted by King's Point; you needed a referral from an influential authority, and I had been granted admission to the school through a congressional appointment. Instead of attending I threw it away, dedicated more to changing a girl's mind than to fulfilling an academic dream.

Only as the end of summer did I finally concede that our romance was over, and with some reluctance I contacted Xavier University, whose recruiting efforts I had ignored until then. In a way, I accepted them more than they accepted me, but in September I began classes there.

And what of the girl who broke my heart? She succeeded at her modeling career, appearing in advertisements and TV commercials. But while riding in an open convertible, sitting on top of the rear seat as the car sped down an open road, the driver was unaware that a recent storm had knocked down some utility poles. No one saw the lowered wire until it was too late, and she was decapitated.

This should have put me back on track to succeed both in the classroom and on the playing field. Unfortunately, it did not. Like many young people encountering the freedom of college life, I had difficulty knuckling down to work. My performance on the football field was disappointing as well, both to the coaches and me. The problem was catching passes with my injured hands. I managed to disguise the difficulty in high school, but this was college football where everything and everyone was bigger, faster, stronger and tougher. I had problems getting the job done, and to make matters worse my roommate at Xavier, Red Kelly, introduced me to Tito Carinci.

Meeting Tito Carinci should have marked a high point in my years at Xavier. Instead, it proved a disaster to my formal education.

Ten years earlier, Tito Carinci had achieved the highest level of distinction at Xavier when he was awarded the school's Legion of Honor. Legion of Honor winners were students who lived a life as close to Christ's, in both spiritual and worldly measures, as anyone on earth could attain. Only those dedicated to piety and devotion in their religious studies, and who achieved victories both on and off the playing field, qualified for the award. After leading Xavier to an undefeated season in 1951, Carinci was drafted by the NFL Green Bay Packers. His professional sports career wasn't nearly as rewarding as his college years, however, and after being cut from the Packers he entered the army. Eventually he wound up back in the Cincinnati area, a changed man.

Somewhere along the way, Tito replaced his ambition for a career in sports with a life of crime, and when I arrived at Xavier, he was managing the Tropicana casino and Glen Rendezvous in Newport, Kentucky just across the Ohio River. Newport was Sin City to residents of Cincinnati, a wide-open town catering to gambling, drinking and prostitution. Since long before World War Two, the Youngstown mob had controlled Newport by paying off key politicians who looked the other way while thousands of Cincinnati residents drove across the bridge to sample pleasures that were illegal almost everywhere else in America.

Tito, who still boasted about his days at Xavier, took a liking to Red and me and began picking us up in his pink Cadillac convertible on Sunday afternoons. We'd ride across the river to Tito's Kentucky ranch, which was always filled with friends and employees from the Tropicana, plus crowds of gamblers, musicians, strippers and prostitutes. I never drank and I never gave in to the temptation offered by the wild girls. Red and I just enjoyed hanging out, watching all the crazy people having fun. It was a window into a different life, one that was endlessly fascinating and diverting, and it made our schoolwork look dull and unimportant. Soon our whole week began revolving around those Sundays with Tito, and the effect on our studies was predictable. By Christmas, I realized there was no way I was going to successfully complete my year, and in January I dropped out of Xavier, leaving my dreams behind me on the campus.

Now that I was no longer either an athlete or a student, I needed two things: a chance to reassess and straighten out my life, and a job. To earn money, I began driving a beat-up Volkswagen van for a local department store, hauling goods back and forth across town. During those days sitting at the wheel, I realized I had to get back into both school and football.

Once again, I pleaded with Xavier for a chance to enroll, and once again they gave in. This time, however, I would have to attend night school, taking classes chosen by the school counselor who believed my primary needs were more spiritual than academic. Every night school class was rooted in Catholic values and practices, and they proved so boring that I thought they would never end. But I hung in to prove to everyone, including myself, that I would be coming back to full-time studies and the joy of football again.

If I could earn a football scholarship at Xavier, I decided, maybe I could earn one at another school, like the University of Cincinnati. It was a long shot, I knew. Scholarship dropouts are considered headaches by coaches and professors alike. With hundreds of students vying for a chance to make the grade, why should any school give a guy like me a second chance? But I knew the football coach at U of C, and he knew my abilities. I talked him into giving me a try-out during spring training, impressing him enough that he offered me a scholarship. I was getting a second chance and this time, I promised myself, I was not going to blow it. I didn't realize how important my determination would be until I arrived at the U of C training camp that summer.

"Training camp" does not describe the place, nor the things I endured over the next three-plus weeks. It was a combination cow pasture, boot camp, and prison located somewhere in the darkest, most remote corner of central Ohio. About a hundred of us were bussed there like raw army recruits and stumbling off the buses we were directed into barracks. For three and a half weeks we were awakened at five every morning, fed horrible food, and sent running through the woods before being taped and dressed for practice and scrimmage. The entire day was spent hitting and running in 95-degree heat and humidity, with breaks for lunch and dinner, where the food was as inedible as the stuff they served at breakfast.

With dinner behind us we wanted nothing more than to crash in our beds, but we were out of luck. First, the coaches held classroom sessions on plays and strategies. Then the real sadists took over.

When the coaches were absent, the camp was run by a bunch of seniors, many of them returning to school after serving a hitch in Korea with the army. Nothing pleased the seniors more than harassing and humiliating the new guys, especially those who had been too aggressive on the practice field. This, of course, included me. More than once, the guy facing me in a practice scrimmage would look up and say, "Cool it on this play, okay kid?" This, of course, encouraged me to hit him even harder than I might have, proving to both of us that nobody was going to be tougher or meaner than me. But after ten o'clock at night, in the barracks after "Lights out," the older guys paid me back.

The seniors would herd the newcomers together for the night's entertainment, which involved humiliating as many rookies as possible. Their favorite game was the olive race.

Stripping the rookies naked, the seniors would place three olives on the hard-concrete floor. Twenty-five yards away, at the other end of the barracks, they would set coffee cups. In groups of three, the newcomers were instructed to pick up an olive between the cheeks of their ass and clamber, stomach up, to the other end of the barracks where they deposited the olive in the coffee cup in their lane.

Humiliating? It was just beginning. It was a race, after all, and the loser in each race had to eat all three olives. If there is an Olympic record for racing naked, facing up and walking on your hands and feet like a crab over a 25-yard course, I'm sure I set it. And broke it, several times. When they grew tired of the olive race, the older players returned to basics, ordering the rookies to crawl past them on their hands and knees while the older guys beat them with sticks. The ones who were struck hard in these sessions were the ones who were most focused and committed, and who refused to give an inch to the seniors and juniors. This, of course, included me. One guy was mean and vicious to me and other newcomers. He was a running back named Joe, and a half-dozen rookies and I planned our revenge. One night we grabbed him, hustled him out of the barracks, dragged him into the woods, and taped him to a tree. Then we all took turns urinating into a bucket, poured it over his head, and left him there until morning. (Joe was never quite as mean again...)

Over a dozen players quit during those weeks at camp, and I was almost a drop-out myself by accident. I became lost in the woods one day, wandering around for hours and convinced that I would never see civilization again. I eventually stumbled back onto the field with mixed emotions. Being lost was no fun, but neither was that football camp.

I counted the days until we returned to Cincinnati. When the bus pulled away, I headed for home and couldn't stop grinning. I had just survived the training camp for twenty-five of the hardest days of my life.

I made the team based on my focus and determination as much as my athletic ability, but things had changed. To overcome my problem with catching passes, the coaches tried converting me to linebacker and other defensive positions. I never complained - I loved

39

the game so much that I would play any position the coaches chose. I also insisted on being tougher and more aggressive than anyone else on the field, partially because I was conscious of my crippled hand. Guys on the other teams, I feared, would think I was a pushover because of my injury, and I would prove that I wasn't. I constantly wore a chip on my shoulder and carried the attitude through every minute of every game. This led to fights on the field and lectures from the coaches about causing unnecessary penalties. I didn't care. If succeeding meant playing the game as though I were a time bomb with a short fuse, that's how I intended to play it. If the other guy got hurt, that was too bad. As it turned out, the only guy who got really hurt was me.

Through my high school years, playing with the old leather football helmets that provided little or no cushioning, I had never been knocked out. The new Riddell helmets, used by U of C, offered more protection, either because I was never fitted properly or I was leading with my head while making plays, I began getting knocked out, even during practice. Sometimes it was just for a moment or two, when I was the only one who realized my bell had been rung, as the coaches called it. At other times I lay on the field completely unconscious while play went on around me. Either way, it began happening more and more often.

Playing competitive sports, at both the university and professional level, teaches you many things. One of the first lessons you learn is Never Complain and Never Explain. You hide your injuries, conceal your weaknesses, and maintain a positive attitude. Nobody likes a whiner, and coaches don't want a complainer. So, I ignored the injuries, shaking my head and telling everybody I was all right, that I hadn't been injured, that I was ready to go right back onto the field again. That's what the coaches wanted to hear, and that's what I told them. After all I had been through, nobody was going to talk me into ending my athletic career. But after my second season, when I realized I was getting knocked out in virtually every practice, sometimes more than once, I faced the facts: I would not play football again.

It was the end of seven years of my life, years when I discovered just who Harold Van Arnem really was, and what he could do. I had changed from a skinny working-class kid to a self-assured young man who could walk into any social situation and feel totally at home and unintimidated. I had distinguished myself with success, and I had embarrassed myself with failure. It was time to set athletics aside and focus on academics.

That was one of the hardest decisions I made in my life. Football had provided both satisfaction and status, and I was losing both. I still wanted to be part of that level of society that lived the good life every day, whose meals consisted of filet mignon and lobster instead of baked beef heart and leftovers. If I couldn't win entry to that world through my athletic abilities, I would get there by being smarter and working harder than anyone else.

With football behind me, I started focusing my energy on school studies and the Sigma Chi fraternity, which invited me to become a pledge in my freshman year. My fraternity brothers elected me first as Pledge Trainer and later as House Manager, an important post within the organization. I took my responsibilities seriously. More seriously, it turned out, than many of my brothers.

This was the early 1960's, after all, when black people in America were demanding an end to segregation. Cincinnati bordered the Mason-Dixon line, and the resistance to integration in the city and surrounding communities remained strong. I had made up my mind years earlier that segregation was more than wrong, it was ignorant. Playing football, some of the best guys I met on the field were black. They were open, honest, and knew more ways of having fun than we white kids, despite being banned from restaurants, movie theatres and restrooms.

We had black players on the basketball courts, the football fields and the baseball diamonds, and we listened to music played by black performers like Chuck Berry, Fats Domino and Ella Fitzgerald. There were many black students in our university, so why didn't we have any black members in our fraternity? After all, the guidelines for a Sigma Chi brother said he must be: A man of good character... A student of fair ability... With ambitious purposes... A congenial disposition... Possessed of good morals... Having a high sense of honor, and a deep sense of personal responsibility. Nothing referred to the color of his skin.

When I suggested inviting a couple of black guys as pledges, the idea was rejected out of hand. Sigma Chi was all-white, and it would stay all-white. That's the message I received.

Okay, I said. I've got a Jewish friend who would be a great pledge. He's not a practicing Jew, so that shouldn't affect the so-called Christian foundation of the fraternity. How about inviting him? Again, the answer was no. No blacks. No Jews. No argument.

My suggestion that the fraternity should start dealing with reality marked me as a rebel, a role for which I never apologized. Someday, I knew, Sigma Chi and all the other fraternities, all the segregated schools and lunch counters, all the restricted golf clubs and movie theatres with a separate "Colored Entrance," would catch up with the rest of the world. I tried to start the ball rolling in the one small corner that I could influence.

I didn't expect to gain a lot of respect, and I didn't. The following year I was nominated to become president of our Sigma Chi chapter, something I had worked hard to achieve, but I was rejected for the post. Someone, it seemed, considered my ideas about integration too extreme for a Sigma Chi president. I was advised to settle for vice president and I did, but a lesson had been learned and the lesson was this: If you stand up for your rights and your beliefs, you become the target of everyone who disagrees with you. And if that person happens to be in a position of authority, you will pay the price, one way or another.

I have never forgotten that feeling of being rejected based on proposing something that was so obviously correct to do. (From that point on, I grew determined to become an entrepreneur in whatever business I pursued. An idea that had formed within me when I learned about my father's experience with the unscrupulous partner). I rejected the idea of working for someone else, someone who would tell me how to think and act regardless of my beliefs. In that way, all my successes and all my failures would belong to me alone, and I would make my decisions according to my own goals, values and dreams. I don't know how many other entrepreneurs chose that path based on a similar experience, but I suspect there are many.

Sigma Chi made another difference in my life. During my junior year at U of C one of the brothers began dating a pretty girl named Karen. I introduced myself and soon it was me dating Karen, and we decided to get married in the summer before my senior year. Our decision thrilled my parents, who were pleased to see me settle down, and alarmed Karen's mother and father when they discovered I was Roman Catholic. As Methodists, they saw nothing but trouble ahead for our mixed marriage. We didn't care. We had a wonderful wedding and honeymoon. At graduation in 1964, with a wife and a baby on the way, I also had new motivation.

Originally, I had hoped to join Xerox, which happened to be the glamour company of its time, making copiers that were becoming as important to the average office as typewriters and coffeemakers. Instead, I accepted an offer from GE, my father's employer, to help launch a new division in the company. It involved devices that had intrigued me for some time. They were called computers.

VAN ARNEM
TECHNOLOGY PIONEER

CHAPTER THREE

GENERAL ELECTRIC
AND THE BEGINNING OF THE COMPUTER INDUSTRY

I cannot claim that I foresaw the impact computers would make on the world. No one can. But more than 50 years ago, I knew they would change things in more ways than Xerox copiers ever could.

During statistics class in university, we used mechanical calculators to calculate square roots, perform long division, and carry out similar tasks. These were noisy machines, as bulky as a television set, with complex mechanisms that threatened to cut off one of your fingers if it got in the way. Computers that could perform the same function electronically instead of mechanically marked a major step forward, even if they were as big as a truck, which they were in the early 1960's. Even then, computers were performing more than simple mathematical calculations, which convinced me that they represented a major growth opportunity.

GE's entry into the computing field involved a substantial commitment in money and resolve, but the payoff prospects were tremendous. The computer industry had been practically created by IBM, who dominated it like no other firm has dominated any business sector. But as one of the largest users of IBM mainframe computers in the early 1960's, GE saw an immediate payback from developing their own units instead of using IBM. Supposedly, someone at GE calculated that the development cost for a GE computer, with a capacity like IBM mainframes, would be recovered in a single year of purchase value to IBM for all the IBM equipment and services used by GE. That's stretching things a bit, but it was probably an added incentive for GE to get into the computer business.

The GE computer division was in Phoenix, and I literally could not wait to get started. In early June 1964 within days of graduating from college I bought a car, a new suit and an attaché case, and my pregnant wife and I set off for Arizona, driving almost non-stop all the way. Reaching Phoenix, we found a cheap motel, and the next morning I set off in the 120-degree heat to take on the world as GE's most promising computer-division employee. Naturally, I expected to be greeted with open arms and an empty desk. Instead, when I finally located the plant and office, the response was, "Who are you?" They had no record of hiring me, and the corporate training program wasn't scheduled to start for another six weeks.

What was I to do in Phoenix for six weeks? "Relax, take a vacation, enjoy yourself," I was advised. Vacation? I didn't want a vacation. I wanted to work. Determined to get started, I insisted they put me to work. And they did. I was assigned to GE's Accounts Payable department, where I spent each day matching approved invoices to purchase orders, calculating taxes and total costs, and ensuring that everything added up correctly. It was basically a make-work job. Since the system already used several stages of manual approvals, I was just another superfluous clerk doing work that two or three other people had already performed. The idea that three or four salaried employees would sit around adding columns of figures to check that the person before them had not made a mistake seems ridiculous today, when the cheapest desktop computer can do the same thing as push a key. But that's what we did. That's what hundreds of us did.

Checking other people's calculations was boring in the extreme. This was not the way to make my mark with the company as I had planned.

When the six weeks were up and the training program began, I joined eleven other candidates recruited for GE's Business Training Course. This was a major achievement at the time. GE's course had been praised by Fortune Magazine as the most advanced and comprehensive managerial, accounting and financial analysis training program of its kind. In many ways, being chosen for a program like GE's was more impressive than earning a master's degree in Business Economics or Accounting.

The course was demanding. You had to be bright, determined and competitive. Three times a week, after working eight to ten hours at our regular positions, we attended night classes for three hours of study and analysis. I wish I could say the classes were stimulating, but they were frankly boring. Fortunately, they proved invaluable in later years when I needed to draw upon all the methods and techniques drilled into us during those night sessions.

Among the most valuable skills I acquired was the ability to organize assets and liabilities, booking them according to GE accounting standards. This was a real challenge. None of us was an accounting graduate – my business major had been economics – and that's precisely the way GE wanted it. The company used a non-standard accounting procedure that confused students who had studied conventional methods. We arrived as clean slates, so to speak, ready to absorb the GE system without questioning its logic or trying to adapt it to the methods we had learned in college.

Managerial accounting covered budgeting, cash management, and cost accounting, all essential to performing vital management tasks. We learned how to create a bill of materials and parts, cost out each component, and add labor and overhead expenses to determine actual product cost. This was tedious and laborious work, especially for a bunch of young guys anxious to take on the world and prove their worth. Only when the program was completed did we realize that we could measure the asset, liability and net cash flow of a corporation – any corporation – and use this knowledge to optimize management of the business.

While absorbing managerial accounting procedures, I realized that these calculations were being performed manually, which meant they could be easily mistaken and were subject to human error. Yet they were among the most critical management functions. They had to be done regularly, quickly and accurately, so they were perfect candidates for computerization by every corporation of virtually any size and in any industry. If computers could do the same calculations on schedule, do them quickly, and do them without error, it would change the way business operated. And that's exactly what happened.

We were all recent college graduates, and none of us had lost the competitive spirit that had influenced our lives in and out of class for the previous four years. We did everything above-board, but every guy knew that the sooner he proved his mettle to the people above him, the sooner (and faster) he would start to rise within the company and leave the others behind. The chance to make our mark came when we were given assignments to pursue outside the classroom. Most of these tasks dealt with active company records and operations. Anyone who could spot a procedure or logistical problem, or opportunity to improve the cost structure, received recognition. While on the job we pored over expense accounts, travel records, consigned stock records, purchase orders, and anything else related to our assignment.

The chance of uncovering anything significant was minimal, so I soon veered off in a different direction. Recalling those first few weeks of reviewing the multi-layered approvals process in accounts payable, I investigate automated methods of doing the same thing. After all, if we were in the computer business, why were we still hand-matching all these pieces of paper when computer cards could produce the same data? I proposed installing an invoice less accounts payable system that would use the original purchase order card to yield a receiver document matched with the goods when they arrived. The receiver card, in turn, would produce an invoice to be paid. This sounds simple and logical now because it's the basis for invoicing systems by every manufacturer, but in 1964 it represented a new concept, the beginning of an Accounts Payable application that thousands of firms were soon to follow in the new automated world.

GE estimated my system would save the company more than a million dollars each year. With those kinds of savings in one area, I began to look around for other applications and soon discovered that the firm held an enormous number of unused airline tickets, representing potential credit from the airlines. The airlines, however, couldn't issue credits until GE identified the tickets, another perfect application of computer technology. On my suggestion, GE installed a program to track airline tickets, identifying those that were never used and generating requests for credit back from the airlines.

These proposals established me as a creative resource, which represented a step above cost accounting. All I had to do was keep working, keep learning, and keep coming up with ideas to save the company money, and I would be given more important responsibilities, which I needed to keep myself competitive and alert.

The company's emphasis on cost-accounting represented the heart of GE's success. Its financial management training program was years ahead of everyone else, and it built the foundation that makes the company still one of the best-managed in the world more than 40 years later. The GE approach centered around this concept: No matter how effective you may be as a manufacturing manager, a marketing manager, or in any other position, if you weren't effective at managing the financial side of things you were a failure. GE was teaching this nearly half a century ago, and it's a lesson that some corporate leaders are still learning.

Many dramatic corporate failures in recent years, such as Enron, happened because the top people did not know how to manage the company's finances effectively. In some cases, they tried to disguise this ineptness with unsavory practices such as setting up reserves and engaging in off-the-balance-sheet investments. They either never learned or totally ignored the lesson I absorbed over 40 years earlier at GE: A CEO's success in an established firm is more dependent on setting a financial plan and maintaining control over it than on any other single ability. GE made this their philosophy within a massive company with dozens of divisions scattered across the country.

GE's traveling auditors, for example, were an efficient way to maintain financial control over operating managers. No matter how many divisions were under the corporate umbrella – and GE probably had more than any other company – nothing escaped the eyes and ears of traveling auditors who would swoop in without notice, scour the books, and identify anything that had a negative impact on the bottom line. That's how a multi-divisional company like GE managed to remain profitable and successful while operating in a wide range of markets and industries with offices and divisions scattered across the country.

By the time you absorbed GE's Business Training Course (BTC) and the financial management skills it provided, you were convinced that you could run a multi-faceted company in any industry. Most of us recognized this fact at the time, and some of the guys saw GE as their corporate home for life and applied themselves to rise as far and as fast as possible within the company.

But not me. I was too impatient to wait 25 or 30 years for the slim chance of grabbing the CEO position at GE. I wanted more, and I wanted it as soon as possible. I was earning $99 a week, and it wasn't going far. My restlessness grew stronger when I began examining expense reports from people in the field. Time and time again I saw receipts for hundred-dollar dinners at places like Club 21 in New York City and the Beverly Hills Hotel. It was taking me a whole week to earn the same amount of money that some top producers in the firm were spending in one night. Why wasn't I enjoying their perks?

Our daughter Aleise arrived in October, and we moved into a comfortable apartment. We were a family with a secure future but progress up the corporate ladder looked slow and painful, and I still had to punch a clock in the office as though I were an assembly-line worker. I wanted to start working in an executive position, taking on responsibility, creating value for the company, and being rewarded with part of the wealth I generated. The truth is, I wanted to run my own show, any show, as soon as possible, and if it wasn't GE or a company as dominant and massive, it would be with some other operation. The real action was happening not where the computers were manufactured but, in the field, where the computers were sold, installed and operated. That's where I wanted to be, and the sooner the better.

The opportunity arrived in a totally unpredictable manner.

Looking around for new methods to apply my managerial

accounting skills and cutting costs, I began examining our records of computer consignment inventory stocks. During the 1960's, the computer market was divided into two distinct sections. One was IBM's, and the other belonged to everyone else. Of the two, IBM's was so dominant it was virtually a monopoly. Everyone assigned to evaluate and purchase a mainframe computer for their company could be assured that they would never be second-guessed for recommending IBM. Any manager who stuck his neck out and recommended a GE, Burroughs, Honeywell or Univac knew that, in the event of a serious problem, someone would point a finger and say, "You should have gone with IBM!" As a result, selling IBM was easy. Selling against IBM was nearly impossible.

Our people in the field were jumping through hoops to overcome this resistance to computers that did not carry the IBM logo, and in heavily industrialized markets where competition was fierce, they would try to generate sales by offering a GE 600-series computer on consignment for a test period. We would install a GE 600-series at our expense just to prove that our machine was more efficient than an IBM for less cost and with better service. After an agreed-upon term, the customer would either return or agree to acquire the computer. As time passed, GE found itself with hundreds of computers on consignment.

The company had so many computers listed as consigned stock that I suspected we could be dealing with a logistical mess and perhaps even a case or two of larceny. It wasn't difficult to imagine somebody in field sales finding a way to make money on the side by taking cash for a six-month consignment agreement. I needed proof, of course, and one day I thought I found it buried among reports from our division office in Detroit. Something among the shipping, inventory, consignment and sales reports from Detroit did not add up, and the more I examined the figures, the more excited I got. Was somebody in Motor City hiding something?

The Detroit division manager was Jim Pompa, one of the youngest and most successful division managers in the company. When I gathered enough information, I phoned Pompa and, speaking with all the respect due to a senior manager, I announced that I was investigating the situation in his division.

Pompa responded to all my questions, then asked me to repeat my name and position. "Well, Harold," he said, "it happens that I'm coming out to Phoenix in a couple of days. Why don't you and I have lunch together and discuss this in detail?"

Later, I realized that Pompa had no plans to visit Phoenix until my telephone call. He knew he had a problem in his division, and he had been looking for somebody with managerial financing ability to handle things. I had not only assessed the situation; I had also chosen to go directly to him seeking an answer. Naturally, I agreed to meet him.

Pompa arrived looking like the success he was. After greeting me warmly, he drove us in his rented Lincoln to the area's most exclusive country club for our meal. He directed most of the conversation over lunch, asking about my background, my training and my ambitions. I explained the issues regarding the consignment stock and how the figures submitted by his division weren't making sense. He agreed with my concerns and assured me he would deal with it as soon as possible. Then, after paying the bill he leaned forward and said, "How would you like to come and work for me in Detroit?"

Was he joking? "In what position?" I asked.

"Division administrator," he replied. "At two hundred a week." Exactly twice as much as I was making in Phoenix. It was an easy decision to make. Within a month, we were driving east again, swinging north towards Michigan in mid-January.

Everything in Detroit was a total contrast to Arizona. We left Arizona on a sunny day with the temperature in the 80's and arrived at Detroit in the middle of a blizzard. The GE Phoenix office had been massive and new; the Detroit division office was small and cramped. In Phoenix, I had a list of specific tasks to follow. In Detroit, I was virtually on my own.

My job title of District Administrator was simply a means of persuading the Phoenix office to agree to my transfer. I learned later that Jim valued my enthusiasm as an asset in Detroit, where the morale of the sales force was low and dropping. My managerial accounting abilities would also help put things in order. But beneath it all, Pompa saw a pretty darn good salesman. As a GE man, Jim knew the importance of accurate up-to-date accounting procedures when it came to management reporting. In those early days of computer development, preparing spreadsheets and calculating earnings and expenses was ideal work for computers. Many of his salespeople could rave about design and operating features of the GE computers, but he needed someone who could present solutions to CFOs in language they could understand and deliver benefits they could appreciate.

First, I had to learn the ropes at the division level. This meant spending a lot of time doing menial tasks in the office, and I hated it. I did learn, however, the value of initiative. When evaluating employees, you can learn more about their value and potential by studying what he or she does when they have time on their hands. Do they stand around the coffee machine gossiping? Do they read a comic book or clean their nails? Or do they hone their skills or widen their product knowledge? All employees find ways to waste time; outstanding employees take initiative.

I refused to wait around while Jim found something for me to do. Driving to work each morning and returning home in the afternoon, I began making cold sales calls on various companies along the route. I didn't present myself as a computer salesman but as a financial guy who wanted to help the company's controller do a better job at getting a handle on expenses and fattening the firm's profit with a GE computer. I never asked to see the CEO or the Operations Manager or anyone else at that level. Why should I? I wouldn't know their primary concerns. But I knew what all controllers worried about, and I could speak to them in terms they understood and appreciated.

This was a major shift in the way most computers were being sold. Usually, the IBM people would stroll into the CEO's office and say,

"We're about to introduce a new line of computers and we'll allow you to preorder your installation." The other guys would say, "We're just as good as IBM, we can solve your problems (whatever they were), and we're cheaper." I didn't talk hardware or costs on my cold calls. I talked solutions to problems that I knew concerned the customer, and when necessary, I wrote programs to meet their unique needs. Many computer salespeople would throw up their hands in surrender when it came to selling against IBM, but that was only one measure of the problem. As a GE salesman, I wasn't just selling against IBM; I was also selling against the CEO, CFO and other top executives of the company because they had all been effectively brainwashed by IBM's multi-level executive marketing strategy, which included hosting senior management at executive retreat functions. How do you sell against that kind of persuasion?

I developed a strategy to exploit IBM's biggest weakness: their over-confidence. An IBM salesman not only didn't have to address a customer's needs in detail, he didn't even have to be aware of them. When a customer asked how IBM would help the firm's inventory problems, the standard reply was: "We have an IBM program for it." The salesperson neglected to say it was an off-the-shelf program that perhaps had no application for the customer's major concerns.

With a few in-house programs to promote on my cold calls, I would request a meeting with the corporate controller and ask him to describe his ideas on controlling inventory and managing expenses, applications I knew were critical in any manufacturing operation. Once I evaluated the problem, I would either modify an existing program or create a new one that would address their problems specifically and run only on a GE computer. Nobody else was doing this.

One of my most productive moves was to obtain a map showing IBM sales territories in southern Michigan. Each IBM salesman was restricted to one sales territory; crossing into another salesman's territory was not tolerated in the IBM hierarchy.

This inflexibility, like the firm's arrogance, struck me as another weakness to be exploited. I noted that a line across the north-west region of Greater Detroit marked the beginning of the sales territory assigned to IBM's office in Flint. The city of Flint was 25 miles to the west and its sales office was tiny. How many IBM salespeople wanted to drive all that way to make cold calls in north-west Detroit? Hardly any, as I discovered when I began visiting companies in that area. In many cases, I was the first computer salesman they encountered. Within a year of arriving in Detroit, I had sold and installed 14 computers, as many as the entire division had sold in the same period. Not bad for someone whose title had nothing to do with direct sales.

My success won recognition from head office, including a trip to Paris for Karen and me, and an offer from the corporate sales department. "You are so good," they said, "that we're going to send you to sales school."

This had to be the silliest thing I had heard. Every other salesman in the division had attended sales school, and I managed to beat them all. Now they wanted me to have the same sales training that proved ineffective for the rest of the sales force. I went along with the suggestion, partly out of curiosity and partly because it meant a week or two in a resort location at GE's expense. I returned from the trip determined to stick with my own sales techniques and make enough money to take care of my family and give them the best quality of life possible.

The more sales successes I scored with GE, the less satisfied I became. I was helping businesses become more independent as they grew and prospered. I saw mediocre businesses grow into profit-generating powerhouses with my assistance. I watched CEO's shape and build their visions, enjoying great satisfaction and enormous wealth. Meanwhile, selling was becoming like homework to me. It was something I had to do, whether I liked it or not.

It was also affecting my home life. When I wasn't making sales calls, I was writing programs for customers. Even my weekends were spent selling; I began joining various associations and organizations, meeting old and new customers, making the rounds in pursuit of a deal. At the time, anyone who possessed even the most basic knowledge of computers, and could speculate on the impact they were making, became popular on the speaking circuit. Invited by Rotary clubs and Chamber of Commerce groups to discuss computers at their lunch meetings, I accepted an offer to lecture freshmen classes at Macomb Community College and other schools on computer basics.

Nothing sharpens your perception of a topic and all its facets better than teaching, and during those sessions I began recognizing the problems and opportunities that computers represented to business at the time. For example, the only way computerization made economic sense to most small and medium-sized business was through time-sharing, when the enormous capital costs could be shared among several dozen users. This was already happening, but things were moving slowly. In addition, writing computer programs was a complex, lengthy process that only a small number of skilled people were able to accomplish, limiting the range of computer applications. Finally, we needed a better method of accumulating, storing and accessing data. Back in the 1960's, this was done almost exclusively on punch cards, which were inefficient and subject to errors.

For those of you who are fortunate enough not to have dealt with computer punch cards, let me explain.

The most common method of preparing data for processing in the 1960's was to enter the information as a code on postcard-sized pieces of cardboard by punching holes in the material. These were called Hollerith cards for their inventor, Herman Hollerith, who developed and patented the idea in the late 1880's. Legend has it that Hollerith was inspired by watching railroad conductors punch passenger tickets. The location of the punched hole identified the passengers' status. If one hole punched in paper could provide information, Hollerith realized, imagine all the data that could be recorded with dozens of such holes. Electromagnetic needles would make a connection through the hole openings, creating impulses recorded by a counter mechanism. When the 1890 Federal census was tabulated in record time, proving the value of Hollerith's invention, he formed the Tabulating Machine Company which, through various mergers, evolved into the International Business Machine Company in 1924.

Hollerith's original card design remained virtually unchanged for years. Each card held 80 columns with 12 punch locations in each column, representing 80 alphanumeric characters. Long after Hollerith cards were replaced by electromagnetic tapes and disks, their influence lives on through standard conventions and file formats. The terminals that replaced the punched cards displayed 80 columns of text, and many programs still use the convention of 80 text columns.

Once the Hollerith cards were punched, they were collated in correct order and stacked until all the data was collected. On the operator's command, the computer "flipped" through the cards, reading the punched areas and calculating the results. One misplaced hole in a single card or a misplaced card in the stack being processed – something that occurred all too frequently – produced an error in the results. We needed a safer, more effective way of storing and reading data.

We also needed a way for multiple users to have easier access to the computer. Too many companies were by-passing the purchase of a computer because the front-end costs were too high to justify the back-end savings. Yet I knew that most mainframe computer installations were rarely using more than a small percentage of their capacity. What's more, the computer should be easily accessible to any user who needed it to perform calculations or obtain important information from its data bank.

If multiple users with remote terminals were accessing mainframes over telephone lines, they could enjoy computer benefits without tying up capital to purchase their own mainframe. Commercial time-sharing represented an opportunity to build a substantial business beyond the corporate bounds of GE, IBM or any other player in the business. I needed to move before others jumped in ahead of me, and this meant leaving the security of GE behind me to launch my own business.

With all the achievements I've made since, I must admit that quitting my job at GE was a slightly insane move. I had a wife and two children, with another baby on the way. I had nothing to sell except myself, and I had nothing to support me except my belief that a means of creating custom-developed programs would kick-start a revolution to alter the way the world did business, and perhaps society itself.

It's stating the obvious to say that computers have changed the way the world works in more ways than we can count. No one could totally foresee the full extent of this revolution, including me. But I had a gut feeling that I was riding a wave whose height, speed and final impact would be unlike anything that has occurred since the Industrial Revolution, in ways that were never anticipated. Only today, when it is almost impossible to imagine the world functioning without computers, can we recognize how deeply they have altered the way that business is managed.

Until the late 1960's, most companies were neither well-managed nor poorly managed. In truth, they were not managed at all. A manufacturing firm's inventory was merely estimated, except once a year when a team of people were ordered, usually on a weekend, to walk through the warehouse and perform a physical count. Taking inventory was one of the least popular employee functions, which almost guaranteed that errors would occur. Financial records were just as difficult to obtain and were almost always out of date. A CFO could smile at the last quarter's profit-and-loss statement while having no idea that the company had begun to drown in red ink since the figures were prepared.

CEOs and CFOs all knew this, of course. They simply learned to live with it. Obtaining even reasonably accurate figures on inventory and cash flow was a labor-intensive job, and every effort towards greater accuracy raised the cost of this data to the point of diminishing returns. How could a CEO justify saving X dollars if it cost 3X to get the necessary information? As a result, planning and budgeting became little more than educated guessing games, and companies remained stifled. Everyone who studies the way business practices were carried out before and after the widespread use of computers focuses on the improvements of speed and accuracy that resulted. In my opinion, the biggest difference made on American business by computers is subtle but far more influential: Computers forced businesspeople to set budgets and make plans. You cannot make the most of a computer by "guesstimating" the data to be entered. Computers don't work like that. They need fixed, specific figures – dollars in sales, units in the warehouse, products on the production line, orders in the basket, and so on. Once company management committed key aspects of its operations to computers, they were forced first to prepare plans and budgets, and later to compare actual performance to the plan. Managing a company in seat-of-the-pants attitude could no longer be tolerated. Computers changed not only the way businesses operated; they changed the way that business executives did their job, and that has made all the difference over the years.

Few people have addressed this business development, and I mention it not only to add some deeper perspective to the changes taking place when I launched my first firm, but to explain how some of us became dedicated to changing the way businesses were managed. Were we driven by a desire to make money? Of course, we were. But we were also motivated, in my opinion, by an almost religious dedication to change the way the world worked. And we did.

IBM remained one of the biggest obstacles to implementing these breakthroughs, and they built barriers against anyone seriously challenging their position through restrictive access. For example, in addition to blocking access to their operational software, IBM prohibited the interfacing of any non-IBM hardware, such as printers, with their computers. Essentially, it was IBM's way or no way at all. In the beginning, this was IBM's strength. As we know now, of course, it proved to be IBM's weakness as well.

VAN ARNEM
TECHNOLOGY PIONEER

CHAPTER FOUR

ME & 24 PHD
THE BEGINNING OF THE INTERNET AND THE CLOUD

Working for Jim Pompa, I absorbed as much knowledge about computer applications as I could. To acquire more would mean stepping outside the GE tent where the emphasis was on hardware development and entering the world of academics where breakthroughs were happening in application and system development. The University of Detroit was a hotbed of experimentation in computers at the time and the dean of engineering, Larry Canjar, introduced me to several PhDs working on various projects. Among them was Dr. Joe Hitt, head of electrical engineering.

Dr. Hitt seemed to have been born for, or perhaps spawned by, the computer age. Dropping out of high school at age 17 he joined the Marines, emerging from that experience with a determination to make the most of his exceptional intelligence, and through the power of his own genius he earned a PhD in electrical engineering at 23 years of age. When I launched my own company to promote computer usage in the Detroit area, Joe was one of the first people I recruited.

Like many geniuses, Joe had unlimited talent for creating new concepts and little ability for dealing with concerns of everyday life. One of his best ideas was to use acoustic couplers to connect the remote terminal to the dial up telephone lines. Selectrics were the first typewriters to use electronic pulses.

We spent a good deal of time and a pile of money but in the end, nothing came of the idea because IBM, who insisted on running a closed system, refused all efforts to adapt the Selectric to a computer interface. It may have been the ultimate corporate arrogance, and in many ways, it was the first step towards the company's eventual downfall. In frustration, we dropped the Selectric adaptation and went with a Teletype terminal and cathode-tube display (CRT) linked to a separate keyboard, which is precisely the format used by every computer built since the mid-1970's.

Joe Hitt introduced me to Jesse Quatse, another genius and pioneer in computer development. Jesse had a PhD in electrical engineering, but his appearance and demeanor were more at home in a Hell's Angels clubhouse than at Carnegie Tech, where he headed their computer engineering lab. Jesse's hair reached to his waist, his nose appeared to have been broken several times in various places, and he spoke in a deep guttural voice. As brilliant in his own way as Joe Hitt, Jesse loved women, drugs and parties every bit as much as he loved working out new algorithms, which probably led to his early demise.

Jesse, in turn, linked me up with Dr. Mel Pirtle, who was the Director of the Institute for Advanced Computation out in California, who grew excited about the possibility of teaming a Selectric with a computer. As bright and innovative as Joe and Jesse, Mel demonstrated true leadership abilities from the beginning. He rarely spoke unless he had something substantial to contribute to the conversation, and his silence was often interpreted as either hostility or disinterest, which was rarely the case.

Joe, Jesse and the others were academicians, working on hardware design and circuitry. (Programs were created on circuit boards with diodes and resistors). I was a practical guy whose focus wasn't on the inside of the computer but on the outside, where the end-users were. As different as our personalities might have been, our approach to finding new, more efficient ways of using computers was a perfect fit.

I had always appreciated the computer's potential as an educational tool, even when promoting them to corporations as a means of improving business management. GE had partnered with Time-Life to launch General Learning Corporation, marrying computer operations with educational needs. GLC provided a link to schools and universities, including Dartmouth, where I met people who would play key roles not only in my career but in the development of computers generally. Several universities were becoming hotbeds of computer development; UC, Berkeley and Carnegie Tech were among the leaders in exploring applications, but Dartmouth led everyone in developing computer time-sharing for faculty and students on-line.

Aware of this wave of advances taking place at schools around the country, I began paying attention to their activity, making friends among the leading professors and exchanging ideas and concepts. Eventually, while still with GE, I was appointed a lecturer on computer development at U of D, a role that brought encounters with several engineering doctoral candidates. At my urging, we began to create a curriculum of courses leading to a doctoral degree in computer engineering.

Almost overnight I was trading concepts and ideas with some of the brightest engineers of their time, all of them PhDs and all of them destined to become legends in the computer industry. Mel, Joe, Jesse and others made up a collaborative group whose engineering research led to several important developments in computer technology, including the creation of the G21 Bendix multi-processor and multi-port TS system, SDS 940, and the GE 440 and the BCC500 (Berkeley Computer Corporation).

My plan was to launch a company that included the talents of these computer engineers, an idea that in many ways excited the academicians more than me. It was fine to have pie-in-the-sky ideas, but I was the only guy with hard business experience. I would be the one to understand the business plan and operations and worry about meeting the payroll. Even while the company was just an idea being kicked around over a couple of drinks, the PhDs were choosing the country club they would join and the expensive cars they would drive. Meanwhile, I kept reminding them that we had no clients to service, no products to sell, and especially no money to spend.

Part of the impetus behind my plans for a company grew out of a discovery made while visiting Dartmouth's computer lab where a new language had been created, one that enabled students to write their own computer programs. The language was simple to apply, provided clear and friendly error messages, required no understanding of the hardware by the user, and offered direct interaction between user and computer. Kemeny and Kurtz called it Beginner's All-purpose Symbolic Instruction Code or BASIC, and it represented a breakthrough in computer programming. Instead of relying on complex pre-written programs with built-in limitations, students could create their own programs designed to meet their own individual objectives. While programs written in the new BASIC language did not operate as efficiently as more complex languages, speed was a non-issue as long as users of time-sharing systems were able to interact with the computer in a conversational way.

At the same time BASIC began opening doors to new application opportunities, the Report Program Generator or RPG was introduced. RPG was a guide that novices could follow when designing and implementing computer programs designed for their own individual needs. Together with BASIC, RPG bridged the gap that existed between the people who could benefit from a computer and the people who operated the machines. I expected everybody on the business side of the computer industry to jump up and down in excitement at the impact this would have. But hardly any did. On the sales side, most remained focused on selling the hardware and hardware which I knew, was becoming less and less important.

With the introduction of BASIC and RPG, my idea of installing remote terminals linked to a mainframe on a time-sharing basis changed from a blue-sky vision to an economic reality. Companies could contract for monthly hours and their own staff, using programs written especially for them in BASIC, could interact with the computer. I began acquiring a library of programs, some from public domain sources and some I wrote myself, all demonstrating not only the benefits of using a computer but the ease with which each company could use it to their advantage. Everything was beginning to make sense, on an economic, practical and personnel level, for an explosion of computer applications in business. I was ready to introduce an interactive solution provider to the Midwest business community and make the kind of business impact I had dreamed about.

CHAPTER FIVE

FORD AND ACTS JOINT VENTURE

In 1968, I launched Applied Computer Time Share (ACTS) to market access to a GE 420 via remote terminals, using the library of engineering, business and accounting packages I had accumulated by then, and all programs were accessible anywhere in the world by dialing up the computer thru the cloud. The business plan I drew up was state-of-art, except that it assumed I had access to a GE 420 computer, which I happened to lack at the time. Fortunately, a solution was at hand.

Before leaving GE, I persuaded U of D to buy a GE 420, followed by extended credit terms for the university. GE was delighted to provide one of their most expensive units to a university known for its team of engineers and for its association with ACTS. The university expressed concern about making such a substantial purchase, but I assured them not to worry about payment. I explained, I was buying the computer, not the university, and I would be generating sufficient funds to cover its cost. Between my assurances and the university's desire to have a leading-edge computer available to faculty and students, the sale was made, and the computer installed. Everyone was happy: GE made a prestigious sale, U of D had a state-of-the-art computer, and I had the computer we needed to launch the time-sharing business.

Applied Computer Time Share (later ACTS Computing Corporation) had three assets at the beginning. One was a determination to turn my vision of widespread computerization into a reality. Another was access to the GE computer being delivered to the University of Detroit, with me as the actual prime user. And the third were the officers of my company, every one of whom had a PhD. They included Joe Hitt, Frank Cain, Jesse Quatse and a few others.

That was impressive, but the assets hardly balanced the liabilities. I had no clients, no income and no place to install the computer when it arrived. I began by searching for a location to house the business. I didn't need a prestigious location or a high-traffic area. I needed cheap accommodations, so I began scouting a rundown part of Detroit near the expressway, adjacent to an area that had been burned during the Detroit riots in the summer of 1967. The location may have been convenient, but it certainly was not prestigious. I didn't care. I needed low price more than high fashion. I passed a real estate office in a low-rise building and, assuming this would be a good place to assess property values and lease rates, I decided to stop and make some enquiries. The woman who seemed to be operating the business appeared distressed and nervous from the moment I entered and asked if any commercial properties were available for rent. "How about this place?" she said, in a heavy French accent. I agreed the building would suit my purpose, but I wasn't looking to purchase. Was she interested in leasing space to me?

Shaking her head, she explained her situation. Her husband had recently died, leaving her with substantial estate tax and other obligations. She had no interest in assuming control of the real estate business, perhaps with the memory of the recent riots fresh in her mind. She just wanted to return to France as soon as possible without the IRS threatening her for unpaid taxes. If I took over the property and assumed the debts associated with it, I could have it.

Naturally, I agreed. We signed a contract, she left for France with her debts and conscience clear, and I took possession of the future headquarters office for ACTS. An assessment of the building's value revealed substantial equity in it – enough for me to borrow $25,000 from the bank against the property's value. The money provided cash to build out the structure to accommodate the GE computer and telecommunications equipment I begged and borrowed materials from various contacts around town, and much of the electrical and mechanical work was done by my brother Ken and other EE students at U of D.

The biggest single expense was the installation of telephone subsystems to provide access to the computer for time-share clients. We needed several datasets, one for each line. Every port providing access to the communication process, or datanet, required a separate modem installation, and we added control processors to interface between the datanet and the users. It was a complex, expensive job, and when all the bills were paid very little money remained to cover my expenses. I didn't care about the slim financial picture, because I expected it to be a short-term concern. I had a complete computer-based communications center, something few people in the world were offering. No one else in the Detroit area, including GM, Ford and Chrysler, had a similar set-up.

With everything in place, I began selling our services, focusing my attention on consulting engineers and accounting firms. I had accumulated various programs from the public domain. I modified them to work on the GE computer. Many of these programs performed engineering and accounting applications, and in my sales pitches, I used them to demonstrate how to perform operations, such as structural analyses that were taking days to complete with slide-rule calculations, in less than an hour. The prospects quickly realized that by contracting computer time through ACTS they could slice their fees in half and still double their profits. One of my first customers was Structural Dynamics Research Corporation which used ACTS to build one of the world's top engineering consulting firms today.

Accountancy firms were even easier to sell, given my earlier work experience. I had another goal in mind, however. Accountants were always advising their clients to cut costs and improve efficiency, and after I demonstrated how to do both for their own firm, the accountants would promote the idea to their clients, generating solid sales leads for me.

Some clients needed a portable terminal installed, along with an acoustic coupler. The "portable" description of the terminals – they were really modified teletype machines – was only effective for people built like Arnold Schwarzenegger. Nobody else could lift them. Everything was relevant, of course, since the computer it accessed was larger than the average kitchen. I would roll the terminal into a prospect's office and, using an acoustic coupler to link the client's dial-up line with my computer, dial my way into the computer, and demonstrate a program's operations. This was revolutionary at the time, everyone wanted to take it home and play games and write simple programs.

Even when the benefits were obvious, many prospects avoided deciding to use the computer. Their problem was computer phobia. I overcame this by expanding the greeting and "hand-shaking" process when a user signed-on. During sign-on, the computer asked the user to identify himself or herself and the computer addressed the user by name through the rest of the session. Later, I added games to the programs, such as a simple version of blackjack, that anyone could play, not to waste time (although it did...) but to reduce the intimidation factor and raise the user's comfort level.

Slowly, we began building a client base, although the promise of big profits remained just that – a promise. I needed to expand my base quickly before others saw the same potential. This meant hiring more people to make client calls, so I asked two GE sales guys whom I respected, along with ten IBM and Xerox people, to join me. The GE people didn't have the sales abilities of the former IBM and Xerox guys, but that's not what I wanted. I was after their drive to succeed.

Each employee I hired put me further out on a limb. I knew I had to stay focused on the goal of getting the most out of the people working for me because if I failed, we all failed. I let nothing prevent me from dropping the poor performers and encouraging the best ones, and sometimes this led to extremes. Questioning one salesman's dedication, I got up at six a.m., parked my car outside his home, and watched to see what time he started work. When he left his house hours later than he claimed, I followed in my car, noting how many calls he made and how many times he stopped to have a coffee and read the newspaper. Later, when he assured me, he had put in a full day of calls without scoring a single sales lead, I confronted him with the facts and suggested he look for work elsewhere.

VAN ARNEM
TECHNOLOGY PIONEER

Was I excessive? Perhaps. But when you're an entrepreneur running on little more than adrenaline and a dream, you become fiercely determined to win and rarely satisfied with anything less than success. It wasn't just a matter of ego or greed on my part; it was a matter of survival. I needed those sales to produce my cash flow, and I needed the cash flow to keep the business running. "Never mind what you did yesterday," I would say. "Tell me what you did today, and what you're going to do tomorrow."

I needed to ride my sales staff hard because I was unable to attract the naturally- gifted salespeople, the young ones who were bright, ambitious and self-motivated. The best salespeople chose IBM, it was safe, and ACTS was a startup. It was a mark of honor to be recruited by IBM, and almost no one turned the company down. After a few years, those same people either squeezed themselves into the inflexible IBM mold, or rebelled against the corporate restrictions and broke away into some other business. In any case, IBM always got the top ten percent of recruits. I had to fight alongside everybody else to hire the cream of the other 90 percent.

I may not have had the best natural sales force versus IBM, but I was offering my clients compatible, easy-to-use on-line computing at an attractive price through time-sharing. IBM did not put a priority on computer time-sharing. It was more interested in selling stand-alone installations, something I was particularly good at. The company declined to be involved in any installation that involved connectivity, because this would have created a demand to interface with non-IBM hardware peripherals and software from its competitors. Coupled with its absolute refusal to permit adaptations to its operating system software, their strategy left little room for competition to establish a foothold except when it came to time-sharing. Other computer manufacturers, recognizing the benefits of on-line computing, developed hardware and software that worked effectively under that arrangement, and nobody did it better than GE. Soon, GE represented my primary competition, and I began to follow their activities closely, looking for any opportunity to score a victory or two.

CHAPTER SIX

FORD ENGINEERING TO ELIMINATE SLIDE RULES

The opportunity arrived in 1970 when I learned that Ford, who had purchased a GE computer with full time-sharing capabilities a few years earlier, had acquired Philco's Aero neutronics and would be installing a Philco 2000 computer to replace its GE 265 system. The Philco 2000 was one of the world's largest computer systems and its installation would make the GE 265 superfluous. Ford would naturally want to spotlight the operation of a product from its subsidiary, reducing or eliminating the GE unit's operations.

This was a chance to gain access to the GE 265 and perhaps a good part of Ford's business as well. I suspected that, as good as the Philco 2000 might have been, moving from the GE system to Philco would take longer than Ford anticipated, because Philco lacked the software developed by GE for Ford's applications.

I saw this inevitable break-in period, between the arrival of the Philco 2000 and Ford's ability to employ all its advantages and benefits, as an open door to an enormous opportunity. Why would Ford want two expensive computers sitting around if they were committed to just one? If I could make Ford an offer for their GE 265 involving a price large enough to benefit them and low enough for me to afford it, I could use my own library of proprietary software, but most important, I could gain access to the entire GE proprietary library which Ford had purchased. Software laws were not established by then and I could acquire GE application software worth millions of dollars which would put me on par with GE with the hardware purchase. That combination would enable me to compete head-to-head with GE, the industry leader in time-sharing installations.

I arranged a meeting with the head of Ford's engineering department and made him a proposition. "You've got a lot of rental credits on that computer," I pointed out. "If it's sitting there unused, they're not making you any money. But if you exercise your credits on the computer and keep it operating here for a while, I'll pay you a premium for access to it, and Ford could wind up making $100,000 on the deal."

The engineer thought this was a terrific idea and referred me to a guy in the purchasing department, who was just as enthusiastic. The purchasing agent promised to get back to me in a few days. I left Ford convinced that I had set up a perfect win-win deal: Ford gets a $100,000 profit and I get both a time-sharing computer system and a software library that was equal to the best in the world at the time.

Naturally, it wasn't as simple as that. Purchasing people love to do deals, even if the deal-making is unfair to the other side, and after I left the purchasing agent's office, he took my plan and ran with it himself. "Actually, it sounded like such a good idea," he told me when I called a few days later, "that we've decided to put it out for bids."

I couldn't believe it. The entire idea had been mine, and now Ford was cutting me out of it? Once the word spread, there was no way I could survive in a bidding war. Everybody else would benefit from my proposal and I'd be left with nothing but a handshake.

Telling the purchasing agent, I was on my way to see him, I jumped in my car and raced to his office, growing more emotional by the minute. "This is unfair," I explained after I practically burst into his office, still trying to control my feelings. "I came up with this idea. I need this computer. If my competition gets it, they'll use my own idea to control my market, especially the auto industry." When the emotional appeal didn't seem to be working, I tried a practical approach. "I'm easy to work with," I added. "Everybody knows that. And if you have problem with the Phalcon, I'll work with you, I'm right here in town, I know this computer better than anybody..."

Nothing seemed to be making an impact on the purchasing agent. Finally, to get rid of me, he made an offer. He would send out a request for bids to purchase the computer. All bids would be opened in ten days, on a Monday morning. If I showed up at the meeting with a check for something over one million dollars, the computer was mine. If I didn't, it would go to the highest bidder. I hadn't yet salvaged the deal, but I at least had won the right of first refusal. That gave me an advantage over other guys I knew would be making a pitch. Unlike me, of course, they all had cash in hand.

I spent the next week calling everyone I knew who might provide the money. I got a lot of sympathy, but not a dime of cash. By Thursday I exhausted all my contacts and was calling every leasing company and capital equipment financing firm I could find in the telephone directory. Back then, the leasing industry was no further along in its development than the computer industry because few firms recognized the benefits of leasing. Most companies either rented from IBM or purchased the equipment they needed, writing down their investment over the years. The few leasing companies who could handle a deal like this were not interested in supporting a company like mine that lacked both a balance sheet and a guaranteed revenue stream. Still, I believed that I could persuade someone to grasp how my deal would work and recognize the potential it offered.

I began working my way through a list of every leasing company in the business, and in each case the person I needed to speak to was either busy or out. I left messages to call me, but none did. Except one.

By now, it was Friday afternoon and I was reaching for people well outside the Detroit area. I placed a call to Data Processing Financial and General in New York City, and to my surprise the CEO not only took my call, he listened with interest. His name was Harvey Goodman, and the more questions he asked, the more he grew interested in the deal. Besides being exceptionally open-minded, Harvey was well-versed in the business, having started his career at IBM. When I explained that Ford would be keeping the GE computer on their premises, although they planned to convert 100 percent of their computing to the Philco 2000, he saw the opportunity as quickly and clearly as I had. No matter how clever and dedicated Ford and Philco engineers may be, the conversion was never going to move as smoothly and quickly as they planned. When things began going wrong, they would need access to the GE 265, and they would have to pay me for it. My company would, to one degree at least, become a partner with Ford Motor Company, raising its status tremendously.

The more we talked, the more Harvey and I connected, first on a business level and soon on a personal level as well. "I've got a great source for the line of credit we'll need," Harvey chuckled at one point. The deal was put together over the weekend and, on Monday morning, I strode into the boardroom of the Ford Credit Corporation where the tenders for access to their GE computer were to be opened and the rights assigned.

One of the first people I encountered was my old boss, Jim Pompa, sitting at the end of the table, waiting to see who would be paying GE for Ford's computer. The rest of the people included heavyweights from Pillsbury, ComShare, Call A Computer and Tymshare, the top I.S. in the USA, and other companies, along with their lawyers, and the president of Ford Credit, Herb Mercer. Other lawyers attended to represent Ford and GE, who were there to object to the idea of Ford selling the proprietary software on the computer, especially if it were to be used in direct competition with GE. (At the time, the issue of software ownership was attached to the computer as a peripheral; today the opposite is true.) Ford's lawyers wanted to ensure that the company wasn't walking into a legal trap. That's when I realized that my idea was creating major issues that had not been dealt with before. Providing computer access to remote time-sharing users was just beginning to expand as a business solution, and my proposal involved new situations that would change the nature of the computer business.

So many people were attending the meeting that various stakeholders crowded every available space to hear how things were to be settled. Many stood against the wall or peeked through open doorways. This was an exciting moment.

At 10:30, the purchasing agent called the meeting to order.

"Mr. Van Arnem has the right of first refusal," he announced, "providing he has funds to cover the purchase price. If he has the one million dollars necessary to make the purchase, he receives the computer access. If he does not, the bids of others will be opened and assessed." He looked down the long table at me. "Do you have the necessary funds, Mr. Van Arnem?" he asked.

"Not directly..." I began.

The Ford purchasing agent waved his hand and muttered, "Okay, let's move along..."

"Just a moment," I interrupted. "Mr. Herb Mercer has agreed to provide the financing to purchase the computer, and it will be leased to me through Data Processing Financial and General." I gestured towards Herb Mercer, president of Ford Credit, who had been sitting silently watching things unfold.

This launched a wave of whispers around the table. None of the other bidders could believe it. They had all arrived expecting to bid against each other, and never imagined that I would walk away with the deal even before they could make their offer.

"I need a check from you," Mercer said to me, "for one million and thirty-seven thousand dollars."

I nodded and withdrew my personal checkbook. Then, as everybody at the table watched either in horror or amusement, I wrote out a check, drawn on the personal account of Harold and Karen Van Arnem on the Birmingham-Bloomfield bank for $1,037,000.

"You've got to be kidding," Joe Pompa said. "We're not taking Van Arnem's personal check for over a million dollars!"

I handed my check to Herb Mercer, who wrote Ford Motor Credit Corporation per Herb Mercer – accepted with recourse, and that was it. Ford Credit would loan the money to Harvey Goodman's firm, who in turn would lease the computer to me on a sale and lease-back basis. I was now the leading computer company inside one of the largest corporations in the world. All of us – ACTS, Harvey Goodman's company, and Ford – would profit from the deal. The only ones who lost would be all the other guys who had shown up looking for a bargain and the GE software. They lost more than a chance to earn large profits; they also lost access to Ford's enormous engineering expertise.

It was one of the most satisfying moments of my life.

My instincts, along with Harvey Goodman's, proved correct. Philco did not get their computer installed and running on schedule. In fact, it took almost two years before the Philco computer was able to perform the same tasks they had been getting from the GE 265 computer. Even then, the Philco computer failed to achieve the level of interactivity Ford expected, and it was eventually replaced without fanfare.

The strategic advantage for me provided by my arrangement with Ford is difficult to overestimate. My acquisition of the GE 265 meant that ACTS was now the only computer time-sharing system fully equal to GE's Information Systems division. The hardware alone, however, didn't make the difference. We would be using software that GE had spent tens of millions of dollars and hundreds of man-years to develop, in conjunction with Dartmouth University, Time-Life, and Bell Laboratories, making ACTS unique in the USA.

Meanwhile, under our agreement Ford had to buy access to the ACTS 265 from me, even while I was selling time-share agreements to my own clients. I was also more than a contractor or supplier to Ford. ACTS worked from inside Ford, where I had a designated parking spot and office facilities for my software technicians. As I predicted, this was proving to be a very good deal, and I had a plan to take things even further.

Over the five years since Ford installed the GE unit, the company had difficulties persuading their thousands of engineers to use the technology. Like most people during that period, Ford engineers preferred to remain hunched over slide rules rather than have the computer perform the calculations. Part of this resistance was due to simple stubbornness, and part of it was attributed to fears that the computer could eventually replace the engineers at their jobs. The biggest obstacle, however, was simple intimidation, which I had overcome with my ACTS clients using conversational interfaces and games.

As soon as I took control of the GE 265's operation, I installed a series of modifications that included the installation of new, more advanced engineering programs. I also conducted free classes to teach the ease and simplicity of using the computers and provided smaller portable terminals for the engineers to carry home with them on evenings and weekends. Eventually, Ford engineers were clamoring for access to the same computer they had shunned for years. This, of course, made Ford incredibly happy, and made me even happier. Now I had over two thousand engineers using the computer instead of the handful who had been employing it earlier. Whenever a Ford engineer accessed the computer to run a calculation, retrieve data, or play one of the games I installed, whether at the Ford office or in the engineer's home, I could bill Ford for the time. Over the 14-month period between that Monday morning meeting and the day that the Philco 2000 finally assumed all the GE's duties, ACTS billed Ford about $1.5 million for access to the computer they had sold me for $1 million.

It was a breakthrough for my company, but it was not as profitable as it appears. Harvey Goodman, as shrewd as any man with whom I have done business, had seen this possibility as clearly as myself, and knew how to take advantage of it. In my haste to acquire the computer at any cost, I had not reached a final agreement on a fixed monthly lease rate. Under our contract, DPF&G had virtually carte blanche to set any rate they wanted.

Soon, Ford management noticed that my monthly billings to them were exceeding $150,000. This was disturbing enough, but they were appalled to discover that most of Ford's engineers were approaching me instead going to Ford's own computer specialists whenever they had a computer question.

By this time, I had developed close relationships with some of the rising executive stars in Ford's Engineering Management Group. Among the brightest of them was Chuck Missler, who recognized the potential that Ford was finally beginning to realize from its computer installation. Chuck eventually built his computer knowledge into a career that culminated in his rise to the CEO position at Western Digital. That was all in the future, however. At the time, I needed his expertise at ACTS, and I persuaded Missler to leave Ford and join us.

From the beginning, Missler and I began planning to acquire a new Digital Equipment Corporation, a new 36-bit computer that would increase processor speeds by a factor of ten or more. The standard measure of computer speeds was Instructions Per Second, or IPS, and a computer capable of delivering 100,000 IPS was considered state-of-the-art. The DEC, however, set the bar ten times higher, providing 1,000,000 instructions per second, true MIPS design. (As an example of the progress made in computer technology, today's leading-edge computers can function at one billion IPS, a thousand times faster than the DEC system 10.) Acquiring a DEC would propel us ahead of anyone else offering time-sharing services.

The key, as usual, was money. It would take millions to acquire and adapt the new computers. I decided that my entrepreneurial success and Missler's reputation as one of the top managers of engineering technologists could attract investors. The best place to obtain advice on setting up a new company and tapping a source of cash would be a large, highly-regarded law firm, and I began discussing our proposal with several in the Detroit area.

One of the law firms was Honigman, Miller and Schwartz, who expressed interest and dangled the prospect of a deal. Time passed while they supposedly shaped an offer. In reality, as I discovered later, they approached Missler behind my back and eventually lassoed the entire Ford team to carry out the same strategy I had developed. Unable to match either their deep pockets or their technology edge, I could not possibly compete with them, and the failure left me devastated. Had we received the capital that was eventually invested in Cyphernetics, an Ann Arbor company that Schwartz and Missler set up, I could have built ACTS into a powerhouse firm like EDS or Computer Science. Instead, Cyphernetics became an important platform for payroll.

It didn't happen, however. I had to step back and vow to fight and win another day – something that occurred a few more times in later years.

CHAPTER SEVEN

FUN AND GAMES IN DETROIT
YPO – BUSINESS – TYCOONS - TRANS AM CHAMPIONSHIP

My deal with Ford over the leasing of their GE computer marked a major change in all aspects of my life. Our family had grown. We had two daughters, Aleise and Heidi, soon to be joined by Heather.

To accommodate our growing family and reflect the success of my business, Karen and I began an extended move into larger and more expensive homes. Our first house, located in an area of Detroit known as Beverly Hills, had cost $15,000. We sold it for $35,000 and, following the rule of purchasing the lowest-priced home in a high-priced neighborhood, paid $40,000 for our next house, which we soon unloaded for $75,000. Now we were living in Birmingham, enjoying a lifestyle that my parents might have described as The American Dream.

Everything comes with a price, and the price I paid was a near-total focus on building and managing the business. I was spending seven days a week on every aspect of the company – making sales pitches for new business, looking for ways to build revenue, searching for wider applications, hiring and training new staff members to market and manage our services, finding new ways to finance our growth, and staying ahead of the competition. The growth in computer time-sharing became explosive. With the expansion came new pricing pressures, because everybody competed to build the largest client base from the same limited market, slashing rates to secure new business. The emphasis on growth over margins meant that our earnings weren't keeping pace with our size, and many of our accounts were billing about $100 a month.

Meanwhile, I was invited to join the Young Presidents Organization, and I quickly accepted. At the time, YPO consisted of CEO's or presidents under age 50, with companies whose sales exceeded $10 million with at least 50 full-time employees, and who had attained their CEO position by age 44. I was 28 and ACTS certainly qualified in terms of sales and employees.

Membership in YPO was originally limited to U.S. companies, which meant that all 500 or so members had a lot of common interests and concerns. (Today, YPO and its affiliate the World Presidents Organization, number over 10,000 members making them probably the most powerful and influential business organization in the world.) YPO was essentially a Who's Who of American business. Among the people I met through the organization were Bill Agee, CEO of Bendix; Dick Manoogian of MASCO; Heinz Proctor, with American Sun Roof; Bill Farley, who bought control of West Point-Pepperell and Fruit of The Loom, Roger Penske, Mike Rose, CEO of Holiday Inn, Bill Davidson of Guardian Industries and Detroit Pistons and many others. I especially remember Bill Agee and his then-executive assistant Mary Cunningham, whom he soon appointed Vice-President of the company. Even then, it was easy to see that Mary was in control of things. Bill, of course, got into trouble, first through his relationship with Mary and later when he tried to acquire Martin-Marietta, a move that wound up damaging Bendix. Bill Farley became a life-long friend, and Roger Penske played a major role in my career as time passed.

The primary goal of YPO was to provide its members with knowledge, connections, and credibility. Many members, despite the business success they might have gained, still lacked extensive track records with banks. Joining YPO offered instant credibility, opening many doors to expansion and new opportunities.

Monthly YPO meetings were entertaining and informative. Key business and community leaders were invited to speak completely off the record – no media coverage was permitted. The speaker at the first YPO meeting I attended was Henry Ford II, who was candid, open and casual in his talk and in his meetings with other YPO members.

I became a big fan and later managed to meet Hank and his future wife, Kathleen DuRoss, at many social occasions.

Along with the monthly meetings, YPO held annual University for Presidents events, providing wider networking and educational opportunities. The first University session I attended was at the Princess Hotel in Acapulco where guests were greeted by the entire Ringling Bros. and Barnum & Bailey circus. Elephants, lions, clowns and trapeze artists met us when we arrived, and the rest of the weekend proved just as spectacular. When we got down to the business sessions, we heard from experts and panelists on management, marketing, manufacturing, economic forecasting, finance, health, estate planning and psychology.

Breakfasts and lunches at the University featured prominent speakers who fielded questions from the floor. The highlight was a luncheon that pitted the newly elected governor of California, Ronald Reagan, against a young black preacher named Jesse Jackson. At the time, Jackson's position was far more radical than it became in later years. Wearing a massive Afro, he was assertive and outspoken in his left-wing views which, of course, were in direct opposition to the conservative Reagan and to 95 percent of the YPOs. It didn't take long for Jackson to realize he was, politically speaking, in a den of lions and he soon stormed out to the applause of the audience. Other YPO University sessions attracted political heavyweights like Henry Kissinger, who attended while honeymooning after his marriage to Nancy Maginnes, and H. R. Haldeman, Richard Nixon's Chief of Staff through the Watergate saga.

After every YPO University meeting I returned motivated to work both harder and smarter, determined to move my company faster and further in its growth and success. The work, and sometimes play, often involved fellow YPO members, including Roger Penske. Roger had maintained a love for cars, especially racing cars, from his earliest boyhood. While still in university working on his B.A. in industrial management, he was winning races as a driver in the Sports Car Club of America (SCCA), the most challenging race car venue of its day. In 1962 he switched to Formula One cars, racing at Monaco and Watkins Glen, and was named Sports Car Driver of the Year by Sports Illustrated magazine.

At the height of his career, just 27 years old, he retired from driving to open his first Chevrolet dealership, keeping his hand in the racing world by launching Penske Racing, which became a dominant force on the Indianapolis 500, Trans Am, Grand Prix and NASCAR circuits.

Among Roger's circle of friends were two other legends in the industry: John De Lorean and Peter Revson. Years earlier, De Lorean had made such an impact working for Studebaker-Packard that GM offered him a job heading any division he wanted. John chose Pontiac, converting an automobile brand considered a housewives' car into the most sought- after street racer of the mid-1960's. Few American cars made a bigger impact on the U.S. auto-buyers' psyche than the 1964 Pontiac GTO, a car that could turn an honest zero-to-60 time of 4.9 seconds. With Pontiac a clear winner, John moved to Chevrolet, where his influence was responsible for building that brand to its highest achievement: In the early 1970's, GM was selling more vehicles from the Chevrolet division than all of Ford Motor Company's brands combined. Dinners with John were never less than interesting, especially when he was accompanied by Christine Ferrari.

John and Peter Revson, heir to the Revlon cosmetic empire, were the two most attractive and eligible bachelors in the country when they invited me to join them on a weekend sojourn to Los Angeles aboard the GM corporate airplane. During the flight, De Lorean removed a stack of magazines from his briefcase. Instead of sports books or business publications, they were recent copies of Vogue, and John began tearing pages out of the magazines and placing them in a file folder. What the heck was going on?

I found out when we landed at Los Angeles, where we were met by an entourage of representatives from Campbell-Ewald, Chevrolet's advertising agency, complete with limousines to whisk us to our hotel. De Lorean handed the file of magazine pages to an agency account executive as he stepped off the plane. "Here are the girls we want to meet," De Lorean said. "We'll be at the Bel Air." The agency man nodded, and sped off on his assignment, which was to round up as many of the models and actresses shown in photographs on the pages of Vogue as he could locate. John had pre-selected his weekend dates, and sure enough many of the women we entertained over the next few days were either the same women who had appeared in the magazine or their clones. I learned this was a routine assignment for the ad agency representatives, the kind of thing you do when your client is Chevrolet and the annual ad budget is measured in hundreds of millions of dollars. I recall a few surprises during the weekend. The most memorable was the appearance of sultry Ursula Andress, who raised the ambient temperature just by entering the room.

My association with Roger Penske triggered an interest in racing, and when Roger introduced me to Marshall Robbins, I had an opportunity to become personally involved. Marshall's father Jim had founded a seat belt company that produced literally hundreds of millions of seat belts for Detroit over the years. Jim Robbins owned one of the major racing teams at Indianapolis through the 1960's, adding Can Am and Trans am racing teams later. After Jim's death in an aircraft accident, Marshall inherited the family fortune, including the racing teams.

Marshall and I began discussing his interest in continuing the racing activities started by his father. I was especially interested in Marshall's Corvette racing team, which included a team of mechanics, pit crew and other people needed to put the car on the track and win races. Marshall and I formed Robbins-Van Arnem Racing. My primary duties at the beginning included signing sponsors for our car, not as easy as it sounds in the days before auto racing became such a huge spectator sport.

Almost every weekend for the next three years, Marshall and I flew in his Jet Commander to a distant racetrack where we joined the crew, who had driven there in Marshall's large Bluebird motor home. My original plan had been to drive the car in races, but I was putting in a full week running my business with no chance to become a driver at a professional level of skill. Instead, I began acting first as a communications link between Marshall and the crew, and later as full-fledged manager. Marshall was a very bright person, but he could never get "down and dirty" with the guys who built and maintained the cars. I suspect his upbringing as the son of a dominant father in a situation where every desire was fulfilled had something to do with it.

As soon as I assumed management of the team, we convinced Mario Andretti's chief mechanic, a man named Spangler, to join us. At the time, Robbins owned two Indianapolis cars with two skilled drivers of their time behind the wheel: Leroy Yarborough and Sammy Sessions. Now we had a true championship team. Robbins used the Indianapolis Raceway Park to test and maintain our cars. He leased Garage #1, a prestigious location. We also leased Indianapolis Raceway Park. When we did, other race teams had to obtain our permission to use the track for testing purposes, something that Marshall either granted or denied, depending on whether he liked whoever was doing the asking.

In the beginning, Marshall and his money provided the best of everything, along with the able assistance of John DeLorean who was always ready to offer critical parts, such as entire engines and transmissions, at the shortest notice. I began test-driving Corvettes on the track, which was great fun although not as rewarding as racing, of course. During 1973 we never finished out of the top five, running against Porsches and BMWs, and that year we won the Trans-Am championship on points. Along with the championship came the right to designate our car #1 for the following racing season.

Several racing deaths in those years turned many people away from the sport, especially sponsors, and even with Marshall's money and De Lorean's support, we couldn't make things work as well as we wanted. In fact, after 1973 Marshall himself lost interest, and the following year I teamed up with Jerry Thompson, a great Corvette driver, and raced Corvettes for another two years. In 1975 during the Dayton 24-hour event our Corvette was doing well until the 23rd hour when the engine gave out. And so, did my enthusiasm for sponsoring race cars.

VAN ARNEM
TECHNOLOGY PIONEER

CHAPTER EIGHT

BIRTH OF SILICON VALLEY
INNOVATION OF CLOUD COMPUTING
FOUNDING OF BERKLEY COMPUTER CORPORATION

Whenever the term Silicon Valley is used today, everyone knows it refers to a region of California circling the south shore of San Francisco Bay. Communities like Livermore, Cupertino and Palo Alto are basically one-industry towns where everyone is associated with some aspect of the computer business. It's an attractive region of the world, but so are areas of Florida, Colorado, New England and other places. How did this small corner become such a hot bed of cutting-edge computer technology? The answer involves ILLIAC, an advanced computer initially developed by the University of Illinois, and some brilliant and eccentric engineers with whom I became associated in the late 1960's.

ILLIAC was the first university-owned computer when completed in 1960. Five years later ILLIAC IV, developed by the university and the Burroughs Company with funding from the Advanced Research Project Agency (ARPA), was introduced as the largest and fastest computer in the world. Measuring 12 feet square and two feet deep, ILLIAC IV marked a number of firsts in computer design. It was the first non-IBM computer to use circuit-card automation, the first to employ Emitter-Coupled Logic (ECL) integrated circuits, and the first to use multilayered circuit boards on a grand scale. Its operational features appear primitive by today's standards, including a RAM of just 64k, a processor speed of 50 kilohertz, and magnetic disk drives that needed half a second to access stored data. At the time, this was true state of the art, it functioned in the ARPANET Cloud.

ARPA had been created after Russia's launch of Sputnik, the

first artificial satellite, as a "technological engine" to keep the U.S. on the forefront of technology, especially where military applications are concerned. Once ILLIAC IV's capabilities were demonstrated, ARPA moved the computer from the University of Illinois to the Ames Research Center located at Moffet Field near Sunnyvale, California. The computer's two primary functions at Ames were to assist in the development of bomb and trajectory equipment for the Army, and to collect seismic data for the purpose of detecting nuclear blasts and determining their location.

The reason for transporting ILLIAC IV to California was to avoid criticism and controversy about its function. This was during the height of the Vietnam War, when every university campus in the country became a hotbed of protest against anything military, and ARPA correctly assumed that the weapons-testing role of ILLIAC IV would spawn violent protest on the University of Illinois campus. Sunnyvale, although just 50 miles from U C, Berkeley, where the most vociferous military protestors were concentrated, had the protection of Moffet Field, a bona fide military base, where the security facilities could be used to control demonstrators.

With the computer installed at Moffet, the military realized that they had the most advanced hardware available; unfortunately, software to run it was non-existent. The University of California, Berkeley boasted a substantial number of computer programmers among its student body and faculty but recruiting them in 1969 was out of the question. The military avoided any presence on the U C, Berkeley campus, probably the most radical of all during the Vietnam War; signing up people to write computer programs leading to weapons development or anything to do with nuclear technology would have sparked violent riots.

Jesse Quatse discussed the situation with me, especially the need for ILLIAC IV programmers and a possible business role for ACTS. He had already alerted me to the scientific possibilities of computing, one that extended well beyond the strictly manufacturing applications I had been concentrating on to that point. Did ILLIAC represent a new direction for our business. I sent Jesse to California with instructions to offer our company's assistance in the project and perhaps earn a government contract or two. As soon as he arrived at U C, Berkeley, Jesse contacted Mel Pirtle, and together they attracted the attention of ARPA, who had a proposal. Could ACTS manage the development of hardware and software that would enable ILLIAC IV to process a number of Department of Defense applications? {see Wikipedia ILLIAC IV}

We sure could, and I was soon on an airplane to California where we established a business model with Mel Pirtle as Chief and Jesse, Joe and a few others as directors. We were facing a two to three-year development period, the majority of the time directed at selecting and installing storage drives, solving interconnectivity problems, and finalizing a thousand other hardware and software concerns, but ACTS was now the DOD Arpanet manager of the ILLIAC development project.

While in California, Mel, Jesse, Joe and I, along with others, began discussing the idea of greatly expanding the number of on-line clients who could access a single computer. At the time, a maximum of 30 or 40 ports were available in the cloud for simultaneous users on a time-sharing computer. Our objective was to create a data-based cloud accessible computer with 500 ports, representing a major advance. Convinced that our group had the talent to achieve this goal, we created a company to design and manufacture a new computer. We designated it the BCC 500, the "BCC" derived from Berkeley Computer Corporation. I held a 20-percent stake in BCC, which received initial funding of $5 million from Harvey Goodman's company and more than $6 million from the University of California endowment fund, an unprecedented move by U of C.

We hired several dozen engineers to design and create the BCC 500, recruiting many from computer engineering classes at U C, Berkeley, Southern California, Stanford and other schools. First, we created an operating system for the BCC 500, one that would improve the throughput and processing executions of 500 simultaneous users. This wasn't merely a matter of writing codes but of actually creating hardwired printed circuit boards and some of the application programs it supported. We rented a dusty old warehouse in Berkeley where programmers sat at long tables working on printed circuit boards. Following schematics written on a sheet of notepaper, the programmers literally hard-wired the code onto the separate circuit boards. Thus, the PCB's provided faster processing than software code.

The design and concept were good. However, the expense and lack of funding disabled our enthusiasm. Inevitably we ran out of money and were forced to relocate the project. Development of the BCC 500 was transferred to the University of Hawaii, where the computer worked effectively permitting user access to data remotely from computers located anywhere on earth that could access networks.

But I'm getting ahead of myself. First, I had to settle a couple of crises back in Detroit. ACTS was doing well in a changing environment. With competition in the time- sharing sector of the business growing fierce, we began shifting ACTS towards a full-service computer operation. My strongest business ally remained Harvey Goodman, the man responsible for helping me make the breakthrough deal with Ford. That experience bonded Harvey and me in a kind of loose partnership, built informally on trust. I leased all of my time-sharing computers from Harvey in an almost casual manner, and Harvey supported high-risk ventures such as the BCC 500. We liked and trusted each other, and although everything between us was handled strictly according to the book, we didn't spend much time worrying about details. Such as, for example, arranging extensions when the original lease term expired.

Harvey had built his firm into an enormous leasing powerhouse, managing billions of dollars' worth of computer leases with a staff of 17 people. Much of Harvey's success was due to the vision he and I shared about the computer's future as a vital management tool. In Harvey's case, he grasped how computers would accelerate the growth of international conglomerates by transferring data from far-flung subsidiaries back to head office in near real-time. This represented an enormous change in managing remote divisions or businesses. Instead of using data manually produced cash flow, financial status, production volume and inventory levels as they were weeks or even months earlier, management could assess and correct problems in real time (NOW) long before they grew fatal, making remote operations more doable. This development was more responsible for the growth and success of global conglomerates than any single factor and made it possible for companies to grow.

Harvey became so successful at generating profit for Data Processing Financial and General that he began investing corporate cash outside the computer and leasing industry, at one time making an offer to purchase the A&P chain of supermarkets and other large corporations. He may have over-reached, however, because somewhere along the line he made a bad decision, and it cost him his job.

Besides concern for Harvey's well-being – which, as it turned out, shouldn't have cost either of us a minute's lost sleep - I began to worry about my own situation. Harvey and I had done deals on a handshake or over the telephone, and many of my leases were running on a month-to-month basis. How well would I get on with Harvey's replacement?

My concern grew when I learned that the man replacing Harvey as CEO of Data Processing Financial and General Inc. was a dyed-in-the- blue-wool IBM graduate named Archie McGill, who had gained fame as the youngest vice-president in IBM's history. Bright, ambitious and talented, Archie had put all those qualities behind an IBM project known as CP67. I knew about this program because it represented IBM's first serious foray into communications time-sharing, and I followed its development carefully. Basically, an IBM 360-65 computer with a communications controller at the front end, CP67 threatened to vault IBM into a leadership position where broad-based computer time-sharing was concerned.

And it might have, until top brass at IBM decided this was not a business they wanted to develop. It was the interconnect that IBM disliked. IBM wanted to have only their equipment connected which was the ultimate doom of IBM'S dominance, and the entire CP67 project, including all the development staff and its guru and leader Archie McGill, were shut down.

McGill's experience with time-sharing suggested that he and I might cement a working relationship as solid and mutually beneficial as the one Harvey and I had enjoyed. But I also knew that a former IBM VP would insist on running things tighter than Harvey had, which meant he would not tolerate the loose arrangement Harvey and I enjoyed. So, when McGill invited me to New York for a business discussion I flew down uncertain what to expect.

My first reaction when I entered McGill's office was, "Another Roger Penske." Both Archie and Roger had the same athletic build and the same sense of pent-up energy that appeared ready to explode if it wasn't put to use. McGill's most apparent quality was his IBM background. He had started his career in the ivory tower of IBM where everything was structured, and everyone accepted the idea that What's good for IBM is good for the industry. Now he had to deal with the real world, and I suspected he might have difficulty making the transition.

Within minutes of meeting me, McGill suggested we walk while we talked. We rode the elevator down to Park Avenue and walked and talked for three hours, non-stop. Nothing firm was determined, except that we made a connection, on both personal and business levels, to be built upon later. I returned to Detroit impressed with McGill and with generally positive feelings about my future relationship with Data Processing Financial and General, but I still wondered about his ability to shake the "IBM is God" attitude.

A short time later, Archie called and asked for a meeting at my office in Southfield, Michigan. How could I refuse?

Archie entered the office bursting with the same energy he had in New York, but his attitude had changed. New York had been a preliminary bout, not much more than shaking hands. This was the main event.

The first thing I noticed was Archie's refusal to sit down while we talked. I kept asking him to relax and make himself comfortable, but Archie insisted on standing over me as he spoke, as though he were the president of ACTS and I was some middle manager. No matter how I tried to persuade McGill to sit down, relax, and talk with me as though we were equals – after all, I was the CEO of ACTS, not him – he insisted on standing and directing the conversation. This was the IBM attitude coming through, and nothing I could say or do was going to change it.

Two things evolved from that meeting. One was the realization that the chemistry between us was not good and would likely not improve. The other was my decision to assume control of a large computer data center that Harvey Goodman and I had launched as a means of squeezing profit from old computers.

When a mainframe computer came off lease and no immediate buyer was available, Data Processing Financial would open a resource center for short-term jobs, using the off-lease computer. These centers were literally walk-in operations for disaster recovery and back-up of data, the latter service an alternative to companies operating two computers. Customers carried or sent their data to the computer's location and waited for the results. If this seems strange today, when every home computer could leave these mainframe calculators in the dust, remember that no secondary market existed for computers back then. Most corporations leased their computer installations, and few were interested in leasing a three-year-old or a five-year-old machine. What's more, these computers were not easily transported in the trunk of a car. An off-lease computer in Detroit tended to stay in Detroit.

I acquired joint ownership of the DPF centers in Detroit. Their large-scale IBM mainframe computers represented an enormous opportunity to expand our services to include test times, back-up services and disaster recovery. I immediately installed a front-end communications controller and began marketing remote access on-line computing via high- speed terminals, printers and card readers in customer offices. With IBM I couldn't offer custom programs written in BASIC, but I could use hi-speed ATT TELPAKA point-to- point connections, capable of transmitting data at 56 kB per second, compared with the ten character-per-second speed available on teletype lines.

The high-speed terminals, installed along with printers generating 600 lines per minute, card readers capable of doing 300 cards per minute, remote MICR readers to handle demand deposits, and communications controllers, all marked a major advance in technology. Naturally, they came with a high price: telephone line access charges ranged from $10,000 to $25,000 per month. I could find a way to make the operation work, but I needed to get out from under Data Processing Financial and General's wing, and away from Archie McGill's domineering management style. Thanks to Roger Penske, I located a solution.

Roger introduced me to Jamie Williams, who had invested in Penske Corporation over the years. A solid member of the Detroit establishment, Jamie and I connected on a personal level from the start. Jamie introduced me to the president of Lear Siegler Inc., which recently had acquired American Metal Products.

Lear Siegler eventually expanded into an international conglomerate, but when I was first associated with the firm its annual sales were less than $500 million. The computing services provided by ACTS enabled the company to launch and complete an aggressive expansion program, acquiring dozens of companies within a relatively short time. Through the 1970's, Lear Siegler grew from a group of 20 companies into a giant firm comprised of over 300 operations and divisions with annual sales exceeding $5 billion.

Like most companies involved in acquisitions, Lear Siegler presented itself to the newly acquired firm as a white knight, prepared to offer management nearly full autonomy in their day-to-day operations. The new member of the Lear Siegler family was assured that the parent firm was pleased with the way management ran things and would interfere as little as possible in future operations. This may or may not have been true, but Lear Siegler management refused to rely on trust alone. They wanted an insight into the day-to-day operations of its divisions, and I provided the window. My firm would be introduced as the Facilities Management arm of Lear Siegler. Our stated mission was to help management of the various divisions to optimize their efficiency where computers were concerned. That was the cover story. Our actual goal was to eliminate the existing division computers and replace them with high-speed terminals connecting division and subsidiary offices to Lear Siegler's computers, providing head office management with access to real-time data on each division's operations. The process was like performing an operation on the company's spinal cord, diverting all of its computer calculations to a new location.

This often-involved stealth tactics on our part. In some cases, we would enter the division offices at night, disconnect the existing computers, and install new terminals with connections feeding directly back to Lear Siegler. When the division managers and subsidiary presidents discovered the changeover, they would call Lear Siegler in panic and anger.

"Van Arnem and his people came in here and changed our entire computer system!" they would practically cry over the telephone. "I'll have him arrested. I'm calling the police!"

As agreed, ACTS and I would be painted as the bad guys in this scenario.

"Did he do that?" the Lear Siegler people would say. "Van Arnem must be crazy. We're after standardization and efficiency, but this could be going too far. Just calm down, don't call the police, and I'll see what I can do."

After hanging up the telephone, the same Lear Siegler executive would call me, congratulate me on a job well done, and identify two more computers to be changed the following week. Then he would gleefully access the computer located in the complainer's office to check on cash flow, inventory, receivables, and other data that had been unavailable until then.

By 1972, our computer services were covering five market sectors, and we were pioneering our way in all of them. We added banking to time-sharing, becoming the only independent computer company in the state capable of providing full banking services, a distinction that later proved disastrous. We were also providing computer services for manufacturing operations on service bureau leases, leased programs, accounting services for franchised and chain outlets including 1500 independent gasoline stations across the mid- west, and resource management for clients who needed computer technicians to assess, specify, procure, install and manage data processing departments.

Thanks to this rapid expansion and an emphasis on client satisfaction, ACTS was rated #17 out of the top 1000 computer firms in the nation in 1972, barely three years after I founded the firm. I was making everyone happy, except for one company that was growing uneasy and envious over our success. Unfortunately, that company was my computer supplier.

Included in my agreement with Data Processing Financial was a clause permitting them to convert my lease payables to them into stock in my company whenever my debt exceeded a certain level. This hadn't been a problem in the past because I was diligent in controlling my A/Ps. It became impossible, however, when DPF announced without warning that they were tripling my lease payments, instantly increasing my debt level to the point where Archie McGill and his people could convert my debt to them into 50 percent of ACTS, essentially controlling my company.

It was a clever move, but it was too transparent. The unannounced tripling of the lease rates tipped me off, and by the time six well-dressed henchmen from DPF arrived in my office on a Thursday morning, I was ready.

Crowded into my office, the leader of the DPF team made his pitch. "You owe us too much money," he said, "and our management has no desire to continue working with you while you head this firm. We intend to assume control of this company, as of today."

"I'm prepared to settle the amount right now," I offered. And I was.

Their response was predictable. They didn't want payment. They wanted the company. And they were determined to get it.

I guess they expected me to call my lawyer, throw a tantrum, or plead for them to just go away, but I did neither. I reached into my desk drawer and removed the keys to the building. "It's all yours," I said. Then I picked up my briefcase, walked out of my office and announced to my staff of about sixty employees, who had been expecting this to happen, that DPF owned the company and I was leaving. Just as we planned, every last one of the employees left with me.

This sounds clever and audacious more than thirty years later, but at the time it was the most difficult thing I had ever done. I felt like a mother walking away from a new baby, leaving it alone on the side of the road.

The gamble paid off. Within a few days the DPF henchmen contacted me, we negotiated a buy-out figure, and I agreed to pay the outstanding debts within six months.

Where did the money come from? Lear Siegler. They had been interested in acquiring a controlling position in ACTS for some time. Either I relinquished my company to DPF, or I sold a majority of shares to Lear Siegler, my largest customer. Either way, I would lose control of ACTS, but at least I was able to choose between two devils.

With that crisis behind me, I resumed building ACTS into the powerhouse company I believed it could be. Our expansion program included assuming responsibility for the aerospace computing network for Lear Siegler, a major player in the space program at the time. Soon we had about 2000 employees, offices in Grand Rapids and Santa Monica, California, and a projected annual income of $100 million. In today's dollars, that would be something over half a billion dollars, and I had just turned 30 years of age.

One of our competitors was Ross Perot, whose Electronic Data Systems (EDS) operation was aggressively expanding in Michigan. Ross and I battled toe-to-toe selling banks and manufacturing operations on our respective facilities management services, which involved assuming full control over all computer operations. I'm proud to say that the only battle we lost to EDS was for Kent Bank, a mid-sized firm in Grand Rapids. With Kent, Perot basically wallet-wiped us by offering trips in his private jet to key employees along with other inducements. We managed to sign about 30 other banks in Michigan, however, and in half of those instances we won out over EDS.

Meanwhile, things in California were accelerating in scope and opportunity. Many of the people we recruited for the ILLIAC project went on to help change the world through computerization. One of them, Larry Roberts, was instrumental in development of ARPANET, precursor of the Internet. ARPANET was originally conceived as a means of transmitting data between computer engineers and operators at various universities, and it is generally acknowledged that Larry's high standards enabled the limited network to grow into the powerhouse it is today.

Larry was impressed with the staff we had assembled in what was to become Silicon Valley to develop BCC 500, by this time much larger in number than we needed. Larry and Mel Pirtle proposed assigning the BCC group to work on the ILLIAC project. The payment they received from the federal government lifted some of the salary and overhead burdens from BCC, which was quickly running out of money, and enabled us to keep the team together for at least a while.

Things were coming together. The Institute for Advanced Computation, where Mel was Director, became a software developer assigned to ILIAC IV, and ACTS was named as the program administrator. We had two projects running in parallel, and among our first duties was to move BCC programmers out of the Berkeley warehouse and into new facilities in Sunnyvale, launching the first software development operation in Silicon Valley.

The ILLIAC IV program grew so complex that it demanded we recruit and relocate more programmers, and within a few weeks we had over 60 former advanced mathematics and electrical engineering students first learning the basic of programming and eventually applying their talents to writing the programs. It was a "learn as you go" operation, and the new programmers quickly realized they were on the ground floor of an industry that would soon revolutionize the world. Before the actual programs could be written, we had to create the computer operating system. Like all the programs, it was hard-wired in registers, since no functional means of storing and immediately accessing data existed for the ILLIAC.

From the first day I met the programmers in Sunnyvale, I was struck by a sudden realization: The federal government could not have hired these people. In every case, the student programmers were revolutionaries in more ways than one. Most of them looked like audience members at a Grateful Dead concert; some looked like the Grateful Dead band itself. Their dress, their mannerisms and their habits represented the counter-culture of the period – anti-military, suspicious of authority, and dedicated to the delights of sex, drugs and rock 'n roll. They worked to the music of Janis Joplin, Jim Morrison and Jimi Hendrix, and when we weren't expressing concern about marijuana smoke drifting through the offices, we were expressing shock at the use of the communications room for quick sex.

We soon learned to overlook these concerns, or as much as we could, because the programmers were proving successful at their work. Besides, we were facing other problems. Chief among them was the question of how to store all the data that would pour into the computer. Hard-wiring the read-only programs made sense, but the ILLIAC would be receiving enormous amounts of seismic information collected from nodes located around the world and down-loaded from satellites, which would feed the computer. How could all this information be stored in an easily accessible manner?

Magnetic storage was the solution, using disks, tapes and cards, but their design and integration to enable the cloud accessibility, was as primitive and limited as the computer. Two nuclear physicists worked for some time on a vertically mounted disk that failed to work due to the pull of gravity on its molecular structure, a phenomenon no one had encountered before. Eventually, a Michigan company called Bryant Disk file developed a horizontally mounted disk six feet in diameter to hold about 10 megabytes of data. The disk spun like a jet turbine, and I always suspected that a major disk failure would spew shrapnel all over the lab, something that actually occurred with a Bryant installation at Ford. Fortunately, no one was injured from the Ford incident, and the disk we used managed to stay in one piece. Later, we installed magnetic cards called race units, which were read-only storage devices with massive (for their time) densities.

My involvement in the operation involved assessing and procuring materials, which meant ACTS became a qualified government supplier, and I was granted top-level security clearance by the Department of Defense. Neither I nor ACTS could have obtained this position without our association with Lear Siegler, a major defense contractor.

It proved a profitable venture for me, for ACTS and for Lear Seigler. Our contract with the government rewarded us with costs plus a fixed fee, an arrangement practically unheard-of today. In addition to the cost-plus fixed fee of 7%, we were also paid as the purchasing agent for all hardware and software we were paid a three- percent commission for all the hardware and support materials I obtained. The contract billed in excess of $100 million and one of the largest commercial and government computing contracts awarded at that time.

This concentration of activity, and the laissez-faire attitude we took to many of the programmers' habits, had an effect on the neighborhood. Programmers began inviting friends and colleagues to check out the area, and most of them were as bright, ambitious and rebellious as the programmers. Eventually a critical mass of highly intelligent people capable of seeing and shaping the computerized future were living and working in this small corner of northern California. When they began launching their own firms associated with computers, the snowball kept building and soon anyone seriously considering entering the computer industry looked first at the southern end of San Francisco Bay, the greatest concentration of computer technologists in the world. It still is, and it all began with the relocation of BCC 500's staff from Berkeley to Sunnyvale in Silicon Valley.

CHAPTER NINE

FDIC MICHIGAN BANKING BAILOUT

Things might have been fascinating in California, but back in Detroit at the ACTS offices they were drifting from complex to fatal.

Our leadership position in providing computer services to banks offered an opportunity to become a leading provider in the industry. It also became a nightmare that I could never have foreseen.

The disaster began with a late-night telephone call to my home from the state commissioner of banking. The Michigan commissioner, a man named Briggs, had just met with the comptroller of currency. Both had agreed to shut down, without notice, all thirty branches of the Bank of Commonwealth in response to the actions of a man named Donald Parsons.

Michigan, along with other states, had unique laws to control banking activities. At the time, Michigan law limited banks to one main office and a fixed number of branches operating within the state. The goal of this law was to prevent large banks controlling a community's financial services while ignoring the individual needs of local customers. Small, locally owned banks, the theory went, would be more sensitive and offer good lending practices to local businesses.

Parsons created a series of limited partnerships to acquire regional banks across the state, all operating under the umbrella of COMAC, a company Parsons controlled. COMAC charged the newly acquired banks above-scale management fees, sucking out the profits and leaving the branches tottering financially. This was serious enough, but when the commissioner refused to allow Parsons to open banks in the Bahamas and other Caribbean countries, Parsons launched a lawsuit against Michigan. That's when the Fed came down hard on him and his limited partnership.

Parsons had consolidated the bank's computer operations with Computran's. The commissioner decided that Computran's association with the banks should end immediately, and I was asked if ACTS were willing to take over the data processing services for all the COMAC banks. Naturally, I agreed, and literally overnight we assumed control banking services for the banks, handling them through our own processing center. We installed code-reading machines that would record data from the magnetic ink characters at the base of every check and transmit the data to us. From there we processed demand deposits, savings transactions, installment loan payments and other banking information, distributing them to the branches through remote high-speed printers installed at our expense.

The initial takeover went as seamlessly as could be expected given the size and complexity of the operation and the short time we had to construct and install the system.

We wanted to retain the existing bank management and staff, but when the banks were immediately offered for sale, the bank employees grew understandably concerned. Unsure of their future and facing the prospect of working for an entrepreneur prepared to demand higher efficiencies, they worried about their job security and the chance that their benefits would be reduced or vanish entirely. Many bank employees decided to look elsewhere for work, their positions filled with younger people and, in some cases, ACTS employees.

This presented its own problems, but the worst was yet to come. Whenever one of the banks in Parsons' chain was sold, the purchase agreement included a freeze on all contracts dating back to Parsons' ownership. I expected this, but I did not expect that the new owners, checking over all the consolidation and distribution of cash handled by Parsons, assumed at least some of it had been spent to prepay the computer and data services ACTS was providing. Those who did refused to pay our invoices.

I had been both flattered and excited by the commissioner's

request to become involved in this project. His selection of ACTS and the trust he displayed in providing virtually a free hand in choosing how to deal with the complex situation brought enormous prestige to our company. Unfortunately, prestige does not equal profit, and in my agreement to assist the state I neglected to ask a basic question: Who would pay ACTS for our services? At the time, it appeared obvious: The banks had been paying Computran, and now they would pay us.

ACTS had performed services as required, and we expected to have our invoices honored. I needed the money to pay my employees for the work we had done and cover the cost of all the equipment and programs we had installed. When the banks refused to pay their bills, claiming they had already paid Parsons and Computran for computing services, I tried explaining our position to them and to the state. We were providing services in good faith, and it was unfair to make ACTS a casualty in the battle between the old owners, the news owners, and the bank commissioner. None of this appeared to have any impact.

Direct requests sent by ACTS to the banks were phrased in the usual strong language from somebody who is owed a substantial amount of money and wants the debt settled quickly. Essentially, the letters stated that I was prepared to "pull the plug."

When no one appeared to be listening and our unpaid invoices kept piling up, I took the only action left and ceased providing services. Overnight, the banks were unable to process checks and deposits along with all the other functions we had been providing, and dozens of banks across the state were forced to shut their doors until the dispute was settled. Timing is everything, and in this case my timing couldn't have been worse. My decision to cut off services to the banks was made just a few days before Lear Siegler, headquartered in California, held a board meeting in Detroit. Lear Siegler took pride in its image as a gentlemanly company in spite of the way it had hired me for the role of bad guy when I made clandestine moves to switch over computer systems in newly acquired subsidiaries – which underlines how much Lear Siegler wanted to be seen as Good Guys.

When several bank owners heard about the local Lear Siegler board meeting, they bombarded the chairman of Lear Siegler, threatening a class-action lawsuit that would besmirch Lear Siegler's carefully polished reputation.

The result was instantaneous. Lear Siegler ordered me to retreat. They would not tolerate the bad publicity that was likely to occur when a group of local bankers, already reeling from the actions of Parsons and the state commissioner of banking, were being abused by a division of a multi-billion-dollar corporation located out of state.

I could not believe what I was hearing. Until that moment, I had received nothing but accolades from Lear Siegler. ACTS had been a jewel in their empire, and I had been a key player in their entire operation. Now I was being criticized for insisting that my company and I deserved to be paid for our work.

While trying to deal with this stunning news, I learned that I was about to be sold down the river by one of my own people. During our expansion program, I had brought Robert Michelini on board, giving him five percent of the company and naming him executive vice-president. Michelini was ambitious and aggressive, which I liked. He was also devious, which I did not appreciate, especially when I learned that he had been undercutting me with Lear Siegler for some time, feeding them untrue stories about my management abilities and values. This, naturally, encouraged Lear Siegler to take a tough stand with me when the bankers complained, and also provided them with someone they could insert into my position as ACTS president.

The entire episode was sickening. I was amazed that Lear Siegler could turn on me for trying to run my company in a business-like manner, and shocked that Michelini could be devious enough to promote himself into the chair I had been occupying. I had built ACTS out of nothing more than vision and sweat, and now it was being taken from me. I could have fought hard to retain my position and my company, but I was tired and disillusioned. I just wanted to end the disappointment.

I resigned from the company, sold my ownership in ACTS and

walked away clutching a million-dollar settlement. Just a few years earlier, I had been focusing on having enough cash to survive from one month to another. Now, in pre-inflation dollars, I had enough money to get me through the rest of my life, if I invested it wisely and lived off the earnings.

But that, of course, was out of the question.

CHAPTER TEN

RACETRACKS - NASCAR

I was ten years out of college and living in Bloomfield Hills, arguably the most appealing neighborhood in the Detroit area, with my wife and four children. I also had a million dollars in the bank. This was the American Dream, and of course I wasn't happy at all. I needed more in my life than playing golf and trading stocks, and I thought I found the solution when I was introduced to Jeff Pierce through the YPO.

Jeff, who looked and acted like the classic Mr. Success, ran a company called Fireplace Corporation of America, a franchised operation that appeared to be profitable. One day a representative from the small local bank I dealt with called to suggest a proposition. Pierce had recently approached the bank looking for some capital for his company. The bank wanted to do business with him, but it was not happy with the security he offered for the loan.

"You know Jeff through YPO," the bank representative said to me. "If you sign your investments as collateral for his loan, he'll pay you interest above the market rate on the guarantee, plus a $2000 monthly management fee." It was offered as a can't-lose proposition, especially with the bank as my partner.

I liked Jeff, I trusted the bank, the interest rate and management fee looked attractive, so I agreed to the deal. This, of course, made Jeff my best buddy. Jeff's company was sponsoring a NASCAR vehicle and soon I was traveling to Atlanta with him to attend a race Jeff had been invited to start. There I was at the start line, watching my investment partner wave the green flag to start the race, and there was Jeff's sponsored car roaring past, driven by Benny Parsons, one of the hottest drivers in the business. I spent the day rubbing elbows with people like Richard Petty, Cale Yarborough, and the rest of those good ol' boys. It was one of those days that shines in your memory, although it wouldn't have been shining quite so brightly if I had known that everything from Benny Parsons' helmet and car to the fuel poured into the vehicle's gas tank was being paid for with my money.

I returned home elated because I had acquired both a good buddy and a good investment. I was wrong on both counts.

About two weeks after arriving home from Atlanta, my first payment from Jeff was due. When it didn't arrive, I called to ask about the status of my loan and received nothing but excuses and assurances. Ninety days later, I heard the inevitable news: Pierce had filed for bankruptcy, and the prospects of recovering any of my money from him or his company were practically non-existent. The bank, of course, called the note I had signed, aiming to wipe out half of my entire life savings.

I suppose I could have traveled the legal route as I did at ACTS, hoping some assets would turn up. Or perhaps I might have considered it just another expensive lesson, as my father had when his partner absconded with the mortgage money many years earlier. I rejected both alternatives in favor of direct action. The bank president, a man named Bud Stoddard, was a neighbor of mine in Bloomfield Hills. Stoddard, I heard, held board meetings in his Bloomfield Hills headquarters every Saturday morning. The Saturday after I received news that I stood to lose every penny of the loan to Stoddard's bank, I went to the board meeting determined to explain my problem and express my dissatisfaction with the bank's treatment of me.

Stoddard looked appropriately surprised when I entered the room where he had been presiding over the bank's board of directors, a group of upstanding local citizens. "What can I do for you, Harold?" he asked when I barged into the meeting.

"It's about my half-million dollars that you want to cover Pierce's loan," I said. "You guys put me into this deal. You told me I could trust Pierce, and you sold me the idea so you could make some money and avoid any risk. Now it's gone bad and you're demanding all my assets to cover the loan you sold me. That's wrong, and I want my five hundred thousand dollars back." The board appeared confused and Stoddard looked embarrassed, but in front of all those witnesses he agreed to look into the matter and get back to me on Monday morning. Stoddard did not discuss the matter any further with me, but when Monday arrived the bank returned all of my money, exactly as I had demanded.

Stoddard and I never discussed the matter again, although we encountered each other at various social functions. I always considered him a good guy, someone who, with a little strategic prodding from me, demonstrated good business ethics.

Sometime later, I became friends with a local baseball hero named Charlie Gehringer. In our age of athletes who chase bigger salaries as hard as they chase the ball, Charlie stands out as a special kind of guy. He spent his entire career, from 1924 to 1942, playing second base for just one major league team: the Detroit Tigers. During that period, he was an AL all-star for six years in a row, won the MVP award in 1937, and never hit under .300. In fact, Charlie Gehringer was so steady his nickname became "The Mechanical Man," an unfortunate title since he was one of the warmest guys I ever met.

Charlie was a member of the Bloomfield Hills Country Club, the most exclusive club in Michigan. All the GM, Ford and other top executives belonged to Bloomfield Hills, so besides being a great place to play golf and enjoy meals, it was the best place to meet the people who ran the automotive industry.

Charlie assured me that his sponsorship practically guaranteed I would be accepted as a member at Bloomfield Hills, and with his status as a genuine local hero I never doubted it. But soon after my name was submitted with Charlie Gehringer's endorsement, I learned I had been blackballed. I could never prove who blocked my membership, but I have long had my suspicions. More than my own disappointment, I felt embarrassed for Charlie, who had promoted me with so much confidence.

Over the years since, the blackballing incident has become more amusing than upsetting, but my success at challenging the bank has grown more remarkable with time. It could never happen today. Banks had little soul back then and they have even less today. To succeed as I did in demanding that a bank act with integrity and responsibility would be as difficult in the current banking environment as flying to Europe by flapping my arms.

VAN ARNEM
TECHNOLOGY PIONEER

CHAPTER ELEVEN

HELLO HOLLYWOOD

With my investments back in my pocket, or at least in another bank, I looked around for other ways of keeping busy and maintaining a lifestyle that neither I nor my family wanted to abandon.

One of the ways I kept busy was through my first foray into the movie business. Nothing I had ever seen on television or in movies to that point had captured the speed, the thrills and the danger of racing.

I was introduced to Claude du Boc, a French film director who had the idea of shooting a feature film on Formula One drivers that would capture the sense of speed that drivers experienced and the dangers they faced. He and his producers obtained permission from FIA to mount 70 mm film cameras on Formula One cars in competition. This was a breakthrough, not only for racing but for feature films generally. Among the famed drivers who agreed to participate were Nicki Lauda; Jody Schecter; Jackie Stewart; Francois Cevert, who had been Jackie Stewart's racing partner; Mark Donahue, a driver for Roger Penske; Mike Hailwood; and Peter Revson, whom I had met on that weekend in Los Angeles with John De Lorean. Actor Stacy Keach was signed to narrate the action.

I invested in the production, and the movie that du Boc produced was both spectacular and tragic. During the filming at least four leading drivers were killed – Cevert, Donahue, Hailwood and Revson – along with an emergency worker and some spectators. The production was released as The Quick and The Dead, later retitled One by One. It is still among the best movies ever made on racing (a DVD was recently issued, this time called Champions Forever) and was the last feature produced by Columbia in 70 mm format. Many of the fatalities that occurred during the shooting were captured on film, making it difficult for some people to watch even to this day.

Bad luck dogged the film all the way through to the distribution deal when it was scheduled to open after another exciting movie. Unfortunately, that movie happened to be Star Wars, which blew everything else off the stage that year. We signed a contract with HBO to show The Quick and The Dead within 52 weeks of signing the deal, but when Star Wars played for 55 weeks, extending beyond the 52-week term, HBO showed it as a new release and wiped out all of our distribution plans.

The Quick and the Dead was the last 70 mm feature released by Columbia and the first to display the studios "sunburst" logo that remains in use today. Larry Spangler, a well- known Hollywood producer and publicist, was involved in the movie. Before The Quick and the Dead, Larry's productions included The Life and Times of the Happy Hooker and Joshua, starring former NFL player Fred "The Hammer" Williamson. Not exactly Academy Award material.

The racetrack film footage proved spectacular, and all of us associated with the movie believed it would win an Academy Award for best documentary. Unfortunately, documentaries are considered box office failures by Hollywood, and Columbia insisted on releasing it as a feature, which meant we competed with every big-budget production of that year.

For the film's premier, the studio set up screenings in Houston and Sacramento in January 1975, a period when I was spending time in Los Angeles with actor George Hamilton. I talked George into coming with me to Sacramento for the screening, where we would be joined by Spangler and Stacy Keach. George, an avid and experienced skier, suggested we stop at Tahoe on the way, get in a day or two of skiing, then drive to Sacramento from there. Before I could express my one serious reservation, George was on the telephone inviting Gray Fredrickson, who had been a producer on several major films including The Godfather numbers One and Two, to join us. He and Frederickson suggested that Rod Stewart and an entrepreneur named

Jim Randall join us.

My serious reservation to George's suggestion that we go skiing was pretty basic: I had never been on skis before. Didn't know the first thing about it. Instead of suggesting to George that this was not such a good idea from my point of view, I began convincing myself that I could probably ski after all. How hard could it be to slide on two pieces of wood down a hill? I was in good physical shape, the same guy who had made all-star teams in football, basketball and baseball. I had good balance, eye-and-hand coordination and lots of confidence. A few minutes of watching everyone else and I was sure to pick up the technique. Or so I told myself.

I had encountered Rod Stewart at Hollywood nightclubs favored by George Hamilton, especially Roxy's on the Sunset Strip. Rod had just broken up with Britt Eckland, and George often brought along his wife Alanna. Rod and Alanna seemed to enjoy each other's company and as things worked out, they eventually married.

A certain aura gathers around people like George Hamilton, Rod Stewart and other celebrities when they appear in public together. Other stars gravitate towards them, and at places like Roxy's we were soon joined by people such as Warren Beatty, Jack Nicholson, Barbara Carrera and others. I especially remember Barbara Carrera. Tall, elegant and stunningly beautiful, she had eyes that seemed as deep as the Grand Canyon. On one of our evenings hitting nightclubs on the Strip, a Star Magazine photographer snapped her and me as we emerged from a taxicab in front of Roxy's. The picture appeared in the next issue causing, as you can imagine, serious problems between me and my wife back in Detroit.

Rod Stewart was as witty as George Hamilton during these outings, tossing lines back and forth to keep everyone laughing. I also remember that he carried himself like an athlete, and in fact he was a great soccer fan and, as I understand it, a pretty fair player as well. I was never as close to Rod Stewart as to George – just close enough to see the star quality that they both exhibited.

At Tahoe, we were all fitted with equipment and introduced to

"Wild Bill" O'Leary, the amateur freestyle ski champion. Standing about 5 foot 10 inches with a full beard and shoulder-length hair, O'Leary had the strength of a bull and, when he was on skis, the grace of an antelope. When Hollywood needed a stunt man for the ski slopes, Bill was the first one they called. The five of us – George, Gray, Rod, Bill and me – set out for the slopes followed by a herd of athletic young ladies prepared to join us on the downhill runs.

Everyone who skis remember their first day on the slopes, and mine was no different – except, I suppose, that I had more confidence in my abilities than others. Even this began to fade as we rode the lift to the top of the hill. I might have been fooling myself and everyone else around me, but I wasn't fooling Bill O'Leary. He sensed my discomfort and stayed close to me as we approached the Black Diamond, the most challenging of all the runs. Barely pausing at the lip of the hill, George shouted, "Let's go!" and everyone pushed off the edge. Including me.

The others began traversing the steep drop, doing smooth parallel turns back and forth across the face of the mountain. I, of course, dropped straight down the hill like a snowball, totally out of control. Behind me I could hear Bill O'Leary shouting "Stop! Fall down!"

Falling down slowed my speed a little perhaps but I was just as out of control as ever. Skis, arms and legs began flailing everywhere, and before I stopped, I was convinced I would leave parts of my body on the hill. Finally, I came to rest. Surprisingly, everything remained attached. I wasn't even suffering a concussion, although my embarrassment level was high. I spent the rest of the day on the beginner's hill with Wild Bill O'Leary skiing backwards to support and instruct me. I've been an avid skier ever since, enjoying the winter breaks with my family at our chalet in Colorado.

Larry Spangler had performed great P.R. work to generate wide press coverage for the premiere in Sacramento, especially when he mentioned that Rod Stewart and George Hamilton would be attending. Everything went well, with one exception. Stacey Keach, who had done a great job narrating the film, checked into his hotel room – and never came out. The movie press met everyone but him. Nobody confirmed this, but we suspected Stacey spent the two days locked in his room not with some young starlet but with a good supply of nose candy. The reviews were generally good and, on the way, back to Los Angeles we stopped for a few days in Tahoe to resume our skiing vacation. This time the sport looked less like a means of suicide and more like a great form of fun and recreation to me.

Much of the praise for The Quick & The Dead was aimed at the director, Claude Du Boc. A very cool guy, Claude might have had a long and profitable career in Hollywood. Instead of finding his fortune in movies, however, Claude saw faster (and bigger) profits in marijuana. Apparently, he accumulated nearly half a billion dollars in dealing the drug before being arrested. He retained F. Lee Bailey to represent him, but Bailey lost two ways: his client du Boc went to prison, and Bailey served six months in jail for dipping into du Bloc's assets without authorization.

CHAPTER TWELVE

BONITA SPRINGS DISCOVERED AND THE FOUNDING OF COMPUTER LEASING WITH MERRILL LYNCH GM AND WESTERN SOUTHERN INSURANCE CO.

My investment in the racing movie produced a good deal of fun but no profit. For that, I explored opportunities in Florida.

A few years earlier, I had met a Pontiac, Michigan lawyer named Chris Powell, who invited me to inspect both a natural phenomenon and a potential investment. Several years earlier, in 1960, Hurricane Donna had swept across Florida between Ft. Myers and Naples, almost wiping out the small town of Bonita Springs and creating a new point of land on the north end of the beach. The land had been when sand was whipped against the shore by the winds. Over the years, the point served as a foundation for other sand carried against the shoreline by wave action, building the point to an impressive size.

Arriving at Ft. Myers, I began questioning Chris's wisdom. In 1969, the Ft. Myers airport looked more like a saloon out of a Hollywood western. I managed to rent a car and drove south to Bonita Springs, which was even less impressive. Most of the population of Bonita Springs were itinerant field workers who resided in the area while waiting for the next crop of fruits and vegetables to be ready for harvesting.

The beach was beautiful, however, and the new point of land sat empty and undeveloped. Chris purchased the 6-acre waterfront site for about $200,000. I kicked in 25,000, making me a 15 percent partner. Chris assumed responsibility for developing the land, and between 1972 and 1975 we built about 300 condominium units and a commercial strip development for the residents.

Everyone has jokes and sad stories about Florida real estate, but my experience was positive and rewarding. Instead of taking a piece of the commercial development profits, I chose some vacant building lots that spiraled in value. Later, I purchased the airport at Punta Gorda for $80,000, and before the deal closed, I had flipped it for $350,000. Hey, this was fun – so much fun that I moved my family there, buying one of the condominiums in Bonita Beach for a mere $25,000. Today, the same condo is valued at $1 million or more.

I enrolled the children in the Bonita Springs grade school and sat back to watch the sun set over the Gulf of Mexico each evening. What followed was relaxing, rewarding... and the most boring year of my life.

The only business with any action in the area was buying and developing land, and I joined in, motivated as much by the need to shake off boredom as make profits. I purchased a few hundred acres and developed them into a light industrial park and an RV camping facility.

I needed something more than Florida land development to maintain my interest, so I approached John Steffens, manager of the Detroit branch of Merrill Lynch. Steffens, whom everybody called Launny for some reason, was a rising star at Merrill Lynch, the youngest branch manager in the company and an absolutely brilliant stock trader. He had provided investment advice for about $300,000 of the money I pocketed after selling ACTS to Lear Siegler, and with his help I managed to double the amount within a year. You could tell Launny was headed for the top almost as soon as you met him and Launny did, rising all the way to the chairman's job at Merrill Lynch.

Through all of this time I maintained my contacts at GM. Within a few months of arriving at Bonita Beach I realized I would want more business action in the future, and the people I knew at GM might provide an entry when I found something to pursue. And they did.

The 1974 oil embargo represented a serious trough in business activity, and Detroit was hit as hard as any region in the country.

Oil shortages, rising interest rates and the first wave of Japanese imports were representing the biggest challenge to the domestic automotive manufacturers since WWII. Most people in the Detroit area were moaning and shaking their heads at the situation. I saw it as a first-rate opportunity.

GM's arrogance in the marketplace was at its highest in those years. About two out of every three cars sold in North America came out of a GM plant, and the company was famous for doing things its way because that's how GM had done things for years. For the most part, GM's policy was to own everything it needed to run the company. Leasing, the theory went, was for small companies with cash flow problems. But by the mid-1970's the company was beginning to experience its own cash flow difficulties, so my timing could not have been better. I pointed out that General Motors did not need quickly depreciating assets like computers on its balance sheet. That was the appeal to GM. The appeal to me was the Investment Tax Credit, which few people knew about and even fewer people were taking advantage of. Under the Investment Tax Credit rule as it existed in 1974, an individual could purchase a computer for $1 million, lease the equipment to another party, and claim an immediate $100,000 tax credit in the first year. A major lease-financing deal with GM would net the leasing company enormous tax-free profits.

I sold GM Purchasing on the idea of leasing their computers and data-processing equipment through a leveraged lease agreement, the first of its kind at the company. With GM on the side as a "hell or high water" guarantor, I went off to find a funding source.

The search took me back to my hometown of Cincinnati where I approached some people I knew at Western & Southern Life Insurance. Life insurance companies are perpetually cash-rich and looking for safe high-yielding investments. That's exactly what I brought them in the form of GM leases and the little-known Investment Tax Credit rule. Here is how the deal worked:

Western & Southern bought AAA investment-grade paper at discounted rates to prime. The GM lease rates included 100 percent repayment of the computer equipment at cost plus a debt rate 100 to 150 points over prime. I sold the leases, picking up the 100 to 150 basis points, plus I owned all the equipment when the lease expired, entitling me to 100 percent of renewal rents and 100 percent of any sale proceeds. What's more, I received 100 percent of the 10 percent investment tax credit, and I was able to accelerate the depreciation rate to produce added tax losses.

"This," the company's portfolio manager said when I laid out GM's side of the deal for him, "is better than a bond!" He was right. In addition to General Motors' participation – and in 1974 no corporation was more blue-chip than GM – we held the computers as collateral.

With Western & Southern providing up to $100 million in cash and me providing the clients and lease management duties. I was back in the business again. Lear Seigler were still running ACTS, and their buy-out of me a few years earlier continued to rankle. That's why I called my new firm The Van Arnem Company. The way I saw it, if somebody stole my company this time, they would have to steal my name as well. Things fell into place in a very big way. I negotiated the first master lease in General Motors history and, in fact, the first master lease with a Fortune 100 company. Under the master lease arrangement, any division of GM wanting to lease a computer or peripheral equipment came directly to me instead of requesting corporate approval. The master lease incorporated terms that corporate had approved, so why bother with repeating the process each time? Everyone loved it – division managers had more control, corporate knew their leases were meeting GM standards, and I was soon managing $100 million in annual leasing from the largest corporation in the country.

Two years later, after I had been handling more than $100 million in leases with GM, its GMAC division invited me to New York on the pretense of providing some financial assistance to my operation. In reality, they wanted to dissect my model contracts and adapt some of the ideas I had pioneered for their own leasing operations.

General Motors was a major breakthrough, but why stop there? I made calls on Dow Chemical and RCA, among others, signing them and other companies to lease-purchase contracts. Each new contract meant an expansion in staff and facilities, and within a few years the Van Arnem Company was among the largest computer-leasing firms in the country.

It didn't take long for others to realize the benefits of the Investment Tax Credit rule, and it took even less time for the federal government to eliminate the benefits in the 1976 tax reform bill. Many people assumed this meant the end of big profits from leasing operations, but they were wrong. Accelerated depreciation opportunities remained in effect, and we structured deals to reap the maximum benefits. We did this by timing annual equity payments to take advantage of accelerated depreciation. With careful planning it was possible to generate write-offs of 5:1 in the first year, 3:1 in the second year, and 2:1 in the third year. This provided only a tax-deferred, not tax-avoidance benefit, which meant the taxes came due at some point in the future. The idea was to properly invest these tax savings over the first three years, generating enough income to offset the taxes and leave a healthy profit.

I kept finding ways to add even more benefits through a complex arrangement employing accelerated depreciation and residual-based financing. When combined with benefits from the Investment Tax Credit rules, while they remained in force, it could generate tax reductions from four to eight times the actual investment. Imagine the appeal of investing $100,000 today and reducing your taxable income by $800,000 tomorrow?

I knew it would work, but I needed independent confirmation, and high-level contacts at Coopers & Lybrand and Touche-Ross, both confirmed it was feasible if the deal were constructed correctly. From there, I went to some bright lawyers and sought their opinion on the legality and structure required. Finally, with both sets of expert opinions in hand, I visited Launny Steffins, my friend at Merrill Lynch, and suggested that his firm market tax-oriented leases to investors.

This was an entirely new idea to Merrill who, except for its real estate arm Merrill Lynch Hubbard, had not strayed from its core business as stockbrokers. Since Hubbard was already involved in financing real estate deals, it seemed like the place to start and Launny introduced me to Les Schoenfeld and Fred Butler, bright and ambitious young guys who loved the concept and agreed to join me as a financing partner. This, to my knowledge, was the first step taken by Merrill Lynch to market capital equipment tax shelters.

We wrapped the full-payout leases into an arrangement that was totally legal under IRS rules yet delivered enormous tax benefits. The deal involved selling the computer to a third party who would sub-lease the equipment to the user over a seven-year term instead of a three-year or five-year term. The investor, thanks to accelerated depreciation plus the Investment Tax Credit rules, would record a write-off equal to several times the original investment. Revenue from the three-year leases was now spread over seven years. Over the same period, you accelerated the depreciation by 250 percent, creating reduced annual lease income and a hefty depreciation during the terms of the lease. The result was a huge reduction in taxes.

The success of these concepts enabled me to build The Van Arnem Company into a powerhouse and altered the face of the leasing industry. Merrill Lynch grew so impressed with the concept that they created M-L Capital, which is now one of the world's largest capital asset financing companies.

I had been commuting back and forth between Florida and Detroit to run things, something I knew couldn't last. Besides, the inactivity in Florida was turning my brain to marshmallow. I had to be back full-time in the middle of the action, and in 1976 I returned to Detroit. The computer industry had matured over the years since I joined GE. Mainframe computers remained, but smaller units located closer to the end-user and far more accessible in operation were becoming the standard. In addition, these "mini-computers" were growing more specialized, with some models created exclusively for scientific applications, and others dedicated to specific non-scientific processes.

The growth brought new manufacturers into the marketplace. IBM remained king, not because of performance advantages but because of the IBM logo on the machine and what it represented to the buyers of off-lease equipment. The key to every leasing deal was the value, if any, of the equipment at the end of the lease. It was difficult to sell used computers from Unisys, Burroughs, Honeywell and other companies, but an aftermarket for used IBM machines always existed, and the buyers were willing to pay market value.

During this period, I learned two lessons that every businessperson needs to absorb at some point in their lives. First lesson: Banks have no soul. My victory over Bud Stoddard's bank a few years earlier was a rarity, achieved mostly because the bank president was a neighbor and I forced a promise from him in front of his own board of directors. Second lesson: Whenever you become involved in a lawsuit, no matter which side of the legal line you are on and how weak or strong your position may be, when you finally get to court the odds become even.

The lessons arrived via one deal I set up with Manufacturers Hanover bank. In 1980, I purchased $20 million in debt from MH, fixed at 11 percent annual interest, and paid a $250,000 commitment fee for the privilege of having the line of credit available. To protect myself, I prudently hired a well-respected law firm to negotiate the deal and produce an agreement that would clearly define the rights and obligations of both sides.

It was a good deal for me because I believed that interest rates were about to rise dramatically, and within a short time they did. Interest rates not only began to take off, they rose faster than any other time in modern history, with annual prime rate levels eventually reaching 22 percent. When the prime started nudging 20 percent, I approached Manufacturers Hanover with leasing contracts worth about $20 million, expecting them to be covered by the debt I had purchased at 11 percent. The 9 percent interest spread, extending over the seven-year leases, represented a potential profit for me (and a loss to the bank) of perhaps $10 million. I approached them with total confidence. After all, I had a commitment letter in my hand that required Manufacturers Hanover to provide me with the money.

But they refused. Time after time I showed them lease agreements based upon the bank meeting its obligation to provide me with funding, and time after time they refused, always finding some reason not to advance the money at the agreed-upon interest rate. With no other way to settle things, I launched a lawsuit charging them with breaking the terms of a legal contract.

I went into the process feeling confident and full of trust in the legal system. I came out of it totally cynical, promising myself that I would never be deluded by contract terms again.

The law firm I had entrusted to draft the contract had done an inept job, but even this might have been corrected if the same firm had been at least capable of conducting an effective lawsuit. They were not. Improper handling of the case by the lawyers, along with a judge who appeared to lack enough business sense to understand the basics of the transaction, doomed our case. I was devastated at the loss, but I took comfort, of sorts, in the lesson I learned. The lesson is this:

Once you launch legal proceedings, you enter a game of chance as unpredictable and risky as anything you might encounter in Las Vegas. The final settlement will be determined by factors that have nothing to do with the merits of your case. Does the judge understand the intricacies of the deal? Will your lawyer choose the correct tactic? Do you have both the funds and the stamina to fight an extended battle? Does the judge like you personally – the way you dress, the way you talk, the way you look? None of these are supposed to have any bearing on a legal decision, but the truth is that they all do.

I was prepared and determined to prove and win my case. Unfortunately, the judge never seemed able to understand our position and an error by my law firm caused us to miss a hearing, which was enough for the judge to dismiss the case. Manufacturers Hanover walked away with millions of dollars that their own contract said had been mine to earn and keep.

Despite problems such as the failure of Manufacturers Hanover to fulfill their obligations, we were proving to be a profitable operation in a highly competitive industry. I was always on the lookout for new opportunities, however, and one of them put me into the air transport business for a while.

Everyone in Detroit was connected to the automotive business one way or another. These connections provided insider news of company problems, which swept through the city like gossip. In the mid 1970's, I heard stories of auto plants shutting down for several hours because a shipment of critical parts had failed to arrive. This was before today's "Just in Time" delivery scheduling and the rise of companies such a Federal Express and UPS. Usually, the problems involved a distant parts supplier to a sub-assembly plant somewhere in the Midwest. Without the critical part, which could be as small as a gear ring or a lubrication seal, the entire plant would grind to a halt at an enormous cost. Even a two-hour delay in delivery of a part worth a few pennies could cost hundreds of thousands of dollars in lost production and overhead. When this occurred, plant managers would scurry around trying to charter an aircraft to deliver even a few hundred of these parts to keep the plant in operation until the full shipment arrived.

"What if I set up an air freight operation to deliver parts on an emergency basis?" I asked one GM executive. He thought it would be a fine idea, and when my bid to secure a contract succeeded, I made a similar pitch to Chrysler, who agreed to sign on. Soon my company Oakland Air was in business, eventually operating a fleet of five Piper Navajo Chieftains, twin turbo-powered aircraft that could quickly be converted from seating eight passengers to transporting a ton or more of freight. I ordered a pressurized version that my family and I could use on weekend flights with one of the company pilots at the controls. I never had any interest in obtaining my own pilot's license.

But I soon developed an interest in something even more risky. Making movies in Hollywood.

CHAPTER THIRTEEN

LOVE AT FIRST BITE
GEORGE HAMILTON

My business achievements were generating interest among various groups and I found myself being invited to speak to their members about computers, time-sharing and leasing benefits. In the mid 1970's one of these invitations came from the College of Financial Planning in Denver, where I flew to attend their annual meeting as keynote speaker.

While there, I had a good conversation with the college founder and mentioned my interest in cable broadcasting and began describing the difficulty of finding suitable shows. My search had taken me to Hollywood on a few occasions, which is where I met with people like Larry Spangler.

"I should introduce you to a friend of mine," the man said. "He's always happy to introduce people to the movie business."

"What is his name?" I asked.

"George Hamilton."

Everyone knew who George Hamilton was, because Hamilton was everywhere – in the movies, on television, and on the covers of glossy magazines, always elegantly dressed, perfectly tanned, and flashing his blinding-white teeth.

I had encountered Hamilton from a distance many years earlier while I was still in high school. Two girls I knew wanted to drive a Triumph sports car to Fort Lauderdale for spring break, but they were concerned about making the drive alone. Would I accompany them, sharing the driving chore? Would you have to ask any 18-year-old boy twice? Once in Lauderdale we separated, and in the midst of other events that week I wandered towards a crowd gathered around a beachfront bar, watching a movie crew and a group of actors. The movie was Where the Boys Are, and the male star was George Hamilton. At the sight of him, girls began crying and shaking hysterically. He was the quintessential young up-and-coming movie star of that period, and every guy on the beach that day envied him. Including me.

By 1975 Hamilton's movie star status had started to fade. Most of his performances were in television productions such as Colombo, Police Story and McCloud. In every other respect, he was still a HOLLYWOOD STAR! He and his wife Alana could be seen attending the glitteriest Beverly Hills events, smiling their brightest smiles at the fans and photographers. I agreed to meet Hamilton, who proved to be as charming in person as he was on the movie screen. This guy, I realized, was smart as well as charismatic, someone who could get anything he wanted from anybody he met. He was so good, I suspected, that even when you knew you were being manipulated, you didn't mind. George proved me correct.

Physically, the man was perfect. He took very good care of his body and appearance. You could not imagine a blemish even daring to mar that ideal skin. The biggest problem Hamilton faced was waking up each day and deciding who he was going to be. He could be anyone he chose or, more important, anyone that others chose him to be for their enjoyment or profit. You want a sophisticated movie star? George is your man. A shy eager- to-please buddy? A smooth-talking womanizer? A hell-raising playboy? A sensitive artist? Hamilton had the whole repertoire at his fingertips. I'm sure other actors have similar abilities, but I doubt that anyone switched roles as instantly, as convincingly and as profitably, for himself at least, as George Hamilton.

Hamilton's marriage was ending, although he and his wife continued to share their house in Bel Aire. The marriage collapse had been triggered by a classic Hollywood event. George and Alana owned similar Rolls-Royces; George's was black, and Alana's was white. One day, after lunching with friends in the Polo Lounge at the Beverly

Hills Hotel, George asked for his car to be brought around, and a valet was sent to "Get the Hamilton Rolls- Royce." A few minutes later, the valet pulled up, not in George's black Rolls but in Alana's white Rolls, which sent George on a hunt through the hotel for her. He found Alana and her lover in one of the small cottages behind the main hotel. I don't know if it was a case of flagrante delicto, but it was clear that Alana and her date, a wealthy European named Flick, were not there to discuss philosophy, and George started divorce proceedings soon afterward.

I assumed George began gravitating towards me because I could be a buddy to help him overcome the stress of his marriage break-up, and we hung out together for a while. Picking him up at his house, I would be stunned some days to see him emerge in a polo outfit. We weren't going to play polo; we were going to have lunch at the Beverly Hills Hotel, or at a little bistro on Santa Monica Boulevard that many of the stars favored. It didn't matter. George wore the polo outfit because he wanted to and, I have to admit, because he looked great in it.

Over lunch, we would be joined by various members of the Hollywood elite including Warren Beatty, Lauren Hutton, Tina Sinatra, Britt Eckland, Marisa Berenson and others. This would be just another normal day. Everywhere George went, excitement seemed to follow him, and he clearly enjoyed every minute of it. Alana treated me well, and I liked her. After their divorce she went on to marry Rod Stewart and bear three of his children.

Did I enjoy hanging out with this crowd? Of course, I did. But I kept my eyes wide open, especially after I expressed interest in financing a movie. That's when I became George's best buddy. George wanted an opportunity to play a lead role in a major Hollywood production, and George always found a way to do what George wanted to do. From my point of view, investing in a feature film looked like a possible way to make some profits and a sure way of having some fun. I agreed to fund a feature movie starring George in a romantic comedy role, and from there everything began rolling like a runaway train. Obviously, we needed a concept and a script, and George suggested Bob Kaufman, who had recently done Freebie and the Bean, Getting Straight, I Love My Wife and Harry and Walter Go to New York.

Kaufman proved to be as brilliant and off-the-wall as Hamilton claimed he was. His first idea was to do a spoof of western movies and Freudian psychology that he wanted to call How the West was Shrunk. When this didn't prove promising, the three of us decided to spend a week in Acapulco where we could stretch Kaufman's imagination and improve George's tan – at my expense, of course. Our first night in Mexico, relaxing over a round of drinks, George began dropping lines in various accents. He knew a number of them, all delivered with convincing style, and when he began speaking with a Romanian accent, someone commented it sounded exactly like Dracula. That's when a light bulb appeared over the heads of all three of us. George Hamilton as Count Dracula – of course! (Actually, I had always believed Kaufman looked more like Dracula, but never mind...) Soon the ideas came pouring out of Kaufman in a stream, prodded by George and me. The film would start by Dracula and his assistant Renfield arriving in New York City.

. "Imagine Dracula showing up at Studio 54 and they won't let him in because he looks too straight," Kaufman suggested. "He's in New York and nobody notices him!"

How would we get him to New York? He would be evicted by the Romanian government, which would seize his castle as a training facility for the Olympics. Why does he choose New York? Because he sees a photo of a beautiful young girl in an American magazine who reminds him of a love, he has pursued over the past 900 years, and she is living in New York City. When he arrives at JFK airport sealed in his casket, it is confused with another casket being shipped to Harlem. Dracula's coffin arrives there in its place and in the middle of the Baptist church service praising the deceased African- American... Well, you get the idea.

Kaufman retreated into his room with his typewriter and emerged three days later waving a first-draft script. As soon as I saw the proposed title – Dracula Sucks Again – I suspected we were in trouble. And we were. The first person I gave the script to for a reading was my 14-year-old daughter Aleise. Big mistake. Kaufman's script was raunchy and perverted enough to earn us an XXX rating if we could release it at all. We sent him back for a complete rewrite, and eventually shaped the movie that became Love at First Bite. Through much of the development, however, we kept the original working title. I often wonder what some of the folks at Bank of America thought whenever they processed my checks made out to Dracula Sucks.

Kaufman's second draft script included sight gags that people who saw the movie still remember. My favorites were when Dracula gets a morning-after hangover from sucking blood from a Bowery wino, and the scene in which Richard Benjamin reaches into his pocket to pull out a cross to defend himself from Dracula and withdraws a Star of David instead.

With an acceptable story in hand, I committed to investing $250,000 in the project. This was enough seed money to prove we were serious, attract the cast we wanted, and attract new investors. Stan Dragoti, an up-and-coming director who came out of advertising and went on to do Mr. Mom and other great comedies, agreed to do the picture. Our original goal had been for Lauren Hutton to play Cindy Sunlight, Dracula's long-lost love. She had other commitments, so we settled for Susan St. James. In the role of Cindy's fiancé and Dracula's sworn enemy we signed Richard Benjamin, who proved perfect. Arte Johnson played Renfield and Dick Shawn was the skeptical detective.

The pace picked up. I was flying to Los Angeles every Friday night, following the progress of the movie through the weekend and returning to Detroit Sunday night. In late July, producer-distributor Joe Cannon agreed to do the movie and sent us a firm letter of intent outlining the details. With production scheduled to begin in the fall, George had a great idea – great for George, that is. "Let's celebrate with a trip to the south of France," he suggested. We could have fun, meet some of George's friends who spent each August there, and maybe create some pre-production publicity. Of course, as the paying partner in the production, I would cover the costs, but I would be repaid out of "first monies," meaning the first income generated by the picture. Or so I was promised.

Well, why not? We were in Los Angeles at the time. I said I needed to stop in Detroit for a day or two, then we would fly to Nice via Paris.

George made a few long-distance calls to France, announcing his imminent arrival, and whatever skepticism I might have had about his influence in Europe vanished when we emerged from the airport at Nice to find a liveried chauffeur guiding us into the longest gold-and-white Rolls-Royce I had ever seen. "Give my thanks to Princess Grace," George said as the Rolls carried us to the famous Hotel du Cap-Ferret. He meant Princess Grace of Monaco, of course. I enjoyed riding in her limousine, but I was disappointed that we never met her during our visit.

It soon became obvious that George was better known and more appreciated in France than in America. Wherever we went, his presence generated energy and excitement, and George thrived on it as though it were the elixir of life. Famous and wealthy people gravitated to his brilliant white smile and his overwhelming charm while I stood nearby, watching the master of schmooze perform with finesse. Sometimes, George would introduce me as his friend or the production partner for his next movie. At other times, I was simply a piece of furniture. Most people, I suspect, believed I was George's strong and silent bodyguard.

One of the people George promised to visit was Brigitte Bardot, who was living in St. Tropez, and after a few days George announced we should travel down the coast to see her. When I suggested we rent a car, George had a better idea, we would charter a boat and sail along the Mediterranean coastline from Nice to St. Tropez. So off we went to find a boat to charter.

We settled on a 50-foot sailboat, which I assumed would be sufficient for a comfortable 25-mile cruise along the Mediterranean shore. Well, it wasn't. August on the Cote d'Azure brings the mistral, a wind that sweeps down from the Alps and swirls in every direction when it encounters the Mediterranean. The trip, which I thought might take two or three hours, took the entire day – ten hours of the worst case of seasickness I have ever encountered. When we finally pulled into the harbor at St. Tropez the setting sun was red, and both George and I were green.

George recovered quickly and was soon posing in his yachting outfit on the deck of the yacht, smiling and waving at passersby. Word spread through the town and each day for a week George stood on the deck of the boat beaming that million-dollar smile, posing for snapshots, signing autographs and pleasing crowds of fans and curious onlookers.

We must have been quite a sight. I had acquired the habit of jumping rope as a means of relaxation, a practice I acquired after watching my daughter Aliese skipping and joined her one day. On the boat, I continued my routine, skipping rope for an hour each morning and evening. Tourists, local media reporters, and nearby yacht owners would wander along the dock to see me, sweaty and skipping rope, on one side of the deck and George on the other side sporting a yachting cap and ascot, as though he were on the cover of GQ Magazine.

Invitations soon began arriving, hand-delivered by chauffeur. We were invited for cocktails here, tea there, and luncheon someplace else. An early invitation requested our presence at a black-tie charity ball at the Royal Palm Hotel in Cannes, hosted by author Harold Robbins and his wife Betty.

"Where are we going to get good tuxedos on such short notice?" I asked George, who smiled and replied, "Don't worry. I know just the man." He led me to a little tailor shop in town, introduced me to the owner, and three days later we walked out with spiffy custom- made tuxedo sets. George was preening, the tailor was smiling, and I was a few thousand dollars poorer.

The most bizarre incident occurred when we encountered Flick, the guy George had caught with Alana in a bedroom at the Beverly Hills Hotel, at one of the parties. Flick was now dating Benito Mussolini's great-granddaughter, a lovely girl whom everyone admired, especially George. Instead of snarling and throwing a punch at Mercedes, George grinned and tossed his arm over Flick's shoulder. After sharing a few drinks, George suddenly snapped his fingers. "You know what?" he said. "Today is our wedding anniversary. Or was. Let's call Alana and tell her how much fun we're having."

Both men ambled away to find a telephone and call Alana back in California. "Just called to say I remembered our anniversary," George said to Alana before describing all the parties he was attending on the Riviera. "And guess who's here to help me celebrate?" He handed the receiver to Mercedes, who added his congratulations and blew kisses over the telephone. It was all nasty fun and games, and one more window into the lives of the rich and famous.

After a week in St. Tropez, we sailed the boat back to Cannes, this time on a much smoother voyage. We went straight from the yacht basin to the Royal Palms Hotel, changed into our tuxedos, and headed for the party. Everywhere I turned that night I encountered a celebrity. Marlon Brando was with three teenage girls, all of them pretty and sexy, and all of them falling over Brando. David Niven approached to invite George and me to dinner at his home the following evening. Most of the celebrities were famous TV and movie stars but some, like Oscar Wyatt, chairman of Coastal Energy, were famous for being enormously wealthy. (Years later, Wyatt was indicted on criminal charges of dealing with Sadaam Hussein during the Iraq oil embargo.)

In between counting the celebrities, I grew fascinated with watching George Hamilton in his element, a performance to be savored and remembered. No one in the world, I am convinced, is better at playing the role of the entertaining socialite. He moved through the party on clouds of air kisses, handshakes, slaps on the back, whispered gossip and laughter. Especially laughter. George was witty and charming to a degree that I never believed any human being could achieve without a script and a rehearsal. Women hung on every word and swooned at every smile, and men marveled at the skill of a consummate professional schmoozer.

After the party broke up, I was ready to return to our hotel room and book a flight home. Along with being tired and missing my children, I was practically out of money, having enriched much of the Cote d'Azure with my credit cards.

"We can't leave without visiting the casino," George said.

Casinos are not my favorite place to hang out, but I recalled that this one had shown Frank Sinatra the door a few months earlier, and I was curious to explore it. Besides, George could be as charming and convincing with me as with anyone else.

The Cannes casino was nothing like the palaces in Las Vegas and Atlantic City. For one thing, it was both quiet and elegant. No background music, no shouts of joy or moans of loss, no flashing neon signs and no slot machines. When you gambled in Cannes, you chose one of two games: either roulette or baccarat. Before you can play either game, you must obtain credit from the house. I received $10,000 credit and was handed $4,000 in cash, which I gave to George.

The casino was crowded and, reflecting the cool sophistication of the place, most of the gamblers either did not recognize George or simply refused to acknowledge his presence. This made it difficult for him to find a place at the baccarat table until he caught the eye of a tall, regal-looking woman in a white silk gown who was wearing enough jewelry to fill a window at Tiffany's, where it probably originated. She was French, and soon she and George were conversing and laughing in her native language as though they were old lovers. George kissed her hand with great elegance and style, and she invited him to play baccarat at the table with her. George was off and running. And betting. And winning!

Baccarat may be a game of chance, but George's skill and experience swung the odds in his favor. He seemed to win over and over again, and soon even the most snobbish of the other gamblers suspended play to watch him. At one point standing ten deeps behind the tanned, smiling and incredibly lucky American. After about an hour's play, I elbowed my way to George's side. "How much are we up in dollars?" I asked.

"Looks like maybe fifty thousand," George smiled.

I was elated. The profit would just about cover my expenses for the past two weeks. But before I could persuade George to cash in the chips and head back to the hotel with me, he stood, raised an arm, and called across the room to the casino manager, "Champagne for the house!"

Almost instantly, waiters appeared from the kitchen carrying trays of champagne flutes and chilled bottles of Dom Perignon, from a great vintage of course. The wine kept coming, and our profits kept going. When things settled down and George began air-kissing the women goodbye, I asked the manager how much the wine service had cost in American dollars. "About forty-seven thousand," he replied.

On the way back to the hotel, George gently scolded me for looking glum. "It wasn't our money," he said. "It was somebody else's money, so it doesn't matter."

I reminded him that our Riviera adventure had been paid for out of my pocket.

"Don't worry," he said. "We're going to make a great movie and you'll be paid out of first money," meaning the first proceeds from the movie's sale.

The next evening, we attended the dinner party at David Niven's house, located on a spectacular point of land in Monte Carlo. Niven was pleasant, but I suspected that George and I were invited primarily because the women guests had pressured Niven to invite us. They wanted to fuss over George, laugh at his witticisms, and sample his inimitable charm. George, of course, did not disappoint them.

"It's our last night here," George said as we left Niven's house. "We simply must go to Regine's."

Through the 60's and 70's, Regine was the reigning disco queen among the jetsetters, and her New Jimmy'z in Monte Carlo was the crown jewel. It seemed that every other car in the parking lot was either a Ferrari or a Rolls-Royce. Inside, the place was spectacular. The dance floor was a massive patio atop a cliff overlooking the Mediterranean. Everyone was elegant, confident, charming, entertaining, and wealthy.

These were special people, blessed with beauty, youth, wealth and energy, the heirs of enormous wealth built up by families in the most glamorous regions of Europe and the oil-based treasures of the Middle East. Their life consisted, for the most part, of being in the right place at the right time among their own class, and in August the place to be was not just on the French Riviera but on the dance floor at New Jimmy'z.

The next day I flew home, arriving to learn that the original motive for the journey – to celebrate Joe Cannon's agreement to finance the picture – collapsed while we were gone. Cannon had backed out.

We began to scramble for another backer, someone who would approve the script, provide the financing and handle distribution. George contacted Mel Simon, owner of a chain of shopping megamalls and whose brother owned the NBA Indiana Pacers basketball team. The former head of AVCO-Embassy Pictures, a sister company of Columbia, Mel had the clout and the contacts to get the movie made, so I felt good about the deal. Until I heard from Bob Kaufman.

Kaufman informed me that my partner George Hamilton was pushing Simon to return my original investment and leave bigger pieces of the pie for himself and Simon. That's the way the game works among many people in the movie business.

To his credit, Kaufman opposed the idea. Later, in an interview with Variety, Kaufman said, "This picture would never have been made without Harold Van Arnem's involvement." Kaufman, of course, was a writer not an actor or producer, and I learned that writers in Hollywood tend to be more honest and direct in their dealings with people.

Hamilton's actions showed his true colors. I must admit I was not surprised, although I was disappointed. George was always looking out for George first, last, and always. Now he wanted me out and himself in as a co-producer, ready to claim a share of the movie profits.

I decided not to fight it, but not to give in either. If they wanted to buy back my original investment, I would sell. But I wanted a share in the equity and screen credits.

We struck a deal, with Hamilton and Kaufman listed as co-producers. I received the title of Associate Producer but, whether by error or intent, my name was misspelled in the movie credits. I also ensured that I would enjoy at least one perk from the film's release when I insisted that the world premier take place not in New York or Hollywood but in Detroit. I had moved from investing in movies to investing in a professional soccer team, and the release of Love at First Bite would occur just as the 1980 soccer season was about to begin, providing a promotional opportunity I couldn't resist.

A world premiere in Detroit would produce a million dollars' worth of local publicity for both the movie and the soccer team. When a deal was reached to launch the film in Detroit, I booked a popular nightclub for the premier party, and invited 600 guests to celebrate the event. Among the attendees would be star players from the soccer team plus Rod Stewart, rock star Bob Seger, director Stan Dragoti, John De Lorean, Roger Penske, some of the biggest names in local football, baseball and basketball, lots of media representatives, and of course the one and only George Hamilton. The next day, the celebrities would attend the opening game of the soccer season. That was my plan.

Detroit had never seen anything like it. For weeks, the media gave the upcoming party enormous coverage. I knew both the movie and the party would be a hit, and for the first time after returning from France I felt good about my involvement in the project.

On the night before the premier, I received a telephone call from George in New York. "I won't be there tomorrow night," George informed me. I asked if something was wrong. Was he ill? Did he have a previous commitment? Had I done something to annoy him?

Not according to George's responses. Then it hit me. "How much do you want?" I asked.

"Ten thousand dollars," he said. "In cash. At the airport."

It took me a moment to get over the shock. George and I may not have been lifelong friends, but neither were we pure business partners. It would never occur to me to squeeze money in this manner from someone I knew as well as we knew each other. He knew I had no choice in the matter. Too much had been invested by this point, in dollars and in my reputation for George not to be present at the movie's premiere.

I agreed to the fee if he would commit to staying an extra day in Detroit to attend the opening game of the Express at the Silverdome. He assured me he would.

George arrived on schedule, pocketed the money, and played his usual role of the suave, witty and sophisticated movie star. The party roared on through the night, and the next day George was gone without saying goodbye, and without attending the season opener of my Detroit Express soccer team as he had promised.

I realized too late that George is a performer, and a very good one at that. He is great fun to be with, and probably gets as much joy out of life as anybody. In many ways, I had played the role that others had played – someone who enjoyed the company of George Hamilton and was prepared to pay for the experience. Was I disappointed at his actions? Of course. Do I regret meeting and hanging out with him? Not a bit.

After all, our relationship produced a movie that brought laughter to a lot of people and is still recalled with pleasure nearly thirty years later.

CHAPTER FOURTEEN

SILVERDOME, NORTH AMERICAN SOCCER LEAGUE, DETROIT AMERICAN SOCCER LEAGUE NATIONAL CHAMPIONS

After Florida, where the living was easy and the energy low, and Beverly Hills and Monte Carlo, where greed was everything and betrayal was just a way of doing business, I was ready to rebuild my life in Detroit. Detroit could be dark and gritty, but it was real, and reality was suddenly appealing to me.

I felt driven by the need to flush out ideas for investment and development. The time spent away from Michigan provided me with a new perspective on things, including opportunities that appeared more obvious to me than to people who had lived among them for many years. One of those opportunities was the Silverdome.

Completed in 1975 at a cost of $56 million, the Silverdome was financed by the city of Pontiac and managed by the Pontiac Stadium Building Authority. Financing had been provided through a combination of bonds, "General Obligation Notes" and installment notes, all underwritten by the city.

Pontiac was no Palm Springs or New York City. Basically, a blue-collar town, it depended on taxes paid by families employed, for the most part, in the automotive industry. Assembly-line workers, secretaries, truck drivers and office clerks saw part of their property taxes and other civic income diverted to the Silverdome. They were proud of being home to an 80,000-seat facility where the Detroit Lions played their NFL games, but that pride came at a steep price, and the price included millions of dollars diverted every year from building new schools and libraries in order to make bond payments on a place that held 16 football games a year plus the odd rodeo or exhibition. I estimated that the Silverdome sat dark and vacant at least 300 days a year, representing a serious drain on the city's tax base. I also guessed that the Silverdome was costing each Pontiac taxpayer between $600 and $800 a year. Since initially funding the Silverdome, the city of Pontiac had abandoned plans to build a new hospital and dismissed police officers and firemen due to a lack of money. Was owning a stadium really worth that cost?

The people in Pontiac benefiting most from the Silverdome were the members of the citizen's group who managed the place. They enjoyed various perks such as free admission to events and represented the wealthiest and most powerful sector of the city. The situation reminded me of the worst aspects of Soviet communism – 95 percent of the people were struggling to provide comfort and luxury for the top five percent of the population.

Government involvement in venues like the Silverdome rarely makes sense, and Pontiac's financing of their stadium made less sense than most. With no incentive to earn a profit, management of the venue becomes sloppy and wasteful, and in the end, no one wins – not the fans, not the attractions, and certainly not the taxpayers.

The more I looked at the situation in Pontiac, the more I grew convinced that private ownership was the answer. I decided I would be the guy to make it work, and I quietly began floating the idea among local politicians and county executives. "How would you feel about someone taking the Silverdome out of the taxpayers' hands and lessening their tax load?" I asked people like Michigan Governor Bill Milliken, Senator Bob Griffin, Oakland County Executive Dan Murphy, and others. All supported the idea of relieving city taxpayers of the burden and providing them with a well-managed stadium facility.

My original plan was to offer $60 million for the Silverdome, a little more than it had cost to build. At the time, the stadium needed a new roof and extensive repairs to the parking lot, expenses I would have to cover as the new owner. Things would not make economic sense on that basis because the Silverdome had only two firm tenants: the NFL Detroit Lions and the NBA Detroit Pistons. The Pistons were only temporary visitors because they were already planning to construct their own facility in Auburn Hills, leaving the Lions as the sole professional team in the Silverdome.

This gave me an idea. What if the Silverdome became the foundation of a wider complex, one that would serve as the venue for other professional sports events? What if we created a critical mass that spawned new activities and attractions? I was looking beyond sporting events towards top-drawer entertainment productions such as the Rolling Stones, whose appearance could easily fill 80,000 seats. A successful complex could be built around the Silverdome with the addition a new sports arena, a first-class hotel, and top-drawer entertainment attractions. Substantial added revenue would be generated by the sale of broadcast rights; any event capable of attracting 80,000 people would be worthy of a major TV production, either commercially or on a pay-per-view basis.

My first concern, however, was to establish a sports presence at the Silverdome. Besides the Detroit Tigers, two professional teams were already hugely successful in the area: the NHL Detroit Red Wings, and the NBA Detroit Pistons, owned by my next-door neighbor Bill Davidson. Back in 1975, I had made a pitch to buy the Pistons, offering $3.8 million for the franchise. A few years later Bill Davidson acquired them for $8 million, and as I write this today the Pistons are valued at about $300 million. That's the kind of return that attracts investors to professional sports teams, especially if the guy putting up the cash is a rabid sports fan. Of course, there is a downside as well. There is always a downside.

The Detroit Lions may have been at home in the 80,000 seat Silverdome, but hockey and basketball are more suited to a 20,000-seat arena. Buying the Red Wings and Pistons was beyond my reach at the time, so I turned to professional soccer.

Despite my focus on business, I still thought of myself as an athlete, and the idea of combining both my business investments and my love for sports was irresistible. None of the existing Detroit professional sports teams was available, but when Roger Faulkner, a local sports fan and promoter, announced that he would be launching a Detroit team to play in the new North American Soccer League, I saw an opportunity.

The NASL was a serious effort to establish soccer as a significant professional sport on this continent, but its birth was inspired less by an aggressive business opportunity than by a defensive strategy. Behind the NASL's creation were a combination of high-profile NFL owners like Lamar Hunt of the Kansas City Chiefs, Sonny Werblin from the New York Giants, and the Miami Dolphins' Joe Robbie. Their partners in the NASL include Lipton Tea and Steve Ross, CEO of Warner Communications, among others. The participation by NFL owners was basically a defensive maneuver. They were spooked by the worldwide popularity of professional soccer and growing interest in the sport among U.S. youngsters. Kids who played soccer in schoolyards, the NFL owners feared, just might grow up to prefer that game over American-style football.

In effect, the NFL owners hedged their bets. By launching their own professional soccer league, the ticket revenues would flow into the coffers of the same owners no matter which game the kids paid to attend. Another professional soccer league, the ASL, already existed, but its teams were in secondary markets.

The ASL struggled from season to season but NASL teams, located in primary markets, were financially stable. The owners and corporate sponsors of NASL organizations had built a strong, stable foundation thanks to the support of corporate sponsors, the impact of a national marketing program, and the attraction of world-class professional soccer mangers, experienced coaches, and gifted players. Most people, including me, believed that the NASL founders were correct: soccer was overdue to explode in America, becoming as popular as it was in virtually every other country around the world. And of all the cities in the country, I believed none was better suited for a soccer franchise than Detroit. Soccer is a blue-collar sport with special appeal to Europeans. Detroit was a blue-collar town with a substantial population of first and second- generation immigrants from Greece, Italy, Poland and the Middle East. On that basis, I decided to invest in the new team.

Roger Faulkner had recruited a Brit named Jimmy Hill as a partner in the new NASL franchise. Hill, a distinctive-looking guy with a jutting chin that made Jay Leno's look anemic, was a powerhouse in English soccer, or football as it's known there. Managing the Coventry football club, he had raised it from the Third Division to the First Division, which is like turning a minor-league baseball club into a major-league franchise. He was also as well-connected in the international soccer world as anyone, and that's the quality we needed to build a team. To serious soccer fans, the presence of Jimmy Hill generated immediate respect for the new organization.

At its inception the Detroit Express, as the franchise was named, attracted good sponsors including the Bonanza Steak House chain and Big Boy Burgers, but it soon became obvious that the team needed an infusion of more capital plus an effective marketing campaign. I contacted Faulkner and provided the necessary funding for the team, qualifying me as both General Partner and an NASL Director.

My interest was not purely business based. I truly loved soccer, although I recognized from the beginning that, even with the large contingent of first- and second- generation immigrants in the Detroit area, it would prove a hard sell. As I always do when evaluating an investment, I focused on the upside. Detroit was among the top five markets in North America, based on income, and no one has ever doubted the city's support for its sports teams. Besides, my investment, while substantial, represented an affordable risk. I went into the project with my eyes open, my head up, and my hopes high. Even while I was immersing myself in the details of running a professional sports franchise, I was still planning an extended complex around the Silverdome.

With hockey, basketball and soccer drawing fans, a 20,000-seat arena could be busy 200 days of the year; concerts, exhibitions and other events would fill out the rest of the calendar. Located on cheaply available land next to the Silverdome, it would create a sports complex as good as any in the country.

It needed one more element, however, and to arrange it I placed a telephone call to Jay Pritzker, founder of the Hyatt hotel chain and operator, among other Pritzker investments, of the Superdome in New Orleans. Explaining my plan to create a sports and exhibition complex around the Silverdome, I pointed out that it would need a quality hotel on the site for conventioneers, sports fan and other people attracted to the entertainment and broadcast production complex. Pritzker remained cautious and skeptical, but I was certain that he would take me more seriously once I had the other elements in place.

After spending time in Florida, away from the mainstream of high-powered business, I was back among the action and totally energized. All kinds of possibilities started opening up in my imagination. The sports complex would lend itself perfectly to a regional broadcast channel, promoting the sports teams and pulling in advertising revenue. I contacted Warner Communications seeking a cable-TV franchise that would provide coverage of events and developments in team rosters, and perhaps carry games associated with all the professional teams appearing at the Silverdome complex. I held several discussions with Steve Ross, who merged Time-Life and Warner Communications to create the first multi-media complex, and the vice-chairman of Warner, Jay Emmett. Both were enthusiastic about the idea of creating a sports network, using the Silverdome as a feed for the Midwest CATV programming needs.

Steve Ross was overflowing with energy and imagination, and he and I were soon discussing ways to combine computer technology with cable services. At one point, I mentioned the possibility of adapting digital data processing to cable broadcasting, a system that would transmit movies and special events programming to the viewer on demand. The technology wasn't ready yet, but I could see it coming, and Steve Ross almost jumped out of his chair at the idea.

Warner was already experimenting with QUBE, an interactive

TV programming system out of Columbus, Ohio and operated by its subsidiary Warner AmEx. QUBE offered 30 channels, including ten premium and pay-per-view networks, along with ten interactive channels via a modem. QUBE provided several programming options including Star Channel, which eventually morphed into The Movie Channel; Sight on Sound, airing music programming long before the arrival of MTV; and first-run movies, sporting events and special programs on Pay-Per-View, similar to today's HBO channel. My suggestion would extend CUBE into a new dimension of entertainment programming, and Warner was the logical company to offer it. As a result of our talks, we formed Warner AmEx Van Arnem, an association that helped to open several new doors in later years.

I began shifting my focus away from a computer-based operation to one more closely associated with entertainment and show business, and I admit that I enjoyed the idea tremendously.

For several weeks I worked behind the scenes, putting together a deal enabling me to purchase the Silverdome and use it as the keystone of the sports/convention/broadcast complex I envisioned. As things heated up, however, word of my plan leaked and spread like wildfire. Most of the rumors occurred during a single week while I was out of town. In the summer of 1978, I used one of the Oakland Express planes to fly with my children to Martha's Vineyard for a vacation. When we returned and landed at the Pontiac airport, hundreds of local residents and an army of TV, radio and press reporters were waiting to greet us. The press was intrigued; the citizens were supportive. "Bloomfield Hills Computer Executive to Purchase Silverdome", the headlines screamed the next day, and the media onslaught continued. This was not all bad, because it provided the means for generating public support, so I agreed to do a few interviews.

When the Oakland Press interviewed me for their Sunday Magazine cover story on my plans for the Silverdome, the reporter asked what I thought I might do to turn the Silverdome around and make it a money-maker. "I'm bringing the Pope in for Christmas mass," I replied.

The editor loved it, and over a photo of me on the magazine cover they ran the headline, "The Pope is Coming for Christmas Mass!" Well, why not? Okay, it was a little over the top, but I knew that nothing would inspire the heavily Catholic population of Greater Detroit more than welcoming the Pope. Besides, a few years later a papal mass was held in the Silverdome, so I wasn't that far off the mark. Unfortunately, the timing could not have been worse.

Just as the magazine began rolling off the press on Friday, a bulletin arrived from Vatican City – John Paul 1, who had mounted the papal throne barely a month earlier, had suddenly died. The magazine had to scrap that issue entirely, redesign the cover, and reprint it entirely. For the first time in the history of the Oakland Press its Sunday magazine appeared on Monday.

Meanwhile, I was not happy with the soccer team. I had invested a fair amount of money in it, partly because so many of the sport's qualities appealed to me – the discipline during play, the physical conditioning that the athletes endured, and the whole atmosphere that floated around a collection of guys who went out onto the field with a single goal in mind and a dedication to helping their teammates share in the glory. Many of the Express players had been First Division players from top divisions in Europe, a credit to Roger Faulkner's management abilities, and I gravitated to them right away, appreciating their skills and understanding their concerns about training, staying in shape, and functioning as a team.

As General Manager, Roger made the key decisions, but I couldn't help offering advice and making suggestions, although I suspect that they distracted him more than assisted him. Roger was always patient and well-meaning, but our UK soccer guru Jimmy Hill resented everything I proposed. In Hill's view, my involvement in the team should have been to sign the checks and shut up, even though we were both general partners.

When I began examining the books closely, I realized why Hill was so upset with me asking questions. Under the arrangement that brought Hill on board (although Hill continued to reside in England), the team was committed to paying him as much as $100,000 for every player who arrived from Europe. It was called a transfer fee, but in my opinion, it was nothing more than a means for Hill to tap into our limited capital. Looking over the books, I calculated that we had paid more than $500,000 in so-called transfer fees to a guy who hadn't invested a shilling of his own money into the operation.

After discussing the deal with other board members, who were as surprised and concerned as me, I instructed Faulkner to pay nothing to Hill in the future. When Hill received the news and learned that I had instigated the action, he became enraged. He persuaded the directors to fire Roger Faulkner and name his son Duncan as the new General Manager. Duncan Hill may have inherited some soccer knowledge from his father, but he knew little about managing a professional sports team and even less about marketing one in the U.S., and within weeks the team was immersed in chaos.

Hill's disastrous influence over the other directors convinced me that the only way I could protect my investment and see the team mature into a winner was to assume total ownership and management of the Express. And that's what I did. I fired Hill and successfully sued him to recover funds missing from the team's accounts. The other investors were annoyed at my heavy-handed move, but I invited their participation in any way they felt they could contribute. The team needed immediate attention from someone prepared to make hard decisions. No one else appeared sufficiently qualified or committed, so I stepped up to assume the role.

It wasn't a difficult decision. As the team owner, I couldn't keep my hands-off things. I just couldn't. I wanted to participate and help the team in every way possible. If I had the skills and experience, I would have been on the field with the rest of the players in every match. I couldn't, of course, but I insisted on being a part of the effort in one way or another.

As I mentioned earlier, I'm a great believer in jumping rope as an aerobics exercise because it combines so many benefits – eye, hand and foot coordination, balance, timing and footwork. I have skipped rope for at least an hour virtually every day of my adult life. Once I counted 60,000 jumps in a single day. Besides its value as a physical conditioner, jumping rope represents a source of relaxation to me, especially when I combine it with yoga. When I spoke to our player-coach Brian Tinnion, suggesting that the players should jump rope as part of their conditioning, he was cool to the idea. If I thought jumping rope was such a good training technique, he said, I could jump rope in the corner and, if any player wanted to go over and skip with me, he would be free to do so. Some did. Most did not. But something worked, because the team led the league in both offensive and defensive categories that year and was the first team to make the playoffs.

We also held friendly exhibition games with local soccer clubs as part of our promotional activities. First-string players sat out of these games to make the teams more evenly matched, and at these events I often played goaltender. I traveled throughout the state with the team on these promotional tours, enjoying the company of the athletes and the response of the fans. Our television commercials even used me as the pitch man, wearing a Detroit Express uniform and inviting the fans to come out for the next game. I was having fun, but I began to wonder if fun was the only return, I could expect from my investment.

I began contacting other NASL team owners, and while I admired the success that people like Joe Robbie and Sonny Werblin had achieved with their NFL operations, I disagreed with their strategy when it came to the NASL. Regardless of the popularity of soccer among school kids, as a professional sport it was an entirely new product, one that needed to be built through generations. The other NASL owners saw things differently. They wanted to field a league of all-star dominated teams, guys who could do things on the field that no American schoolboy could even dream of doing. Pele, the greatest soccer player of all time, played three years for the NASL New York Cosmos, and the league was filled with million-dollar-a-season players. Our own star performer, Trevor Francis, had been the first British soccer athlete to earn one million pounds Sterling in a single season, and he won the scoring title that year with 54 points despite starting after the season had already begun.

Soccer fans loved to watch Pele and others perform. But the stars overshadowed the teams, and none of them inspired American youngsters to dream of playing in the NASL the way they imagined joining teams in major league baseball, the NFL, the NBA or the NHL. "You know what you have here?" I said at one point. "You have a league full of Harlem Globetrotters, except they play soccer. Now, a lot of people enjoy watching the Globetrotters play, but only about once a year. We need people to come out a dozen times a year, and this all-star approach isn't working."

In some ways, the league had been set up to prevent, not encourage, American kids from becoming players. One rule dictated that the starting eleven players of every team had to include three Americans out of about twenty players on the squad. The rule treated Canadian and American players equally, and with professional soccer more firmly established in Canada than in the USA, more Canadian-born players of professional caliber were available. This meant that some NASL franchises could recruit three Canadians and field a team without a single American on the entire team.

CHAPTER FIFTEEN

AMERICANIZATION OF THE US SOCCER ASL CHAMPIONSHIP

I loved the game, and I wanted other Americans to enjoy it as much as I did. More than that, I wanted American kids to grow up with the talent and ambition to become professional soccer players, something they would never acquire under the NASL rules.

As long as the NFL owners were running the show and disagreeing with me, I knew I could never get the rules changed. So, I changed leagues.

The American Soccer League had been around since 1933, although an earlier organization with the same name had been launched in 1911. In the late 1970's, the ASL struggled against the NASL the same way that the old American Football League remained in the shadow of the NFL before joining it. With teams in several secondary markets, including Columbus, Rochester and Nashville, the ASL lacked the prestige – not to mention the money – behind the NASL. I didn't care, because the ASL was grass-roots soccer in this country. It was the league that stood to attract American kids to the sport at the professional level.

It seemed to me that the ASL represented the best hope for establishing professional soccer in America. Their approach, I believed, would help create a grass-roots movement that would eventually produce talented local players and produce a true Americanization of soccer. Moving from the NASL to the ASL was like switching a franchise from major league baseball to AAA level. But if I were to field a viable pro soccer team in Detroit, there appeared to be no other choice. Losses kept mounting, budget forecasts were either non- existent or out of control, and both our salaries and overhead costs were much too high. The only way we could hope to survive was by scaling down both our salaries and our overhead to a manageable level. With that objective in mind, the move to the ASL was fairly easy. Besides, I suspected that the NASL would soon close up shop, and that's exactly what happened later.

I approached the ASL with an offer to move the Detroit Express to their league, and a suggestion that it restructure itself to promote a grass-roots strategy. Instead of following the rule of insisting that each team must have three American players, I proposed reversing the concept: Each team could have only three non-Americans, and this time "American" did not include Canadians. The three foreign players would undoubtedly be the most proficient, but their American teammates would learn by playing alongside them.

In the short term, this would provide a significant reduction in the league's operating costs because most American soccer athletes simply wanted a chance to play and would accept a lower salary for the opportunity to get on the field during a match. Over the long term, I expected a few native-born stars to emerge, which would inspire other boys to move into soccer at the professional level.

The other team owners agreed, I assembled a good board of directors to help run things, and we all looked forward to the coming season with anticipation and hope. Had I known more about the other team owners; I would have had much less of both.

To put it gently, the other team owners were simply not good businessmen. They either lacked the money they claimed to have, or they simply refused to pay their bills. Too late, I realized I had made the leap from associating with a group of business people with deep pockets but no experience with soccer, to a gang of guys with lots of passion for the game but not much else.

At least we had an opposition team for every home game, but this was often thanks to my generosity. More than once during the first season, I received a telephone call from the owner of a visiting team announcing that he had no money to fly his team into Detroit for the next day's game. I had gone through this with George Hamilton and now here it was again. The only way to avoid disappointing fans of the Express, especially those with season's tickets, was for me to cover the opposing team's travel expenses. And I did. Once, when we were about to take the field at an out-of-town game, a posse from the local sheriff's office arrived to seize the home team's equipment for failure to pay their bills. The owners even refused to pay the salary of the league commissioner, Mario Machado. Mario, who had established himself as a popular TV and game show host, was experienced in dealing with the media and dedicated to helping soccer grow into a major sport in the U.S. One of the reasons for handing Mario the commissioner's job had been to give the ASL some badly needed credibility. Now some team owners were expecting him to work for nothing.

Mario resigned, of course, and the other owners elected me chairman of the league. I wasn't so much flattered as frightened. Now I risked being sued by anyone with a grievance against the American Soccer League, and their numbers were legion.

I accepted the position, partly to satisfy my ego I suppose, and partly to implement my own ideas about developing youth soccer in conjunction with a professional level team. I gave it a good shot but trying to persuade the ASL owners to agree on anything that related to good business practices was impossible. Eventually it dawned on me: The only way to turn my vision into reality was to own all the teams in the league.

This was not as outrageous as it appears. I had already covered unpaid bills and travel expenses for other teams in the league, and some owners already had given up on their operation, the league, and soccer in general. I could acquire the teams with assistance from local sponsors who would cover start-up costs in exchange for marketing and promotional opportunities. Each club would be placed on a balanced cash flow program and establish an association with local youth soccer organizations. Locally, the Express would provide training clinics for the youth teams, host their appearance at the Silverdome, tie in local sponsors to the youth events, and cover the games on the local CATV channel.

I almost pulled it off.

About two-thirds of the owners either agreed with my proposal or simply didn't care. Price wasn't much of a consideration; most were anxious to get out of the sport but didn't know how to do it without appearing like a loser. I suggested they could either admit failure and fold up teams they had spent years promoting, or permit me to assume ownership, leaving local fans to assume the previous owner had made a legitimate sale.

I tried changing the game to make it more attractive for American fans. Europeans appreciate a good defensive game, but Americans want to see scoring, and soccer scores are notoriously low. I reduced the field size in the Silverdome, moving the goalposts closer together. It worked. That year, the Express set a record for the average number of goals scored per game. One by one, I began approaching the owners of teams who were privately spreading the word that their franchises were for sale. Some of these were NASL teams. If I could move just a couple of NASL teams into the ASL, I would add prestige to our league and make it easier for others to join us. I made my first approach to Peter Pocklington, owner of the NASL Edmonton Drillers and the NHL Edmonton Oilers. Pocklington was riding high with a young Wayne Gretzky, who was about to lead the Oilers to a string of Stanley Cup championships. Caught up in the NHL excitement, Pocklington was becoming frustrated with his soccer franchise, and I flew to Edmonton to discuss assuming control of the Drillers.

Like other people I encountered in professional sports, Pocklington was a unique character. He had positioned his desk atop a riser at one end of his large office. To reach his desk you literally had to walk up steps, as though climbing a mountain to meet some fabled guru, so you felt small from the moment you entered his office. But he was a charming and entertaining guy, full of energy and ambition, and we got along well. After the preliminaries were finished, Pocklington made his offer. I could have the Drillers gratis. One signature on a contract and the team was mine. Free. With one catch. (There is always a catch.)

"You have to buy my Learjet. At a discounted price, of course," Pocklington said.

"Your what?" I asked.

"My Learjet. You buy the Learjet – I promise you'll pay less than market cost – and the team comes with it. You can sell the airplane later and I guarantee you won't lose money on the deal."

I couldn't believe it. I had flown to Edmonton to buy a soccer team, and I could be going home with an executive jet. "Why are you being so nice to me?" I asked.

Pocklington explained that he had an image to fulfill in his hometown as a shrewd businessman, and he didn't want it known that he had given away the soccer team. It would mean Pocklington had failed at something, staining his reputation. But if he could announce that he had sold the team for a reasonable amount of money, it would sound as though he had completed just another wise business deal. No one, of course, would have to know he used a free Learjet as an incentive.

I began offering objections. I didn't want or need a Learjet, and I wasn't interested in selling it to get my money back.

"Can I announce the deal?" he kept asking me. I wasn't prepared to go with any deal until I had a chance to evaluate the opportunity of attracting other teams to the ASL. I avoided saying either yes or no, suggesting he give me the night to sleep on it and we would meet at his office the next morning.

I arrived the following day to find a crush of media people and television cameras outside Pocklington's office. Had he bought some other sports team? I wondered. Was he launching a new political campaign (the previous year, Pocklington had sought leadership of Canada's federal Conservative Party)?

It was neither. When I entered Pocklington's office, he introduced me to the local media as the new owner of the Edmonton Drillers, and drew my attention to a gang of lawyers standing around, waiting to draft the legal agreements.

I was annoyed, but Pocklington was a brash, likeable guy, and as somebody who had been brash when circumstances required, I couldn't become angry when Pocklington acted the same way with me. When the press began asking for details, I replied we were still working on details of the arrangement, which appeared to satisfy them.

"We don't have a deal," I reminded Pocklington after the press and lawyers left.

Pocklington assured me that I couldn't lose by purchasing his Learjet and taking the team as an incentive. "Fly back to Detroit in it," he said, "and get somebody there to appraise it. It's worth $750,000 easy. By the way," he added, "I'd like you to take the Drillers coach and a few key players with you, if you don't mind."

Flying directly home to Detroit had its appeal, because it had taken me about twelve hours, changing planes twice, to reach Edmonton from Michigan. I wrote Pocklington a check for $5,000 as a security deposit and to cover the cost of fuel and rode back to Detroit with six members of the Drillers, planning to arrive in time for an Express playoff game that evening. As soon as we landed at Pontiac airport, we were surrounded by local media who wanted me to confirm that I had just purchased the Edmonton Drillers. Pocklington had alerted them, of course, and when I kept trying to avoid commenting on the story the reporters turned their attention to the Edmonton coach and players. It was all a clever plan by Pocklington to pressure me into buying his team. Unfortunately, the only things it did was draw attention from the important Express game that night.

If the jet had a market value of $750,000 as Pocklington claimed, I had assured him we had a deal, but the Lear was assessed in the U.S. at barely $500,000. Too bad. I might have been part of the first transaction in professional sports where you buy an entire team and get an executive jet free. Or was it the other way around?

Meanwhile, I was busy assembling other teams for the new league. The Lipton Tea Company, owners of the Jacksonville Tea Men, was anxious to dump their investment and we worked out a tentative deal. The owners of franchises in Oklahoma and New York City came on board with me, prepared to "warehouse" their franchises until the new league set- up was established. Other investors claimed they were interested in launching teams.

Unfortunately, when it came time to stop talking big and start writing checks, my potential partners were unable to come up with the money. I had a league on paper, but none of the teams could afford to put players on the field. I began approaching companies that would benefit from sports sponsorship, including Dr. Pepper, Coca-Cola, Budweiser, Frito-Lay and others. By this time, it was clear to everyone that the NASL was doomed. In my view, this meant soccer fans across the country would turn to the ASL. The sponsors saw things the other way; they believed the death of the NASL proved that soccer had no future as a professional sport in America.

Back in Detroit, my plans for buying the Silverdome were running off the track as well. I had strong support from William Milliken, the Governor of Michigan, Robert Griffin,

CHAPTER SIXTEEN

AFL-NFL-STRIKE GAMES

But a new opportunity soon arose when NFL players went on strike just a few weeks into the 1982 season. In mid-September, after just enough games to whet the appetite of millions of fans, the football players walked off the field in a contract dispute with the owners. A few weeks later I received a telephone call from Shelly Saltzman, a boxing promoter and broadcaster. Shelly had an interesting proposition: those millions of football fans were being starved from their favorite game. They wanted to see NFL-level football so badly that it almost didn't matter who was playing. So why not satisfy their need with a series of all-star games, played in half a dozen major cities and carried on network television?

I agreed that it sounded like a great idea, and the next day Saltzman flew in from New York to discuss it with me as a potential investor. Ed Garvey, president of the NFL Players Association had already given his blessing to a schedule of six games played in Washington DC, New York City, Las Vegas, Los Angeles, Atlanta and Detroit. Five investors, putting $50,000 each into the pot, would select the players for each all-star team and cover the cost of uniforms, organizational expenses and other costs. Ted Turner had agreed to televise the games on his TNT channel. How could I resist? I was having fun with the soccer team, but football remained my first love, and I was being offered an opportunity to become a combination NFL team owner and league commissioner. Look out, Pete Rozelle!

Speaking of Rozelle, he was outraged at the idea, and began launching a series of court restraining orders on behalf of the NFL team owners to prevent the all-star series from happening. Threats of legal action began descending on me and the other partners, but

Garvey and the NFLPA kept encouraging us to go ahead with the schedule. Besides maintaining interest in the game, Garvey and the players knew the series would put pressure on Rozelle and the owners to settle the strike. Things came together quickly. The opposing teams were chosen, the players agreed to participate, uniforms were designed and produced, the stadiums were booked, and local sponsors were lined up.

Our first game was set for RFK Stadium in Washington, and I talked my daughter Heidi in to attending the game with me. Heidi wasn't a big football fan, but I convinced her to come because it would be an historic occasion. I expected to participate in a full-fledged NFL game with roaring crowds and marching bands, and that Heidi and I would watch the entire proceedings from an exclusive owner's box. But when we arrived, all we encountered was chaos. In the locker rooms, both teams were mixing and laughing it up as though it were all one big bachelor party. Cases of beer were stacked against a wall and tables were spread with all kinds of food and snacks. Players were swigging the beer, wolfing down the food, slapping each other on the back, and generally acting like a bunch of good ol' boys at a barbecue instead of fierce professional football players preparing to knock each other down on the football field.

When I finally found Shelly Saltzman, he looked even more upset than I felt. Shelly had just received a restraining order preventing us from selling tickets or even admitting fans to the stadium. Dozens of the game's most famous and gifted athletes would play and nobody would be there to watch it! Millions, however, would be able to watch it in their own living rooms because the restraining order did not apply to Ted Turner's broadcast deal. So, Turner would make money from the game sponsors and we would sit in a silent stadium.

Saltzman and Turner reassured me and the other investors that the restraining order applied only to this first game. We had five more games in the series to make money from our investment. This calmed us down a little, although we really didn't have much choice.

I decided to exert some privileges as an owner and returned to the locker room where the players were suiting up. Quite a sight greeted me there. The best football players in the world were wandering around with a beer in their hand, laughing and slapping each other on the back as though this was a bachelor party. Where was the intensity, the competitive spirit, the will to win that is part of every game worth watching? It wasn't in that locker room, and my heart began to sink.

Things grew really weird at kickoff time. To me and every other fan, NFL football means cheering crowds, brass bands, waving pennants, dancing cheerleaders and an electric atmosphere. None of this was present that day. Just twenty-guys with beer foam on their jerseys, trying to work out plays. The guys were out of practice and a little out of shape. Sitting in the stands that afternoon had to be one of the strangest experiences of my life.

At half-time the National All-Stars were leading 17 to 7, and I entered one of the locker rooms just as Ted Turner appeared with a big grin on his face and carrying a bucket of ice-cold Budweiser. The players laughed and worked their way through the beer as I stood thinking about the money I had invested and my commitment to funding another five games. But if this game didn't improve, nobody would be attending the later games, which meant my money would be disappearing as fast as the Budweiser.

Finally, I stood in the middle of the locker room and asked for everybody's attention. Nobody else was going to shape these guys up, I realized, so it would have to be me. "You guys aren't giving one hundred percent," I lectured them, putting on my best Vince Lombardi voice. "The punt coverage is really bad and both lines, offensive and defensive, aren't maintaining aggressive contact..."

That's about as far as I got. A roar of disapproval from the players drowned out the rest of my words just as Roy Jefferson, a former Washington Redskin receiver who was filling in as a referee that day, pulled me aside and told me to shut up, since I obviously didn't know anything about football.

Perhaps my words made some impact, however, because the

second half of the game was played with more energy than the first, and the game ended with the National All-Stars winning 34 to 24. After the game, both locker rooms were even more raucous than before, with more Budweiser being consumed. Everybody congratulated each other, promising that the following week's game in Los Angeles, where we expected a stadium full of people, would be even better.

The following week began with enthusiasm and hope. Advertisements and promotions for the Los Angeles game began appearing, and our lawyers expressed total confidence that the restraining order barring spectators would be lifted. Then, in the middle of the week, it all came crashing down. After assuring us that every scheduled strike game would take place without question, Ed Garvey signed an agreement with Pete Rozelle to end the strike. The Los Angeles game was cancelled.

Today, if you search for any evidence of the 1982 All-Star series during the NFL players' strike, you will find nothing on the record. As far as the NFL and the major TV networks see it, the whole idea never existed. The game in a silent stadium never took place, the colorful NFL-AFL uniforms were never created, and the gallons of Budweiser were never consumed in the locker rooms. But it all happened. I was there, watching my $50,000 vanish before my eyes. In a way, it was worth the money to say I was an NFL team, owner. For about four weeks.

CHAPTER SEVENTEEN

AMERICAN SOCCER LEAGUE NATIONAL CHAMPIONS

With my plans for creating a sports complex around the Silverdome gone, I focused attention on the soccer team. In every respect but one, the team was a success in 1982. We set an attendance record and finished atop the league. We also achieved status among Detroit's establishment. When companies like Budweiser printed posters celebrating the city's professional sports franchises, the Express was right there with the Lions, Tigers, Red Wings and Pistons. Unfortunately, the financial picture was not nearly so bright, and I was still pulling money out of my own pocket each week to meet the team's payroll.

In the playoffs that year, we defeated New York to move into the finals against Oklahoma. The crazy schedule had us playing Saturday night in Oklahoma City and Monday night back in Detroit. We won in Oklahoma, and I knew our chances of winning the whole thing back in Detroit two nights later looked good, but I couldn't bear the thought of winning the championship in a Silverdome that was 90 percent empty, as it had been during our regular season. I wanted the place crowded with screaming, enthusiastic fans watching the first Detroit professional sports team to win a championship since the 1968 Detroit Tigers. How could I ensure it with less than 48 hours' notice?

Detroit has always been a great sports town, but it is also known as Motor City, and on Sunday morning I turned to the automotive industry for help. My first call to Joe Campana, VP of marketing for Chrysler, paid off. Joe and I had connected when I was doing my time-sharing at Ford. When I suggested Chrysler could benefit from sponsorship, he loved the idea and saw an opportunity to pull thousands of local citizens into Dodge dealerships. "Leave it with me," he said.

I still don't know how he did it, but Joe managed to have 300,000 tickets printed and in the hands of every Dodge dealership by 9:00 a.m. the next day. That's when one of the biggest advertising blitzes in history broke on every radio and TV station and in every daily newspaper across south Michigan. Dodge dealers had bought out the Silverdome, the ads proclaimed, and every sports fan in the Greater Detroit area would receive two free tickets to the ASL championship game that night just by visiting a local Dodge dealer.

All day long, people visited Dodge dealerships for their free tickets, taking time to check out the new cars, read a brochure and perhaps even arrange for a test drive. The Dodge dealers loved the campaign, and it remains one of the most successful local one-day promotion in Chrysler's history. That evening, I arrived early and sat in my box looking down at the lower level of the Silverdome. On other game nights I might watch 7,000 or 8,000 people file in. That night I sat grinning as the entire lower bowl filled with over 35,000 people, and they all waved banners and cheered as the Express took the field. This was the kind of enthusiasm expected if the Red Wings were playing in the Stanley Cup, but it wasn't the Red Wings – it was the Express, and this was soccer, not hockey. I wasn't making a nickel from the free tickets, but nobody in the crowd knew or cared. They were enjoying a great show and Detroit was getting a boost to its civic pride.

The first half of the game included some of the most exciting soccer I had ever watched. At half-time the score was tied 2-2, and the crowd was frantic. Nobody in the stadium was as pumped as me. I raced down to the dressing room and collared Brian Tinnion, our player-coach, just as he stepped off the field and lit a cigarette.

Tinnion's smoking habit had driven me nuts all year long. He wasn't the only guy on the team who smoked – half the players did – but I argued that he should set a standard for other players to follow. We were trying to influence American kids to identify with new sports heroes, playing soccer instead of football or baseball, and the players and their coach were smoking cigarettes every chance they could get.

"You've got to put more pressure up front!" I shouted at Tinnion over the roar of the crowd.

Brian began walking away, trailing a plume of tobacco smoke.

"And we need more shots on goal! They're dribbling too much, they have to start passing and shooting and get rid of the ball!" I kept shouting at him all the way down the corridor and into the dressing room, where most of the players were lounging around.

Tinnion collapsed on a bench. I kept waiting for him to say something to the team – discuss strategy, praise some players, admonish others, lead them in a cheer, anything. He did nothing, except drag on his cigarette. I couldn't stand it.

"Okay, listen up everybody," I said, standing in the middle of the room. Tinnion was slumped behind me, fishing for another cigarette. I waited to catch everyone's eye.

"This is the time to stay focused," I said in my best Vince Lombardi style. "We are forty-five minutes from winning a championship. You will remember this day for the rest of your lives. But you're not there yet. You need another forty-five minutes of playing like champions to become champions!"

The only reaction my rant seemed to be generating was a few smirks from some of the players, and I realized that Tinnion was mimicking me behind my back.

"All right," I said. "Let's get serious. If you guys don't win tonight, you're fired. Every one of you. I'll never talk to any of you again. And what's more, you won't get paid next week!" Then I stormed out of the dressing room. I had used my ultimate weapon. Unlike other teams in the league, the Express had never missed a payroll. As I left, I could hear the players whispering among themselves, looking concerned. It worked. We scored two unanswered goals in the second half, winning 4 to 2, and the Detroit Express became the 1982 champions of the American Soccer League.

At the end of the game, the Silverdome was a mad house. In a city desperate for a win of any kind, in almost anything, this was like capturing the World Series, the Stanley Cup and the Super Bowl all in one.

The Express was front-page news in all the papers, and the leading story on radio and television. The governor called to congratulate me, and the state legislature issued a proclamation recognizing the achievement. For a few days at least, the city of Detroit floated on a cloud created by a team supported by less than 10,000 fans for an average game.

All this attention was late in coming, but I enjoyed it nevertheless. We had set ourselves a goal, and we achieved it. After the excitement faded, I realized that I took greater satisfaction not from winning the championship but from the impact we had made over the years on boys and girls who loved soccer, especially underprivileged kids to whom even the smallest gesture was important. During our ASL days I estimated that the Express had performed for 200,000 children, who watched and learned from skilled athletes. We also gave away an estimated 40,000 soccer balls to schools, clubs and children all across southern Michigan. That, in itself, makes the whole experience somewhat satisfying.

CHAPTER EIGHTEEN

HEIDI:
THE INTERNETS WOMAN OF THE CENTURY

All my activity during the years after returning to Detroit from Florida – the building of my company, the frantic commuting to Los Angeles and back, the pressure to make the Express a winning team and establish soccer as a professional sport – came at a price. And the price was my marriage.

In 1980, Karen and I had agreed our marriage was over. The effect on our children was as devastating as divorce is to any family.

When it comes to praising my kids, I'm no different from any other parent, especially those with children who have experienced divorce and remarriage. Karen and I had four children, and each was unique. Aleise, our first, was born in 1964. Heidi arrived in 1965, Heather in 1969, and our son H.L. in 1974. Parents cannot say they love one child more than another without being unfair to the other children and perhaps untrue to themselves and their family.

Of all our children, however, Heidi stood out as the most stubborn, most determined, and most insistent on exploring her freedom. She had the darkest complexion, reflecting Karen's features. Her other qualities, including her height – at age 16 she was five feet, ten inches tall – and especially her stubbornness, probably were acquired from me. She also had great athletic ability and participated in every sport that interested her, always with great success.

All children explore their independence at some point, but Heidi demanded hers almost from the day she was born. Nobody could change her mind no matter how hard they tried. I know, because while she listened to me and respected me, I could never shake her determination that she was right, and the rest of the world was wrong.

When she was twelve years old, I bought her a motor scooter, and as soon as she learned to ride it, she took off for parts unknown. Most twelve-year old's would travel only as far as a friend's house to show off their new toy. Not Heidi. She rode that scooter so far, she became lost and telephoned me to come and get her. I had no idea what Heidi would do with her life as an adult, but when my gift to her on her sixteenth birthday was a car, I worried a little about her brashness. Would she be responsible behind the wheel? I had reason to worry. But not about the car. When our divorce became final, Karen received all my assets, including the Florida property, with the exception of The Van Arnem Company and the Express soccer team. Under any accounting method you can name, the soccer team was not an asset but a liability.

Running my company following the divorce proved difficult and painful. The difficulty arose because it wasn't easy to focus on business dealings when my personal life was collapsing around me. The pain arrived when I discovered the guy I had appointed CEO for the firm had been conspiring with Karen to take the company from my hands, giving him control and giving Karen more of my assets than the court had awarded.

The result was an extended period of deep depression, a feeling I had never experienced before. I attempted to deal with my inner turmoil by buying a boat. I had no idea how to navigate on the water, and no inclination to sail further than the nearest Great Lake. Nevertheless, that summer I purchased a 46-foot Bertram yacht christened Sonny Express, which I kept anchored at The Old Club on Harsens Island in the St. Clair River. Set among several undeveloped islands, The Old Club had been established in the early 1900's by early automotive pioneers in the Detroit area and it remained a beautiful secluded place close to the city. It was my "hideout" and the Sonny Express was my means of escape.

The owner of a boat anchored not far from me was Warren Avis, who launched Avis Rent-A-Car in 1946. Warren's innovation, and the key to his early success, was to offer car rentals not from downtown locations, where everybody else in the business was located, but at airports, starting with Detroit's Willow Run Airport. Warren, who long ago sold Avis for a hefty sum and was living off his investments, had just married a stunning young French actress named Yanna Elbin. He enjoyed travel but he never flew first class on long flights. Instead, he would buy three adjacent seats and stretch across them with a blanket and pillow, enjoying a better sleep than the first-class passengers trying to get comfortable in a single reclining seat.

Warren was no more experienced at boating than me. In fact, I believed I could handle a boat better than him. So, when I saw Warren weaving his Chris-Craft out of the marina and up the river towards Lake Huron on his way to Mackinaw Island, I decided if he could do it so could I, and I spent much of the summer exploring the nearby waters in Lake Huron and Lake St. Clair. The beauty and tranquility of it all was relaxing, especially when my children were with me.

CHAPTER NINETEEN

JOCKEY CLUB, DETROIT RED WINGS, ABBA

The following year, I shipped the boat to Florida and anchored at a berth in The Jockey Club, a Miami marina favored by "The Beautiful People." A boat near mine was owned by the Bee Gees, who threw great parties. One night I met a lovely blonde Swedish woman on the Bee gees' boat. She had a young child with her and, like me, had recently undergone a painful divorce. She told me her name was Agnetha, and a few days later we had lunch together, this time with my children along. On the way back to the marina, she asked me to stop at a local music store where she could purchase some cassette tapes. While in the store she almost shyly showed me a record cover of the group ABBA, and there was Agnetha – a member of one of the biggest singing groups in recording history. In spite of her fame, she was among the most natural, unaffected people I have ever met, and I don't know why I didn't pursue a relationship with her.

The Jockey Club represented a weekend escape for me. From Monday to Friday, I remained in Detroit running my company, watching over my soccer team, visiting my children, and looking for ways to acquire another professional sports team with a better promise of profits than the Express. Berthing my boat at The Jockey Club provided a great opportunity, because two other yachts anchored there were named the Red Wing and Blackhawk. Blackhawk belonged to Bill Wirtz, owner of the Chicago NHL team, and Red Wing was Bruce Norris's boat. Bruce's family had owned the Detroit NHL team since its inception and gave their name to the league's Norris Division, but in the early 1980's neither the team nor its owner was in very good shape.

Bruce Norris was on heavy medication to dull the pain of a severe arthritic condition. The effects of the medication on his liver, along with years of enjoying alcohol, were responsible for his death just a few years later.

This was the year after the Express won the ASL championship, a time when I should have been building on its success and pursuing my plan to turn the league into a force that would propel soccer into a professional sport. Perhaps it would inspire American kids to dream of being soccer stars the same way they dreamt of playing major league baseball and football.

But my enthusiasm for soccer in general, and the ASL in particular, was beginning to wane. Within a few weeks of the championship game, I realized that nothing outside Detroit had changed. The other teams were still refusing to pay their bills, and the owners were demonstrating the same low-life behavior and lousy business practices that concerned me in the past. As much as I loved the sport and the team I assembled, and as much as I wanted soccer to succeed at the grass roots in this country, I just couldn't see myself doing it with my ASL partners.

The Detroit Red Wings, however, were another matter.

The Red Wings, one of the proudest franchises in professional hockey, were beyond the glory days when Gordie Howe made the team a perennial contender for the Stanley Cup. Howe had retired ten years earlier, and with him went much of the Red Wings' success as a team and a business. Season ticket sales were hovering around 4000, no one appeared happy with Ted Lindsay's management, and the operation was essentially bankrupt. Valued at perhaps $10 million, the franchise had a debt of roughly the same amount and was facing the prospect of another losing season.

I approached Norris about buying the team, and he agreed on condition that I assumed the $10 million debt. Norris's price was double the debt, making it a reasonable deal on the surface, but I wasn't aware how serious the cash flow problems were. In any case, I needed deeper pockets than my own to acquire the franchise and keep it solvent during a turn-around period, so I approached

Detroit business people as potential partners. The owner of a local toy store chain, and several traders who had made fortunes recently from the gold exchange, pledged financing. I also recruited two key management guys to help run the operation. Don Canham, a local legend as athletic director for the University of Michigan, would bring a winning tradition to the group. Linc Cavalieri, the Red Wings VP, supported my purchase proposal.

I attracted other investors with a system adapted from my experience at leasing computers. Depreciation losses from leased equipment would offset net earnings, providing a built-in tax shelter that over time would increase in value to an enormous level. This was an unusual move back then; in fact, I believe we were the first to offer such a plan to investors in professional sports teams.

Everything was coming together, and I began working towards the June 1st deadline set by Bruce Norris to close the deal.

CHAPTER TWENTY

HEIDI SHOT AND QUADRIPLEGIC ADA FOUNDING- ENTREPRENEUR

One evening in March, I was preparing to attend an evening event on behalf of the upcoming Special Olympics where I was to be one of two MC's. While getting dressed in my black tie and tuxedo, my mind bounced back and forth between the details to be worked out on the deal to purchase the Red Wings and the comments I would be making from the podium during the charity affair.

Suddenly, someone began banging insistently on my front door, and I opened it to find several police officers, their cruisers parked at the curb with flashing blue lights. They practically burst into the room and began hustling me out the door, telling me I had to come with them right away. Was I being arrested? No, I was informed. It was worse.

"Your daughter has been shot," they told me, and we roared off to the emergency room at St. Joseph's Hospital in Pontiac.

The story came out in small revelations from the police, and in greater detail from others later. It was so outrageous that I have difficulty dealing with the facts to this day.

A girlfriend of Heidi's had confessed that she had nothing to wear to the upcoming Spring Prom. Heidi, as generous as she was determined, volunteered to bring one of her own dresses to the friend's house, suggesting her friend try it on. If her friend liked it, it was hers for the prom. Tossing the dress in the back of her car, Heidi drove to the friend's house where, walking down a corridor, she passed the bedroom of her friend's 12-year-old brother. Living with their working single mother, her brother was home unsupervised.

Somehow, the boy got his hands on a .22-caliber rifle. Reclining on his bed, he aimed the weapon at Heidi as she passed his open door. "Stop or I'll shoot," he called to her.

Before Heidi could respond to what she assumed was a silly joke, he pulled the trigger and the bullet passed through Heidi's neck, severing her spinal cord as cleanly and completely as a scalpel.

"I felt as though I had been electrocuted," Heidi recalled later. "My legs just gave out and I was suddenly on the floor. It felt like I wasn't breathing."

At the hospital, still trying to grapple with the news, or as much of it as I had been told, a doctor almost ran into the emergency room, gripped my shoulders, and began to shake me. "Your daughter has been totally paralyzed," he said. "She will never use her body again. Understand? We are trying to save her life. That's our only priority now!"

To this day, I do not know if this was his method of forcing me to deal with a nightmarish development or if he was losing control of his emotions the same way he expected me to do. Whatever his intent, I remained stunned when I was finally permitted to enter Heidi's room.

She was placed in a Stryker frame, a device that enabled her to be turned front to back and side to side. The sight of my daughter in such a contraption was chilling enough, but as I watched her body shook with waves of spastic motions. Each time they flowed over her tears would pour from her eyes until she fainted. I began demanding an explanation, and a surgeon took me aside to provide me with the facts of spinal cord injuries.

With an injury like Heidi had suffered, portions of spinal cord tissue remain suspended within the spinal column. Those above the break remain connected to the brain; those below it are connected to the motor operations of the body.

The spinal cord is basically a two-way transmission wire that carries sensations from the body to the brain and sends impulses from the brain to the nerves and muscles. Jagged ends of Heidi's severed spinal cord were connecting from time to time and, just as with bad electrical connections, power would flow like a shower of sparks for an instant. When this happened, Heidi's body was wracked with pain, the agony so intense that she would pass out.

"Do something," I told the surgeon. "Give her morphine or something, enough to dull the pain."

He shook his head. "We can't," he said. "We need to monitor all of her vital signs for a while. Medication might conceal something we need to know."

I cannot begin to describe what it is like to see your child disabled in such a manner and undergoing terrible agony that neither you nor the medical professionals can relieve.

Anyone who thinks a spinal cord injury is simple, if devastating, has never watched a young person undergo the transformation from active, lively human being to a quadriplegic. Everything in the body is affected, not just the limbs. The doctors were concerned about Heidi's breathing, convinced she could never breathe without assistance again. They worried about brain damage due to a lack of oxygen, and they warned me that her internal organs would likely suffer damage. All of this happened in one instant, one microsecond, when a foolish young kid fired a weapon that should never have been in his possession. Over those first days I didn't know whether to cry with grief or explode in rage.

I visited Heidi every day she remained at St. Joseph's. The hospital was about five miles from my home, and for every visit I made to her bedside I ran all the way. I wanted to feel pain for Heidi; I wanted to somehow share some of the physical agony she was enduring. By running that full five-mile distance I would experience pain while dissolving some of the anger and frustration I was feeling.

Eventually we moved her to the Craig Institute in Denver, a facility specializing in the treatment of spinal cord injuries. By a strange coincidence, she was placed in a room next to Gary Stroh, a member of the Detroit Stroh Brewery family and an attorney of my brother-in-law Phil Kessler. Gary had suffered an injury similar to the one Christopher Reeve would endure several years later, both of them thrown from horses. I have always been fascinated by the contrasting reactions between Gary and Heidi following their injuries. At age 50,

Gary assumed his life was effectively over; at age 16, Heidi believed her injury had simply thrust her in a new direction, and she remained in Denver for a year and a half, learning to deal with the new person she had become. Gary gave up. Heidi grew more determined.

Whenever I visited Heidi at St. Joseph's, at the Craig Institute in Denver, and later at home in Detroit, she demonstrated more strength than I had a right to expect from her – in many ways, more strength than I had myself. She never complained about her situation, and she always expressed concern for my health, well-being and happiness. She only became angry if someone expressed pity for her. She did not want to be pitied. She wanted to be successful and, perhaps, envied. More than anything else, she wanted to be viewed not as a freak but as a normal person.

No matter how much I tried to imagine what it was like to go from an active and healthy 16-year-old to a totally dependent quadriplegic in an instant, the challenge was beyond me. I would begin to feel perpetual rage, frustration and depression. If Heidi felt those emotions, she concealed them completely. In many ways, the injury did not depress her; it elevated her to a godlike status. Whenever I visited her, I forgot my own problems because Heidi would not let anyone be depressed in her presence. She remained cheerful and kind, and after the physical effects of the first round of medications wore off, she became more beautiful than ever.

She also stunned the medical profession by learning to breathe on her own, something the doctors believed impossible. It would not be the first time Heidi surprised the world. She also learned to employ biofeedback, enabling her to write with a pen and use a computer keyboard.

Heidi's injury and her response to her disability removed any chance that I might ever feel sorry for myself. From the day of her injury, I saw that we cannot be certain of anything in this life because we never know what may occur in the next minute. That's not a pessimistic view; it's a healthy one. We need to exert all the powers available to us right now, and not waste them. Heidi proved that philosophy, and I live it.

Heidi had never considered the problems facing people with disabilities, such as access to public buildings, before the shooting. Why should she? Almost no one else did in the mid 1980's. Side-effects of the gunshot wound, beyond the basic one of near-total paralysis, remained forever. Until her blood-flow stabilized, she continued to have spasms that would lurch her out of her wheelchair and onto the floor. A few of the effects of the blood-flow problem were startling. For example, at times one side of her face would be a deep scarlet red and the other side would turn almost snow-white

After completing high school, she attended Oakland University in Rochester Hills, Michigan, graduating cum laude, and announced plans to attend law school. Things were merely difficult for her in high school and university; in law school, they became impossible. The school provided neither disabled parking nor facilities for people with disabilities and offered no evidence that it gave a damn about the needs of people like her. She could not attend classes because, with no elevator or other lifting device, she couldn't reach them. After a year of frustration, she abandoned plans to become a lawyer. I assured her that this was fine with me because I never liked the profession very much anyway.

We discussed what she should do next, and somewhere along the line we combined two interests. Hers was travel. Mine was helping her gain the financial independence she desperately craved. If her injury taught us anything at all, I suggested to Heidi, it proved that we never know what is going to happen next, so we had better be prepared. One way to prepare for the unexpected is to make money. A lot of money.

Among my investments was Fugazi Travel, a long-established travel agency based in New York and Boca Raton, Florida. It didn't take Heidi long to launch her own travel service, Travel Headquarters, specializing in arrangements for both able bodied travelers and disabled travelers. Travel Headquarters represented a dramatic breakthrough for people suffering from various disabilities. The travelers needed to know that the elevators, corridors and doors could accommodate motorized wheelchairs, that tour buses could handle wheelchair-bound passengers, and dozens of other concerns that never occur to those of us with full mobility. Even with pre-boarding assistance, for example, people in wheelchairs had difficulty reaching their seat, which was almost always at the rear of the aircraft. Heidi began addressing these concerns, first with information and education, and later with demands and persuasion.

Travel Headquarters grew quickly under Heidi's management. It soon occurred to Heidi that if she and her staff could satisfy the needs of disabled travelers, they could meet the expectations of senior corporate executives. She made a pitch to top-level management at GM, Ford and other local corporations, who agreed with her, and soon Travel Headquarters was booking trips and accommodations for business leaders in the Detroit area. Within a few short months of launching her firm, Heidi was managing a staff of 16 travel professionals.

Her success with the travel operation energized Heidi. She became instrumental in the design and passage of the Americans with Disabilities Act (ADA), promoting the inclusion of people with disabilities into day-to-day society. The ADA recognizes that people with disabilities have special needs to make their workplace more accessible, but it is difficult for many people with disabilities to find employment because of the negative perception that employers have of them. Heidi's efforts to shape and implement the ADA also influenced the creation of the President's Committee on Employment of People with Disabilities.

There was no holding her back. She began writing a column on the challenge of disabilities in both the Detroit Free Press and the Detroit News, and President Clinton recognized Heidi's selection as Entrepreneur of the Year, representing over 56 million Americans with disabilities.

With the rise of the Internet, Heidi spotted another opportunity. The Internet, she recognized, represented an ideal way for the disadvantaged to obtain access to vital information and communicate with each other about critical issues. Beyond the access benefit, Heidi saw a method of using funds more efficiently. Involved in fund-raising drives since her college days, she had been dismayed to see how much of the money designated to assist the disability community and find a cure for paralysis was spent on peripherals like advertising, offices and administrative materials. Finding a way to avoid these costs would make more money available to assist people with disabilities, and the Internet was the answer. She grew so convinced about the value of a website dedicated to people with disabilities that she sold the travel agency to her employees and started iCan.com. To fund the operation, she prepared a 40-page business plan, sent it off to a few investors, and received all the start-up money she needed almost overnight. I provided office space and network computer server time, but Heidi insisted on handling all her cash needs without me. As usual, she wanted to do things her way, and she did.

Soon she had a staff of 22 web designers, editors, assistants and technicians, and iCan.com became involved in activities far beyond even Heidi's dreams. Corporations like Ford and GM began consulting her about vehicle design and sensitivity training for employees dealing with disability issues, and millions of Americans accessed the site to exchange views and search for advice, guidance and materials related to disabilities. AOL was so impressed they made iCan.com an AOL keyword for disabilities, one of the first keywords used by the service. She also founded the non-profit Heidi Van Arnem Foundation to Cure Paralysis, and even patented and began marketing The Slinger, a lightweight lifting device for use in place of the sliding board used to transfer.

Every encounter with her was another eye-opener to me. She hated the wheelchair and worked from a sofa, sitting upright with her legs crossed. I would often enter her office to discover her with a telephone receiver held against each ear, carrying on two conversations at once, usually with a governor, a mayor, the CEO of some large corporation, or anyone she needed to help her reach her goal that day.

She took great delight in every achievement, and always seemed to be in competition with me. Calling me on the telephone she would say, "Hey, dad. Have you ever had your picture and a profile of your company in the Wall Street Journal?" before telling me to check a certain page of that day's issue. Naturally, I would, and there would be a photo of my daughter smiling back at the camera and a story about all the things she had accomplished and her plans for the future.

Heidi's skill and determination changed the world in many ways and at many levels. She founded the Heidi Van Arnem Michigan Youth Leadership Forum and was appointed Michigan Commissioner on Disability Concerns. Michigan passed new laws to protect the rights of the disabled, and established a state Department of Disabilities, both in Heidi's name. After her tragic passing, The Heidi Van Arnem Foundation launched the annual Heidi's Dream Ball, a black-tie gala to honor extraordinary individuals and businesses that open doors of opportunity for people with disabilities, and raise money to fund research in finding a cure for spinal cord injuries. Typically, Heidi's Dream Ball generates in excess of $100,000 per event, and among the recipients of the award was the late Christopher Reeve, a good friend of Heidi's.

Heidi was named Evan Kemp's Entrepreneur of the Year and Ben & Jerry's Citizen Cool. She also won the General Motors da Vinci Award for Information Technology, the first Small Business Development Lifetime Achievement Award from the Michigan Commission on Disability Concerns (MCDC), which the organization immediately called it the Heidi Van Arnem Award, and Oakland University's prestigious Odyssey Award.

Heidi's story appears in a display at the Liberty Museum of Philadelphia that honors 200 outstanding Americans of the 20th Century, where she is recognized for her achievements and advocacy of the disability community.

The honors poured in, and while my daughter's achievements no longer surprised me, I was constantly amazed at her ability to deal with issues of disability and communicate their importance to people. In 2000 I accompanied her to San Francisco, where she was named one of the Internet's top 25 women of the century, based on the success of iCan.com. Among the others sharing the stage and honors with Heidi were Carly Fiorina, CEO and President of Hewlett Packard; Dawn Lepore, CIO and Vice Chairman of Charles Schwab; and Linda Sanford, General Manager of Global Industries at IBM. During the ceremonies that evening, I realized that Heidi had become a legend.

Before her introduction, the audience watched a film on Heidi's life, followed by a speech delivered by her that was so eloquent and moving that everyone in the building – including me – was dabbing tears from their eyes. "Look at me and treat me as normally as possible," was the core of Heidi's talk. It is a request that every disabled person in the world wants to make, but I truly believe that no one has made it with more impact than Heidi, and she made it with more than words – she made it by living her life in a manner no one could have expected before that horrible day in March 1983.

Heidi may have believed that her survival and success following the shooting meant she was less vulnerable to physical dangers than other people. Perhaps that's why she ignored an infection. What could harm her now?

The infection spread, complications developed, and on Sunday, November 11, 2001 Heidi died at William Beaumont Hospital, Royal Oak, Michigan. She was 35 years old.

While in the hospital, Heidi was declared one of two winners of Office Depot's Businesswoman of the Year Award. The other winner was Madeline Albright, the former Secretary of State for the USA. The formal presentations were made two weeks after Heidi died. In the spring of that year, Heidi had been presented with the national Wyndham Women on the Way Award, another in a long string of awards, in New York City.

"It's appalling to think about the lives and dreams wasted, and the frustration that resonates through our community, due to, so much missed opportunity," she said when accepting the award. "This is what keeps me going and focused on doing everything in my power to bring about change."

My daughter Heidi brought about more change, in more ways, than anyone I have encountered.

CHAPTER TWENTY-ONE

DETROIT GRAN PRIX
CHRISTIE BRINKLEY-OLIVIER CHANDON

During the first weeks of Heidi's recovery from the gunshot wound, I was reminded of my commitment to purchase the Red Wings. Of course, the monumental deal that would have defined me as both a businessman and a sports enthusiast had shrunk in importance. I suggested that Mike Illich, the founder of Little Caesar's Pizza and a neighbor and friend, assume control of the team. The move represented both a good investment for Mike and a great promotional opportunity for his company, and he agreed. At the first game of the season that year, Mike introduced me to the crowd. I walked across the red carpet and onto the ice accompanied by my seven-year-old son H.L., who was both exhilarated and frightened out of his wits. It was a memorable moment for H.L. and a kind gesture by Mike.

Sports continued to fascinate me. I was no longer interested in sponsoring race cars, but I still loved the sound of motor racing and the skills of the drivers. In the mid 1970's I had approached Mayor Coleman Young with the idea of laying a racing circuit in downtown Detroit, similar to the circuits in Monaco and elsewhere in Europe. In our case, however, we would race cars made right there in Detroit – GMC Camaros, Corvettes and Firebirds against Ford Mustangs and Dodge Chargers.

The mayor agreed it was a perfect way to showcase the city and its most famous products, and one Sunday morning the entire circuit was cleared for us to run a Corvette along the entire length with Bill Bonds, a local TV sportscaster, shooting film footage from inside the car. Eventually, the idea grew until, in 1982, the Detroit Grand Prix was launched, becoming one of three Formula One venues in North

America. Unfortunately, this gave exposure to European cars and not Detroit-built vehicles as I had proposed, but it brought the city some much-needed publicity.

My racing activities introduced me to a number of owners and drivers, and among the most memorable was Olivier Chandon, son of the family that produced Moet-Chandon champagne. Olivier enjoyed life as much as any man I ever met, and his life included beautiful women – including Christie Brinkley, his girlfriend at the time. Most men dating Christie Brinkley would stop looking, but not Olivier. Every attractive woman caught his eye, and he was ready to turn on the charm.

One day I was visiting him in New York and the three of us – Olivier, Christie and me – were strolling past Saks Fifth Avenue when Olivier spotted a pretty young woman entering the store. Making some sort of excuse he slipped away, followed her in to the store, and got her telephone number. By the time he returned, Christie had figured out what he was up to and began screaming and hitting him with her handbag, right there on Fifth Avenue.

Their relationship was passionate and stormy. One minute they were physically hitting each other and the next they were pawing at one another. Olivier raced around the city on his motorcycle, wearing a sports jacket and jeans while Christie, in a flowing dress, clung to him from behind. They would go anywhere they wanted, along the sidewalk, up and down stairs, in and out of buildings. They were living a movie in real life, an adventure film that you just knew was going to end badly.

He brought Christie to Detroit during a Grand Prix race, and when they arrived at my home my seven-year-old son H.L. became totally speechless at the sight of Christie. She really was that striking. Later, I walked with them towards the V.I.P. section of the track, and she created more shouts, screams, whistles and moans than any of the famous Grand Prix drivers. She loved the attention, but she was absolutely mad about Olivier.

They broke up the following year when Olivier became involved with the daughter of the president of Venezuela. Olivier headed for Florida to test a new Porsche in early March 1983. The track was wet, the car was unfamiliar to him, and after a couple of circuits he lost it on a curve. The Porsche flipped and landed upside down in a rain-swollen gully. Olivier survived the crash but unable to release his seat belt he drowned before help could arrive. Christie was devastated by the news, and many who know her well said she took a very long time to get over Olivier's death.

Around the same time, I encountered another strikingly beautiful woman. Divorced from Karen, I was living in Bloomfield Hills across the road from Jim McDonald, president of GM. I drove a black Ferrari previously owned by rock superstar Bob Seger, traveled in limos accompanied by athletes, business executives and attractive women, and hosted endless parties that probably appalled many of my older, more sedate neighbors.

The house welcomed a constantly changing cast of houseguests, a mix of professional athletes and various girlfriends. One of the guests was Eric, a young American who had given up professional tennis to play soccer on a minor-league team. One day, Eric announced that he knew a terrific young woman, originally from the Detroit area, who had moved to New York City and recently returned to Michigan. Eric suggested I meet her.

"Invite her over," I said, thinking little more about it. I was frankly skeptical. If she was so terrific, I thought, why would Eric suggest that I meet her? Why wouldn't he keep her for himself? The next morning, a Sunday, I opened the front door to find a vision smiling back at me. Dressed entirely in a white dress, with the sun behind her, I was stunned by her beauty and the warmth of her smile. This was the woman Eric had mentioned. We introduced each other. She told me her name was Bridget Sahline, and she proved to have as much personality as she had beauty.

I had planned a party after the game at Tiger Stadium that evening, and I asked her to join us. She did, and her presence made an impact on everyone who attended. All the men were intrigued. All the women were jealous.

I didn't realize it at the time, but my bachelor days were over. Bridget and I were married and today we have three boys: Adam, Max and Sean. The tale remains a lesson on how your life can change in the time it takes to ring a doorbell.

CHAPTER TWENTY-TWO

WORLD'S LARGEST TECHNOLOGY LEASING CO
FINALCO ACQUISITION OF A PUBLIC COMPANY
WESTERN SAVINGS AND LOAN

The ASL finally folded that year. With it went the Express and my dream of promoting soccer as a grass-roots sport. The truth is, I was relieved. Sports, movies, TV syndication, none of it mattered to me anymore. When I looked around for new business opportunities to keep me busy, earn an income, and satisfy my need to build and operate something bigger and better than anyone else in the field, it was easy (and almost a relief) to return to equipment leasing.

Over the 20 years since I walked into GEs newly hatched computer division in Phoenix, things had changed in a manner no one could have predicted. IBM had introduced their PC three years earlier, a machine capable of doing everything the original mainframe computers had been doing at 1/20th the cost. While mainframes remained necessary for many functions, PCs were popping up on desks everywhere. Obviously, the concept of time- sharing, with its limited speed and costly access, was becoming as old-fashioned and impractical as using a horse and carriage for transportation.

Tax laws were changing as well. The IRS kept threatening to eliminate the accelerated depreciation provision, wiping out many of the leasing tax benefits that had been available to individuals. When the new rules were adopted in 1986, and the residual value of mainframe computers dropped to a fraction of their original estimate levels, leasing companies began collapsing everywhere. Most people saw this as the end of an industry. I saw it as an opportunity to play a different game under the new rules, picking up good companies and their massive portfolios at bargain prices.

The opportunities came from companies that kept plunging ahead while denying the reality around them. Large corporations are notoriously slow to react to changing environments. Even while tax benefits were vanishing and technology was racing ahead faster than anyone could have imagined a few years earlier, corporate giants could not recognize the prospects these changes represented. I could, and I began taking action.

I focused on technology leasing companies because that's the business I knew. With high overhead, dropping residual values, and leasing companies that tried to paint a pretty financial picture by inflating the residual values of equipment under lease, I expected some substantial firms would soon become available at bargain prices. And I was right.

In 1986 I began looking closely at Finalco Inc., the world's largest computer leasing company, located in Maclean, Virginia. An over the counter publicly traded company, Finalco had been founded as a capital equipment leasing operation in 1968 and had acquired almost $10 billion in leases. When the tax reform law virtually eliminated tax benefits, Finalco management refused to deal with the issue. In my opinion, they were acting like the crew of the Titanic, heading full steam towards an iceberg with nobody willing or able to turn it around.

I had established a connection with Finalco a couple of years earlier when I began buying leases from them at less than market value. On a visit to their head office, I saw that the executive management team, installed by a consultant acting on behalf of Finalco's bank, was running the place as though it were a non-profit institution instead of a publicly traded corporation that owed a duty to its shareholders. Meanwhile, costs were spiraling out of control and assets were shrinking. I picked up some good bargains there, but I knew the company could not continue in this manner for long. I launched an investigation into the firm, looking for the source of such bad management, and discovered that some officials with Western Savings & Loan were making major corporate decisions, most of them unwise. What was going on here?

Western S&L, led my Gary Driggs, held shares in the name of a recently fired Finalco president and some other former top management members who had pledged their shares to the S&L as collateral for loans to buy shares in an IPO sale. This was in addition to Western's 20 percent ownership of the company. When Finalco share prices fell, the loans became under-collateralized and Western management stepped in, seizing control of a majority of Finalco's outstanding shares.

This looked intriguing, and examination of the company's K1 financials proved even more interesting. According to Finalco's own figures, filtered through my evaluation of their lease agreements, the company's value was about $15 million but they were holding leases with residual values of about $60 million.

I contacted Fred Hoops, a brilliant maverick lawyer I knew. Together we concocted a plan to acquire controlling interest in Finalco. My first step was to visit the former CEO whose company shares, representing about 25 percent of the firm, were in the hands of Western Savings and Loan, which was about to foreclose on him. I offered a combination of cash plus a promissory note in exchange for the shares, the note to be paid when I completed my acquisition of the company. Eventually he agreed because, frankly, he had nowhere else to go.

Next, I approached other ex-management members who were in the same position and made them a similar offer. This took more work than expected, but thanks to some brilliant strategy from Fred Hoops by late 1987, shares representing 56 percent of Finalco were in my hands instead of in the hands of Western Savings & Loan.

This did not make me popular with the S&L. Western had about $10 billion in assets, which is not nearly as impressive today as it was twenty years ago. The firm valued their investment in Finalco at about $22 million, which showed up as hard assets on their balance sheet. Applying the S&L guidelines that required firms to hold three percent of their outstanding loans as net capital, this meant the $22 million in Finalco permitted Western to loan 33 times that amount, or over $700 million. Without the Finalco shares listed in their asset base, the S&L would be forced to lower their outstanding loans by almost three- quarters of a billion dollars.

Scrambling around to preserve their asset base, Western wanted the Finalco equity converted to a debt because the actual equity value of the shares was less than $3 million. Converting their $3 million in stock value into $22 million in secured debt was clearly illegal. To help carry off the deal they hired John Cotton, a heavy-duty takeover artist whose first action, supported by members of Western's management group, was to attack me personally, telling Finalco employees that they would suffer if I were to assume control of the company. The slander had no effect on the overall situation. I had covered the debt of the former Finalco officers, and the bank should relinquish the shares to me.

On January 13, 1988, my son Adam was born at 9:00 a.m., the first child for Bridget and me. At noon, the same day we sealed the agreement with Finalco, transferring 56 percent of its shares to a partnership I had created to do the deal. Within three hours I had launched a new family and a totally new direction for my career, this one at the helm of a publicly- traded company.

Later that week, my lawyer and I arrived at Finalco's head office to attend a scheduled board meeting, routine action for a guy who controlled most of the company. As soon as we stepped into the building, a security guard ordered us to leave. "Wait a minute," I said, "I'm the new owner of this firm!" Unfortunately, I wasn't paying his salary, and we were forced to leave.

Western's top executives had good reason to keep me from looking too closely at Finalco's operations and records. As I learned later, Western had been concealing a few facts from the SEC, and they were quite rightly concerned that I would reveal their secrets. Permit me to see the books, check the records, and perform an audit? Not on their life.

Nearly three months and about $500,000 in legal fees later, I reached an agreement with Western that acknowledged my position as co-chairman but denied me a position as officer of the company. To run the company that I owned, on paper at least, I had to find a CEO acceptable to both Western and me. Both of us finally agreed on Jim Boris, who recently had held the president's chair at Paine-Webber. Boris, a Vietnam vet, once planned to become a doctor but he switched to a business career when he saw a bigger earnings potential there.

During our discussions, Boris demanded a $1 million annual salary, more than twice as much as I had expected to pay him. We settled on $750,000, which was still too high in my opinion. Of course, since we were both co-chairmen, I could claim the same salary level, and I did. Boris had a background in finance, but he knew little about the complexities of Finalco's business when it came to understanding lease structures, computer technology, equipment values, tax implications, and other critical issues. I expected to guide him in his decisions for the first few months, but within weeks of moving into the best corner office in the building – I was assigned an over-sized broom closet down the hall – he appointed a former cohort at Paine Webber, who was as inexperienced in complex leasing agreements as Boris was, to become COO.

It didn't take long for the new COO to begin objecting to my presence in meetings, especially when I questioned management's elaborate luxury car rentals and expensive business trips. They were spending money as though it were going out of style. Had it been their own money, they would have been more frugal. None of my concerns made an impact on either man, and I soft-pedaled them until an incident with our public income funds occurred.

Finalco had joint-ventured with the brokerage firm Raymond James, with Finalco acquiring leases and managing the assets, and Raymond James raising money and issuing reports to investors. About six months after Boris came on board, Raymond James offered to buy the income funds, a move that I opposed. I wanted a qualified and accurate appraisal of the funds' value before I could agree to dispose of them. Raymond James' offer was tempting, but I didn't want to risk losing future business from the lease customers. I needed time to consider all aspects of the deal before making a decision.

That's when Jim Boris and I tried to fire each other, creating a stand-off that could only be settled either by my abandoning ownership of the company or Boris choosing to quit.

The experience with Boris illustrated the difference between entrepreneurs like me and by-the-book executives like him. I could start new ventures or turn bankrupt companies into going concerns. I could also manage an existing company, expanding it into new markets and generating profits over time. Most managers can do the second thing, but they are hopeless at doing the first, and that's where Boris and his team discovered their limits. They had tried running Finalco as though it were a solid, mature company with the cash flow of IBM. It was not. The company needed major surgery if it was to survive, and they weren't equipped to perform it.

With Boris gone, I reshaped the operation while ignoring threats from Western Savings & Loan. Adding up the number of people on our staff list, I counted 400 full-time employees, about five times more than we needed. Of those 500, about two dozen were in-house lawyers and paralegals, yet we were spending $500,000 a month on outside legal services. This was a problem to be dealt with, but my initial concern was the top executive group, including the COO, CFO and a couple of others, that Boris had brought in and who remained after his departure. Their loyalty was to Boris, not to me, and none of them fully understand the business anyway. Replacing them with my own team was a necessary first step, and I took it as soon as possible.

Key to restructuring the top management group was Phil McKnight, who I moved into a senior position and later installed him as President and CEO. Phil had been the moving force behind ITT's Global Electronic Messaging Network, the dominant provider of fully integrated world-wide technology services. Before that, he had developed the world's first home computing and electronic messaging network and pioneered on-line office automation solutions. Phil's background provided a chance to reduce my dependence on leasing and replace it with technology-based services, a move I had seen coming for some time. I needed him to help me slim down Finalco and prepare for the switch to technology, and after hearing my offer he willingly and enthusiastically took charge. We went to work, meeting and shaping things, putting in 18-hour days, often seven days a week.

Beyond over-staffing, Finalco was managing more than 900 syndications and over 21 public income funds, acting more like a conglomerate of financial services than a leasing company. Those public income funds remained a problem. They were being sold through agents to IRA holders across the country, despite the fact that they were not good investments for people building a retirement nest egg, in my opinion. Their returns remained sub-par because computer technology was moving faster than anyone could have forecast a year or two earlier, cutting deeply into potential residual values. People were buying the funds on the basis of past performance levels before the technology wave arrived, and the funds could never match those returns in the future. When it came time for me to sign the annual report detailing their performance, I refused to do it. I killed the funds, paying close to 100 cents on the dollar to investors, hoping they would move the money to more suitable vehicles. Most did.

With the income funds gone I focused my efforts on Finalco's future, which appeared less and less likely in Virginia. A year earlier, Bridget and I had purchased a small farm in Virginia from Susan Ford, the daughter of former president Gerry Ford. It was a lovely place, with horse barns and green pastures. We also had a winter home in Ft. Lauderdale. The winters in Virginia were milder than those in Michigan, but they were still winters. I began missing the year-round warmth of Florida, and in the midst of redirecting and reshaping Finalco into a profitable entity, I speculated on the idea of returning to Florida permanently, taking the company with me. Why not? I was enjoying my job. Why couldn't I enjoy my surroundings as well? Not everyone in the company would relocate with me, but perhaps that was a good thing. Only the employees who were dedicated to the company's future and who enjoyed working with me would come along. It sounded like a good method of winnowing the firm down to a smaller, more dedicated core of workers. This was especially important in Virginia's Fairfax County where, thanks to restrictive labor laws, dismissing employees was becoming neither easy nor inexpensive.

CHAPTER TWENTY-THREE

EXODUS TO BOCA RATON

In early 1989, I selected five key people at Finalco and asked them to join me for a management meeting in Florida. We flew to Lauderdale, checked into the Bahia Mar, and gathered in a meeting room where I announced the purpose of the trip: The company would be moving to Florida. Our objective was to scout a location to work and live for those employees and their families who wanted to come with us.

We used the simplest of techniques, renting a car and driving around the area north of Lauderdale, and settled on the Boca Raton area. IBM, which maintained a presence there for many years, had recently announced they were vacating the area, producing a temporary glut of both houses and office space that dropped prices dramatically.

I discovered just how dramatically prices had fallen when I spoke to the local Chamber of Commerce a few days later, announcing my decision to move to Boca and hire perhaps a hundred or more employees. As soon as I stepped down from the podium, I was approached by agents offering me commercial space, and as I stood listening to their pitches, the prices dropped. The first offered quality space at $15 a square foot, the next said he could match the space at $12 and another undercut him at $10. In the end I took the entire 100,000 square foot facility that had housed IBM, getting it for about $1.50 per square foot. The extent of this bargain is best measured against the price I had been paying in Maclean, Virginia: $30 per square foot. In fact, the savings in Florida office space cost covered our total relocation expenses.

About 200 employees and their families made the move to Boca. Traveler's Insurance handled the necessary arrangements, and nine months after that first visit to Boca everything and everybody was in place, an amazing piece of logistical planning. I am even more proud of the fact that the relocation occurred in the midst of major changes conducted within the company's operation. With overhead and operating expenses reduced, a smaller employee group, a decrease in our debt load, and a new operating plan and budget controls in place, Finalco managed to produce a profit for the first time in three years. We also settled a few outstanding lawsuits in the bargain, and as 1990 approached I launched my plans to reinvent the firm.

Finalco was now a liquidator more than a leasing company, which is one reason I wanted the 100,000 square foot IBM building with its 48-foot ceilings. I wasn't interested in new leases, nor was I interested in raising public money. I wanted control over a market based on liquidating off-lease equipment, an industry with the potential of expanding to enormous size.

Soon the old IBM space was filled with used and refurbished capital equipment, including computers, aircraft parts, telecommunication devices and even modular buildings. We knew how to market these items, most of them available to us at prices reflecting their diminished residual values, and we set out to buy companies and the off-lease equipment at bargain prices. With a new location, reduced overhead and tighter controls in hand, I hired two former Finalco employees who had been dismissed by previous management and who knew the business as well as I did. They came aboard, moved their families to Florida, and together we identified companies that fit our growth strategy, eventually buying Pacific Telephone Finance, Bell Atlantic Computer Products, AmEx Technologies, and others. The actual value of the companies we brought under our corporate umbrella was about $3 billion. We acquired most of them for next to nothing.

How were we able to strike such great bargains? We had three advantages: agility, expertise and location.

Most of the companies were subsidiaries or divisions of the same firms I described as steamships, unable to maneuver and meet changing conditions until it was too late. The parent firms saw them only as liabilities and were becoming nervous about carrying them on the books. Their inventory included leases on products whose book residuals were out of touch with the real market values, and management didn't know what to do about it.

We did. We had the expertise to valuate and remarket the equipment at a profit. Even if the parent firms were able to move quickly and correctly to dispose of their leasing inventory, close up shop and cut their losses, their profile and location often prevented them from taking this step. Large mid-west and north-east companies were finding it difficult to close operations and dismiss employees without generating negative PR, along with pressure from elected officials and labor advocates demanding large severance payments. But as a smaller company located in a state with little union support, we could take over the operation and close the shop without problem. Employing this tactic, we expanded our portfolio until we became the largest dealer in off-lease equipment and high-tech parts wholesaling in the world, picking up distributorships and marketing expertise in the bargain.

We were dealing with leases on a wide range of equipment from several of the biggest and best firms in the business. Assuming control of PacTel's Select Leasing, we picked up 6700 leases on computer and telecommunications equipment with an original cost of $100 million. Leveraged leases from First Interstate Bank of Denver brought in leases on commercial aircraft, railway locomotives and mining equipment costing over $166 million, and Home National Bank in Massachusetts had capital leases on equipment valued at $30 million. Other acquisitions, including Pacificorp Financial Services, Interlogic Trace Incorporated, and R. J. Leasing represented another $150 million in computer and telecommunications leases. We purchased them all for a fraction of their real value.

Growing so big and so fast was quite an achievement but dealing exclusively with leasing meant too many limitations to growth, so in 1992 I liquidated Finalco and created Gemini Equities. Within two years, Gemini was the 20th largest capital asset funding in the world. The spreads between access to capital and lease returns were rapidly shrinking, and while I remained in the industry, I began searching for the next stage in the computer revolution. It proved to be, of course, the Internet. Around this time, I was introduced to Tom Benham, a former IBM employee who decided to stay in south Florida when IBM vacated Boca Raton. Tom and a partner had launched a local Internet service called Cybergate to serve individual users. When we met, Tom was working out of a ten-foot-square office with his computer installed, literally, in an adjoining closet. The concept of a World Wide Web (WWW) had just appeared, and I could see it expanding the concept of the Internet into a totally new dimension of telecommunications, with a potential literally to change the world.

Benham and I soon reached an agreement. I purchased his partner's interest in Cybergate for $300,000, provided Benham with office space in a building I owned in Hillsboro, and granted him a $1 million loan to create an Internet-based communications center. The ink had barely dried on the contracts before AOL roared into Florida, seeking to wrap up the entire state as AOL customers. We fought back with billboards all along I-95 saying AOL is a great place to get started BUT..., followed by all the benefits of Cybergate.

The day after the campaign began, we received ten calls, followed by 50 the next day, 100 the day after that, and soon over 500 each day, all of them wanting to be Cybergate subscribers. We had a winner!

By now it was clear that many of the ideas I had proposed years earlier, including movies on demand and other entertainment/communications services, were about to become a reality thanks to the advent of high-speed connectivity. While Cybergate was proving a great success, my strategy was to use it as a bridge while I moved the firm from leasing mainframe computers to providing customers with local area networks (LANs) and wide area networks (WANs). The customer base was already available in our leasing portfolios. Next, I needed a captive hardware source to pull things together into a vertically- integrated service.

CHAPTER TWENTY-FOUR

MEMOREX TELEX-CIS

I found it in Texas, where Memorex Telex, a huge company with annual revenues of over $2 billion, was liquidating its leasing operations under Chapter 11 bankruptcy protection. Like many firms successfully launched when the computer revolution was young, Memorex was not as nimble when developments began outpacing the ability of management to follow them. It was an unfocused company, and I decided to restore its focus.

Admittedly, two billion dollars in annual revenue was larger than anything I had tackled before, a fact that did not intimidate me but made a few Memorex people unhappy. In search of funding, I visited Manhattan-based investment banking firms. And in search of credibility among the unhappy Memorex principals, I recruited Bill Packard from Unisys to help manage the changeover. Packard had grown disillusioned with the direction of Unisys, second only to IBM in size when it came to mainframe computers, and he agreed to meet me in Dallas. I offered him an equity position in the new company, but my investment bankers were not the right fit to assume the risk they believed that Memorex Telex represented. In the end, Packard and I accepted a management contract to operate the firm under Chapter 11, with the understanding that it was an interim agreement until we obtained control.

Meanwhile, other things were happening. A year earlier, I began exploring an opportunity to acquire Ultimate Computer Leasing from AmEx Germany. UCL was categorized as a leasing bank with $1 billion in computer leases. I also planned to pick up Continental Information Systems out of Syracuse, NY, a giant bankruptcy operation that ironically was also under Chapter 11 protection.

Reading the business press each day, many people may assume that acquiring companies the size of these two firms is similar to buying a house – you size up the place, get an appraisal or two, round up a source of capital, then negotiate and settle on a price. When the target firms are essentially bankrupt, the process must be simplified, right? If only it were that easy.

In the case of both Memorex and CIS, I did all the work upfront; neither trustee appeared anxious to hand over the company for a fair price and move on. It soon became clear that both trustees had other ideas in mind beyond their legal responsibility. The CIS trustee worked against me in order to gain full control of the firm's assets for himself. What other conclusion could I reach when the court would agree to my terms on one hand and the trustee would reject them on the other hand? The CIS trustee fought me so long and hard to derail the deal that when I was offered the company's European operations with headquarters in the UK and France almost as a consolation prize, I accepted. I didn't give up; I simply planned to merge them with UCL's German operations.

Battling the CIS trustee drew attention away from Memorex Telex, where things were going from bad to disastrous. If the fit with the investment bankers had been bad, the fit between me and Bill Packard grew worse. Packard, I realized, was a one-man band. He wanted total control and full recognition for everything that was happening at Memorex. It took several months to realize that I would not own Memorex after all. Nor could I have run it with Packard at the helm anyway. Chalk up another one to experience.

CHAPTER TWENTY-FIVE

ENTRY INTO EUROPEAN UNION
AMERICAN EXPRESS, CREDIT LYONNAIS, ZURICH REINSURANCE

Like it or not, I was now running a company with strong links to the European market. CIS operations in France and the UK represented a beginning, and I was continuing to assess the lease holdings of AmEx in Germany. My activities there uncovered other companies whose leasing portfolios were facing the same fatal crunch that had struck American companies a few years earlier. While my eye was still on Internet opportunities, I just couldn't cut loose entirely from leasing, because the value of a lease base both from a current cash flow from renewals and residual sales and the acquisition of a new computer user who I could sell my consulting and network services.

Credit Lyonnais, the largest French bank, unloaded its leasing arm Locinfor to me, a company with operations in France, Germany and the UK. Meanwhile, I sent a team to Wiesbaden to assess the portfolio of Universal Computer Leasing, the German AmEx division. With expertise and long hours of hard work, these portfolios could be quantified accurately according to equipment and associated residual values, lease expirations, potential add-ons and new business potential.

The summary presented to me on UCL was not pretty. The company correctly boasted that it had financed leases on $780 million of capital equipment, but our estimate of the residual value of that equipment after debt was negative value. What's more, UCL was facing potential litigation that threatened to produce negative cash flow.

I informed AmEx that I was prepared to discuss the acquisition of UCL, and a meeting was scheduled at the London offices of Lehmann Brothers, an AmEx subsidiary. The president of American Express bank parent of UCL, a young man named Bloomquist, arrived with his entourage, all smiles and brimming with confidence. We exchanged the usual pleasantries before he asked me how much I was prepared to offer for UCL.

"We're not sure we can offer you anything," I said. Bloomquist blinked but kept his smile. Had we changed our minds about doing the deal?

"No," I explained. "We're interested in purchasing UCL but the portfolio relative to debt has a negative value. I began reviewing the findings of my evaluation team, admitting that the company's $780 million in leases was an impressive number, but the residual value of the equipment was practically nil. Liabilities were substantial, and if all the legal challenges against UCL proved successful, they could balloon by as much as $25 to $50 million negative. "You can't just liquidate this company," I explained. I didn't need to remind him that liquidation or bankruptcy was out of the question because a registered bank in Germany could not file bankruptcy, but I could if necessary. Bloomquist appeared overwhelmed.

"What are you telling me?" he asked.

"I'm telling you that UCL has an apparent negative value of $25 to $50 million," I answered.

"That's impossible," he replied.

I explained that it was true and, if he would like, my people and I were prepared to review every lease in UCL's portfolio, establish its value, put an accurate evaluation on the residual value of the leased equipment, and explain how we arrived at our figures. That would take all weekend.

Bloomquist objected. I agreed. But if he wanted proof, we would provide it. So, we weren't prepared to make an offer to buy? Bloomquist asked.

No, I explained, we were not. But if AmEx would provide financing to meet forecasted shortfall and assume all the liabilities, since AmEx was a bank, and UCL as a division is a guarantor of all UCL liabilities which could be substantiated along with disposing of equipment coming off the leases.

He asked for a chance to discuss the situation in private with his staff. I agreed, and Bloomquist led his group out of the office, returning with a proposal: they agreed to our deal emphasizing our assumption of all liabilities and other governess issues.

We all agreed.

After weeks of attorneys and agreements we owned UCL. AmEx was happy to have the company off its books. We were happy to have it on our books, because over the next year or so we made about $8 million from the operation. We negotiated existing leases with new and add-on equipment with power house companies like Beyer, Daimler Benz, etc. We discovered non-booked leases and millions in off lease equipment that was still in place and not billing. It was a home run, but I don't think possible in the arms of AmEx.

Bloomquist was a smart, ambitious young guy who went far in AmEx. Later, when I met him through social contacts, I confirmed a suspicion I had when he responded to my news that UCL had no positive value. Had he known it all along? Of course, he had.

Later, in negotiations to acquire another leasing firm in difficulty, I encountered a similar situation with a much different outcome.

The company was C.O.S., the largest technology finance company in Europe and a publicly traded company owned by a consortium of major Swiss financial institutions that included Zurich Reinsurance, UBS, Swiss Banc Corp and others. The consortium partnered with C.O.S. as a leasing source for their computer and data equipment, and the company's board of directors consisted of Chairmen and CEOs from the banks, investment firms and insurance companies representing the backbone of the Swiss nation.

When bids were invited for the firm's assets we applied and won, based on our success with AmEx, CIS and others. I was pleased and the C.O.S. executives were so delighted that they invited Bridgette and me to spend some time touring the region around Zurich, where we were hosted at several dinners. As part of our commitment, I agreed to move to Switzerland during the first 2 years of our transaction.

C.O.S. wanted $150 million for a company with leased equipment valued at $1.5 billion according to their books. In my bid, I agreed to assess the company's worth according to Generally Agreed Accounting Practices (GAAP) as practiced in the U.S. The agreement also noted that C.O.S. would be required to pay me a break-up fee if they withdrew from their side of the deal. This was a fairly standard requirement, one that I insisted upon based on my experience in similar situations. This would protect our effort and due diligence and force them to sell the company at an exact purchase price. If they refused, they would have to pay me $5 million for my effort.

As part of due diligence, I sent a dozen staff members to Switzerland to examine the lease agreements and value the residuals. Their conclusion was stunning but not surprising: instead of the $150 million book value stated on its annual reports, C.O.S. was basically worthless. The residual values of equipment under lease were inflated according to our calculations and offset by accumulated debt. Liquidating the residuals would just cover the debt, producing zero net worth. The administrative overhead, over staffing, over spending had eaten all the cash and some residual borrowing.

A date and time were set for a meeting where we would present our offer to purchase the firm. The meeting reinforced an aspect of doing business offshore that I had observed for some time: the smaller the country, the weirder the times for scheduling meetings. In this case, the meeting was set for 9:30 in the evening.

My team and I arrived on time and, along with pushcarts filled with files, we entered a massive boardroom crammed with C.O.S. executives and representatives of their auditing firm, Price Waterhouse. After the usual pleasantries and introductions were exchanged, Julie, our controller, revealed a series of charts and began explaining our research and conclusions. With each revelation I watched tension and disbelief build on the faces of the C.O.S. owners.

Halfway through Julie's presentation, the chairman of Zurich Reinsurance, who was also the chairman of C.O.S., interrupted to ask if he and I could have a private conversation. I agreed and followed him out of the room into the hall.

Outside the meeting room he turned to me with a scowl on his face. "What is going on here?" he demanded.

I explained that our due diligence revealed an overstatement of residual values and an understatement of the company's debt, erasing the stated book value of the company. "I have a contract that says I will pay you the book value of the company," I reminded him, "and we have determined that the book value is zero."

I asked him, "If I am only fractionally right how could you not disclose the actual book value?"

"Are you suggesting that we are lying?" he sputtered. Before I could reassure him that our figures were accurate, he grew more enraged. "There is no Securities and Exchange Commission here," he pointed out.

"We take care of things ourselves. We are not litigious like you people in America!" I suggested, "without revealing our assessment that the residual values have been overstated."

I had heard that the Swiss are cool, calm and controlled, and perhaps they are. But not this man, and not this time. He claimed we were accusing C.O.S. of misrepresentation, and finally exploded. "The deal is off," he almost shouted, "You and your people must get out of here now!" I still had a contract which required COS to sell at book value (GAAP) or pay me $5 million. We struggled to find a law firm who would file a lawsuit against the Swiss establishment. We did. The law firm filed a claim on behalf of Libra (LGS), the European holding. The case was so clear cut that we persuaded them to work on a 100% contingency for (1/3 of the proceeds), and we won.

VAN ARNEM
TECHNOLOGY PIONEER

CHAPTER TWENTY-SIX

TELECOM DEREGULATION IN EU
EUROPE'S LARGEST NETWORK INTEGRATOR

In 1996 high speed connectivity was becoming a requirement for all enterprises. Competition and supply of bandwidth communication equipment technology was exploding in North America. Europe was still controlled by Telecom monopolies, France Telecom, Deutsche Telekom, British Telecom, etc. European wide telecommunication deregulations will take place on 1/1/98. LGS was preparing to compete by 1/1/98.

One of the leading data solution providers in Europe at the time was the Italian company Olivetti. I flew to Milan and met with the head of Olivetti's Computer Systems and Service Division. We agreed to meet in the United States, and I invited him to Florida with his teenaged daughter to stay on the corporate yacht. Dubbed the Quintessence, this was a 75-foot Cheoy Lee, very fast, with five bedrooms, and 3,000 sq. ft of living space. We visited South Beach, Miami and Ocean Reef Yacht in Key Largo, Florida before getting down to business. In our discussions I agreed that LGS would purchase Decision Systems International (DSI), Olivetti's networking services in Europe.

DSI was a substantial operation, employing 500 people located in 40 sales and service offices across France, Germany, UK, Spain, the Netherlands, Belgium and Luxembourg. Their staff included over 250 systems engineers servicing IBM platforms, although the company also had strategic partnerships with Novell, Microsoft, Compaq, Oracle and Bay Networks. Revenue for the previous year totaled more than $125 million. With DSI, I could see the synergies begin to work. All the leasing customers under my umbrella could become service customers, and all the service customers could be wooed to become lease customers.

The picture grew brighter when I flew to Paris and began negotiations to purchase Thomainfor, a subsidiary of the massive French company Thomson-CSF. France had nationalized Thomson-CSF in 1982, and by 1997 the French government had decided to spin off various subsidiaries to private enterprise, enabling the company to focus on core activities of electronics and defense. Thomainfor was even larger than DSI with 1300 people serving a customer base of 14,000 companies virtually everywhere in Western Europe, making it the largest network-related customer base on the continent. It was also a major money-loser for the French government, one practically begging for effective management and a clear corporate focus to turn it around.

I had traveled from Cincinnati to Phoenix to Detroit to Virginia to Florida, and now to Europe. In January 1997, my HQ was in the Bristol Hotel in Paris, where I began experiencing all the machinations involved in purchasing and managing a European company, complicated by the fact that Thomainfor remained part of the French government. I managed to close all two deals for DSI and Thomainfor within months. This would have been a remarkable achievement in the U.S., and it was even more impressive in Europe. I gave Phil McKnight due credit for all the organization, energy and patience he applied to make things happen so well in such a short time. If only the rest of the exercise had gone as smoothly...

Although LGSI now controlled companies with total annual revenues of almost $500 million, European rules prevented me, as an American, from serving as an officer in the firms or even from drawing a salary. I managed to skate around this madness thanks to my Irish grandparents. On the basis of their origins, I applied for and was granted Irish citizenship, enabling me to draw an income from the companies I was so busy managing.

It soon became apparent that the French workers at Thomainfor wanted nothing to do with LGS on the basis of our American roots, my ability to move quickly on deals, or perhaps just the way I dressed. The firm was dominated by the CGT, a socialist/communist-based union representing its maintenance workers. CGT union executives were outraged at the French government for selling the company to an American, and they did everything in their power to derail the deal. The union leaders knew every labor law on the books and every way to apply them. A string of special meetings was called, pulling all the union members off work without notice. Added to the disruptions was CGT's application of a peculiar French law permitting the union to demand that an independent auditor conduct a statutory audit whether company management agreed or not to determine financial viability.

To provide me with a cushion of time for moving Thomainfor from a money-losing operation to at least a break-even point, the deal involved 100 million francs, provided by the French government, that would fund the payroll for six months. By that point, I expected to have reduced the overhead and the synergy of DSI and Thomainfor working together would begin to kick in, improving earnings and profits. It was a good plan. It would have worked.

CGT kept throwing every available obstacle in my path, and within 6 months of closing the deal we would be running out of cash. In desperation, I called for a meeting with Thomson management to discuss the situation and look for a solution together, but within minutes of meeting them I had a clear picture of the real situation.

The French bureaucrats running Thomson had insisted on placing the six-month payroll funding agreement in a sidebar to the actual body of the contract. That was fine with my lawyers, who determined it was still enforceable, but it provided a convenient public relations exit for the French government. Whether they had planned it from the beginning, or they arrived at the conclusion after the fact, the Thomson people wanted the deal to fail under my management. Thomainfor had been a candidate for bankruptcy over an extended period; only by declaring insolvency and starting over with a clean slate did the company have any hope of stemming its losses as a nationalized entity. The bureaucrats running the company knew it, but they couldn't make it happen. Private enterprise could do what a government bureaucracy could not. But a government bureaucracy could not permit a nationalized corporation to grow broke because the unions would simply demand the government throw more taxpayers' money at the problem. The French government knew it was in a quandary. It would take a private corporation, preferably foreign and ideally American, to assume control of the sinking ship, which would sink anyway. Once things settled out, the government could re-enter the picture as a white knight and rescue the firm, imposing all the measures that the private owner had proposed. That's why the promise to provide six months' payroll funding was fixed as a sidebar; the French government could state, with a straight face, that it was not part of the original contract.

Business is business, and you need both a hard nose and a thick skin to succeed in it, as I learned over the years. But I had never experienced such a Machiavellian plan before, and I refused to accept the idea that I could be used so blatantly. Uniting the various company divisions into one firm would produce better service for our customers, more profit for the corporations, and greater job security for the employees. With enough effort, I believed, I could convince everyone involved that this was a goal worth aiming for.

So even while persuading Thomson to live up to the payroll funding arrangement I began bringing management groups together in a series of meetings to discuss the merger. The location of these meetings was always France because, as a government-funded corporation, Thomainfor owned spectacular facilities that would have been unaffordable for most well-managed private corporations. Over a hundred managers from the UK, Germany, France, Spain, Netherlands, Switzerland and Belgium arrived to hear the merger plans and discuss ways of making it work to everyone's advantage. That's when I discovered Rule #1 about doing business in Europe. According to this rule, World War Two may have ended 60 years earlier, and the European Economic Union may have created a free-trade zone, but you can't stamp out old problems quickly or easily. From day one, the management meetings looked more like raucous sessions at the United Nations instead of a collection of players on the same team.

Everybody in the room, it seemed, hated the French. The only people disliked more than the French were the Germans. Among all the people hired to mold the groups into one cohesive unit, I was the only one they viewed in a positive light. The younger, more ambitious people loved the idea of fashioning the company into a European powerhouse, and even the most negative managers were affectionate towards me compared with the French unions, who launched an offensive not only in my direction but in the direction of my family.

Bridget and our children arrived in Paris from the U.S., having completed their school year and prepared to settle down in a house I had rented from a Polish professional tennis player Wojtek Fibak who was also the wealthiest man in Poland. On that same day, a thousand union members paraded along the Champs Elysée carrying placards declaring LGS Pigs Go Home! A photograph of the marchers appeared on the front page of La Monde, welcoming my family to their new life.

Things grew worse. Working late one night with my management group, we discovered that unionized workers had soldered the metal doors shut, locking us inside. The following week our Mercedes was trashed – the windshield broken, and the tires slashed – and one evening Bridget, the boys and I returned home to find someone had broken into our house. When I began asking myself if whatever I was attempting to do could be worth the price my family was paying, we moved out of Paris and took up residence in London.

The discussions with Thomson kept dragging on and the money kept flowing out. When Thomainfor's 1200 service engineers stopped coming to work, creating an enormous problem for customers that included many French government departments, they essentially won. Based entirely on their dislike of LGS and our plans to expand Thomainfor, their union brought France to a standstill. That's when

I was forced to declare Thomainfor insolvent.

My disappointment was deep, of course, but it didn't last long because it was soon replaced with fear. Under EU law, any operator of a private corporation who fails to declare bankruptcy at the point where the company is unable to meet its financial obligations becomes personally liable for the corporation's losses, and the losses include wage and salary obligations to employees. This meant that I faced the risk of paying $200 million in Thomainfor losses out of my own pocket, a charge I could spend the rest of my life fighting in court. Fortunately, we battled and won this case thanks to a reasonable French judge and a good French law firm. But until the settlement was reached, I spent many sleepless nights worrying about the outcome.

Life went on, and I refused to dwell on the unfairness of it all and the money I had wasted. I planned to handle the European operations from London where I created a new firm, Total E, an umbrella over our multiple companies. With the loss of Thomainfor our annual sales volume dropped from $400 million to about $100 million, and our employee list was reduced to 600 from 3500. Still, we remained a force in Europe with a strong presence in the UK, Germany, Switzerland, France, Spain, Belgium and the Netherlands. We had been awarded over 500 network contracts amounting to over $200 million in network services provided by LGS and Telecom Italia.

Expansion prospects loomed, and I decided to take the company public, working through Robertson Stephens, a subsidiary of BancBoston. The Robertson Stephens people valued Total E at $500 million in order to raise $100 M for 20% of Total E with a go-public value of $1.5 billion. Retaining 80% which represented the vast majority of shares, I calculated a potential net worth from them of more than $1 billion. On that basis, I turned down an offer of $25 million for a ten percent share of the company.

Robertson Stephens planned a two-stage issue of shares, raising $25 million in the first round and $100 million in a second issue, and I went to work with my staff preparing the prospectus needed to accompany the issue. In April 1999 we were ready to go forward but no one had called from BancBoston for some time, nor could I reach anyone at Robertson Stephens. Finally, I got the news: Robertson Stephens was placing on hold most new IPO's indefinitely, including Total E. Meeting after meeting, and delays, we remained hopeful that Robertson Stephens would surely go forward after all the promises and commitments made by Robertson Stephens officials to the dozen plus companies, we had acquired on the promise that we were going public. Is it possible that the deal is off? The deal was off. In place of a possible $1 billion net worth, I had a $20 million out-of-pocket loss.

Could things get worse? Of course, they could.

Phil McKnight had been a key player in my European expansion efforts, and while I managed to shrug off the string of disappointments, I began to suspect they were changing Phil. Our relationship to this point had been in some ways like a general and a lieutenant plotting strategy and executing tactics, my position as the general reflecting the fact that I owned five times as much of the company as he did. In other ways, it was more like two old friends making their dreams come true together as business partners. We liked and respected each other, and Phil worked as hard as anyone to build the company into the powerhouse we both wanted it to be. The withdrawal of BancBoston from the plan to launch a public issue marked a change in Phil's attitude. Instead of a trusted lieutenant, Phil began acting like a general totally in charge of the troops.

Around this time, I began discovering things about the company that had not been disclosed by Phil in our gathering of material for the public offering, a fact that may have been responsible for BancBoston's sudden lack of interest. Phil had great talent and a lot of energy, especially when it came to marketing and promotion, but taking the company public required a more nuts-and-bolts approach than a marketing strategy. I also needed someone with the skill and experience to pull it off.

In search of help, I turned to a Texas-based management planning outfit that specialized in transforming and restructuring technology-based companies. Impressed with their track record, I hired the consultants, Woodrow Buckner. Their objective was to bring all of the European partners together and ensure they worked effectively as a team.

I made this decision on my own. When I informed Phil about it, his reaction was more like a jilted lover's than a professional businessman. Phil accused me of not trusting him and leaving him out of the picture, and he insisted that I cancel the contract with the consultants.

I refused. "Let's bring them in and see what they can do," I responded from Florida, where I had gone from London. "We need a new plan and we need to involve all country execs. We need for them all to buy into a resurrection. All countries must reach break-even at once."

Phil's answer was to fly to Florida and make outrageous demands. He wanted to be appointed CEO with a $200,000 increase in salary, he wanted the consultant contract spent, and he wanted several other things that would cost money without bringing a benefit.

I answered his demands as much as a friend as a boss. I explained that the company was under a great deal of pressure, both internally and financially, and this was not the time or the way to deal with these changes. Nothing could shake his determination. He resigned, and I returned to Europe to pick up the pieces all over again. I suspect he knew more about Problems in Germany and The Netherlands. He also knew without some meaningful capital input very soon it was going to be very difficult to install new business and placate the recent acquisitions that were not going to be public.

Looking through the detailed records behind much of Phil's activities, I uncovered a terrible mess. Our German operations, which Phil had constantly assured me were in good shape, were in reality a disaster. The company owed $10 million in back taxes, a fact that Phil had hidden from both me and the people at Robertson Stephens. Of almost $20 million I understood were in the coffers of the German company, perhaps $3 or $4 million remained.

I needed more capital, and I approached Parcom Ventures, a Dutch firm located in Amsterdam that specialized in providing short-term funding. We agreed on a $10 million investment from Parcom, one I believed they were making as a reasonable investment and nothing more. It took me a while to realize that Parcom wanted full control of my company. Over 30 years of business experience in America and Europe had ensured that we had a great deal of experience when it came to business deals, but my encounter with Parcom was a total revelation in the steps shrewd people will take to grab all the assets they can seize. Perhaps, boasting a Dutch background myself, I simply believed they would not act like a pack of sharks with me. But they did. Had I followed Vito Corleone's advice in The Godfather to "keep your friends close and your enemies closer," I might have avoided a disastrous experience.

Parcom's first move was to secretly approach the manager of Total E operations in the Netherlands, which was the country Total E Holding Company domiciled, proposing that he assume direction of the division on his own. Naturally, the manager thought this was a fine idea, especially with Parcom promising its full support.

Parcom managed one of two venture funds holding shares in my company, and they contacted the principal of the second fund to recruit him in their takeover plan. The principal, who was also CEO of a publicly traded computer service firm with which I had been negotiating a merger, began cementing a personal relationship with me, winning my confidence and trust.

Then, out of the blue, the manager of my Netherlands division handed me an ultimatum: Either I provide him with near-total control, or he would resign. With all of my other concerns, I agreed. He was a capable person and I did not need the distraction of searching for and appointing a new top-level manager.

Meanwhile, the European bankers were playing their own game, offering to provide more funding if I altered the structure and operation of the company according to their directions. By this time, Robertson Stephens was completely out of the picture and the only source of venture capital I had was Parcom. With Parcom holding the reins and providing management advice, I agreed to declare certain divisions insolvent as a means of maintaining the rest of the corporation.

Obviously, I was not fully knowledgeable about the difference between corporate law in the U.S. and similar laws in Europe. In most parts of Europe, it is possible for an individual to force a company into liquidation and arrange for someone else to acquire its assets without the company gaining protection under a European version of Chapter 11 rules in the U.S.

Following the advice of my contact at Parcom, I hired a bankruptcy trustee to manage the assets during a restructuring period while I worked with Parcom in an application to the British courts to have control transferred to them as my investment banker. This, I assumed, would be a temporary situation. I had a letter of agreement with Parcom that stated the company would be jointly owned between us until Total E paid off its financial obligations to Parcom. It represented a reasonable decision because I was paying Parcom hefty fees for their consultancy work. And the application was successful.

Let me rephrase that: Parcom was successful. Once the assets of Total E were within Parcom's control, they cut off all contact with me. I had paid them generously to finesse my own company out of my hands and into theirs.

In hindsight, it was clear to me that the Europeans had collaborated to obtain control over TOTALe and all the assets it possessed. My buddies at Parcom, who wined and dined me, arranged golfing trips and flattered me with compliments about my business acumen, persuaded the Netherlands manager to blackmail me at a vulnerable time. They worked with the banks to force concessions from me in a desperate move to retain control; and they had partnered with the trustee to set up court decisions that handed the assets to Parcom. All this happened while I was being billed monthly fees for their consulting services.

I know all about hard-line tactics of business deals, especially where the assets are valued in hundreds of millions of dollars. I have played that game myself, taking every legal advantage in negotiations and strategies where it profited my company and me. But I can say that I have never considered using the tactics that my European "partners" applied, one based on misplaced trust and deception. Nor would I. If those are the new rules of the playing field, I am prepared to look for another game.

Many of the companies I had assembled and restructured continue to operate successfully, their profits now directed into the coffers of Parcom and its parent ING bank.

Legal advisors have told me that I have a case against Parcom on a number of points, and that I should launch civil proceedings. I considered taking action, but my experience suggests it would be a waste of time and money. As I discovered with my suit against Manufacturers Hanover, in civil lawsuits the odds begin at 50-50 no matter how strong or weak your case may be. Thus, you don't want to be on right side of suit because you have a 50% chance of losing. Everything else is a matter of luck, according to the skills of the lawyers, his resources experience and relationship with the judge, legal advice you obtain and the judge appointed to your case. Then there is the matter of deep pockets – the deepest pockets almost always win. Besides, my unfamiliarity with the nuances of European civil law versus the same law as practiced in America had already cost me dearly. Was I really prepared to spend years commuting back and forth to Europe in pursuit of a satisfactory settlement I was unlikely to receive? I was not.

I turned the company over to a liquidator based in the UK who supervised the break-up of the corporation. This proved to be a good move, because I avoided being mired in all the complexities of dealing with all the different rules regarding employee rights and a host of other concerns. Through the liquidator, we worked with each individual company manager, encouraging him to clean up his operations and prepare the company to operate as a viable independent corporation. Most of them did, and I understand they continue to function to the benefit of their customers and employees.

Well, I was a Billionaire on paper for a few months and my consolation prize was that I came back home to good old USA avoiding any lawsuits. I guess most people would have been devastated but I quickly moved on to the next journey that God had in store for me.

WOW! What an experience! Breathing without pain thank the Lord I searched for what assets were left over and began again. Real Estate and Yoga.

CHAPTER TWENTY-SEVEN

DISCOVERING DELRAY

We returned to America with another lesson learned, and an expensive one at that.

Fortunately, our domestic operations had continued to operate effectively and in fact had generated enough income to more than offset the losses suffered in Europe.

It didn't take long for the next opportunity to present itself. By this time, the dust had begun to settle from the tech stock collapse of 2000-2001 and a lot of publicly traded companies were selling at bargain prices. I began searching for companies, in any industry, that appeared to have a good balance sheet, good cash flow, healthy assets and potential growth. We explored several of them including Cybergate, whose parent had filed for bankruptcy since my involvement. In most cases, we were facing a hostile takeover situation, and when we faced a risk of litigation and a need to inject more capital into an uncertain situation, we chose not to pursue the deal. We always managed to make a little profit on each venture, however.

After some time, the idea of dealing with threats of legal action and corporate insiders following their own agenda destroyed my enthusiasm for new business ventures. Instead, I grew intrigued by a business I had once found boring but now appeared interesting, exciting and profitable: Florida real estate.

I began focusing on Delray Beach, a small community about midway between Ft. Lauderdale and Palm Beach. Lauderdale and Palm Beach were already dangerously close to being over-developed. Delray, however, offered a fair amount of available land, a good infrastructure, and beaches that were just as appealing as those in its better-known neighbor communities.

Most Delray residents could be classified as either senior citizens or members of an expanding Haitian community occupying the old downtown core. Every spring the senior citizens installed their hurricane shutters and took them down at Thanksgiving. Otherwise, not much happened. Good restaurants and new commercial development were non-existent.

It took Delray Mayor Tom Lynch to breathe life into the town. An insurance man with entrepreneurial spirit, Tom set out to resurrect Delray, and he did. Today, Delray Beach is arguably the hottest town of its size in Florida, offering a fair amount of available land, a good infrastructure, and beaches that are just as appealing as those in its better-known neighbor communities. In my view, Delray represents the profitable future of South Florida, and an almost sure bet for developers.

While the rate of increase in the value of South Florida land may vary according to economic conditions, the market value will almost certainly never decrease from today's prices. Market watchers have declared in the past that the price of Florida properties along the oceanfront and the inland waterway had reached its peak value, and over and over again the price has started rising again, perhaps after taking a breather or two. It may reach a plateau, but it hardly ever drops. I know because I have profited from this fact. Here's how:

A local businessman in Delray told me about an oceanfront property that appeared to be well-priced at $750,000. I soon discovered that the woman selling the property had made a previous deal with another buyer to transfer it for $650,000. This deal, she assured me, had fallen through when the purchaser failed to meet his obligations before the contract expired. This meant that the property came with an attached encumbrance but, accepting her assurance that the other buyer had no case and attracted by the development opportunities, I submitted an offer to purchase the land for her asking price.

As expected, the other side took legal action, claiming their earlier offer entitled them to the land. Meanwhile, I began drawing up plans for development of the property. Almost two years passed before the case was sent to mediation. At an all-day session nothing was achieved until, late in the afternoon, one of the lawyers from the other side approached me and asked how much it would take for us to sign off on the deal and basically walk away, leaving the earlier buyer to acquire the property.

Almost with thinking I replied, "Five hundred thousand dollars." The lawyer laughed as though I had made a joke and left the room.

About ten minutes later, the lawyer returned. We had a deal. I transferred the right to purchase contract to his client and within a week his client delivered a check to me for $500,000. That's the way Florida real estate goes sometimes. After so many other occasions when legal actions had left me high and dry, this one felt like a winner. But an even more rewarding one was unfolding. It was late, but it was better than never. Much better.

Several years earlier, in the mid-1980's, I sold about $10 million in leased computers to a man named Wagner, who wanted to use them as a deferment against a tax liability of about $5 million. I structured some wrap leases that enabled him to defer his tax payment, and in return he was to pay us over a five-year period. After the first year's payment arrived on schedule, we sold the balance of his note to a bank at a discounted rate, providing us with cash and enabling the bank to earn some interest income.

Wagner defaulted on his next payment a year later, and the bank pursued us for payment, meaning we were facing a loss of over $4 million. I had already written off a major amount of cash on my soccer team, making this blow difficult to absorb. I sued Waggoner and, in the suit, I was partnered with Key Bank of Buffalo, New York; Key Bank was a 60 percent secured debt holder and I was a 40 percent secured debt holder. Wagner declared bankruptcy and once again I found myself on another very slow train winding its way through a legal landscape. This one took over six years.

Wagner had assets in Alaska, and Key Bank and I retained a law firm in Anchorage to explore the prospects of claiming anything of value that was in Wagner's name. Alaska may be large geographically, but from a business and legal standpoint it's like a small town where everyone knows their neighbor's business. Our lawyer, a bright guy named George Lyle, noted that Wagner's brother in-law happened to be the state's attorney general. Digging a little further, Wyle learned that Wagner had arranged to transfer his assets to a number of people, keeping them out of the hands of creditors while he sought bankruptcy protection. This represented an illegal conveyance of assets a serious breach of law made more intriguing when it appeared that the attorney-general himself was part of the scheme.

Among the assets were 30 to 40 oil leases on about 120,000 acres of oil fields, and at our insistence and court approved, the assets were transferred to Key Bank and to me. I set the leases aside, ready to chalk the experience up as yet another lesson, when monthly royalty checks began arriving. The first checks were so small – about $1000 – they seemed like a joke, or maybe just a mistake. But month after month they began growing and soon, we were receiving royalty payments of $50,000 every month. The checks cover oil production of about 30,000 barrels per day, but tens of thousands of acres in the area, known as the Fiord Field on the North Slope near Cook Inlet, remain untapped. Sometimes you fall into a ditch and come out smelling like roses...God always takes care of me, but never lets me get too far ahead. He wants me hungry.

Even a mini paradise like Delray Beach can have its dark side, as I discovered a few years ago. The episode was made especially painful because my intentions had been to help both the city and people with disabilities such as my daughter Heidi. As it unfolded, all I received were bruises and a visit to police headquarters.

It began with an offer to assist Mayor Tom Lynch in his efforts to promote Delray Beach. Thanks to Tom's vision and enthusiasm, a 7000 seat Delray Tennis Center had been built as the home of the Virginia Slims Tennis Tour. The stadium was ideal for tennis and little else, so when Virginia Slims cancelled their sponsorship of professional tennis, the facility sat empty for some time. I suggested that the town convert the stadium into an entertainment complex, a mini-Silverdome that could be the center of various events. With the growth of cable television, I revived my idea of combining a concert venue and a TV production facility, broadcasting on a pay-per-view basis.

Tom loved the idea, and my first move was to contact Don King, who had recently moved to Delray Beach. King and I talked about the idea, but nothing panned out. Still believing in my vision, however, I signed a five-year personal contract to lease the Tennis Center and produce at least one major event there annually. Everyone except the city's director of Parks and Recreation, who I suspect resented the idea of me encroaching on his turf, supported me.

When I heard that disco queen Donna Summers announced that she was coming out of retirement, I negotiated a deal to bring her and her band to Delray Beach for a Mother's Day concert. My marketing instincts told me that kicking off a major production in a new venue would be a hard sell. The fact is that Delray represents a wide-spread market, meaning we would have to attract people from as far away as Lauderdale and Palm Beach, complicated things even more. That's when I thought of Heidi.

Having dealt with her paralysis and grown determined not only to overcome it as much as possible but to build a career by helping others in a similar situation, Heidi brought both the contacts and the commitment we needed. She contacted Mark Buoniconti, who had broken two vertebrae in his neck while making a tackle in a college football game. The injury severed his spinal cord, leaving him with the same degree of paralysis as Heidi. Mark and his father, football hall of famer Nick Buoniconti, co-founded The Miami Project and the Fund to End Paralysis. I agreed to donate any positive cash flow the event produced to these organizations.

While trying to set up an event with boxing promoter Don King, I had developed a friendship with another King, this one named Roger. Roger was chairman of King World, the largest and most successful distributor of TV shows in the business. Every time you watch Oprah, Jeopardy, Wheel of Fortune or a dozen other shows, you're in the audience of a King World presentation. When Roger learned of the show and the benefits it would provide people suffering from the same limitations as Heidi and Nick, he agreed to produce television commercials and promotional material aimed at building an audience for the Donna Summer concert. Everything appeared to be coming together. On a beautiful evening in May, with a full moon shining down from a star-studded sky, over 7000 people filled the stadium to see and hear a terrific performance by Donna Summer and the outstanding musicians and dancers backing her up. By the third song, the entire crowd was on its feet clapping and singing along, right through the encore. By every measure except one, the concert was a great success. Unfortunately, the one way it didn't measure up was in the cash register. We lacked control over income and expenses, and the result was a net loss. This disappointed Heidi, Mark and others as much as it disappointed me, but I was determined to try again.

Over the next several months, I produced various concerts at the Tennis Center, this time with tighter controls on the money to generate contributions to The Miami Project and the Heidi Van Arnem Foundation to cure for paralysis. The high point was a concert with the legendary Ray Charles; the low point was one featuring soul performer James Brown.

Brown had nothing to do with the disaster. The problem began with many of his fans and ended with an out-of-control cop, whose sense of authority was greater than his intelligence, and my opponent in the Parks and Recreation department, who continued to resent my involvement.

Under my contract, the city of Delray Beach assumed responsibility for maintaining security at the concert, and they hired local police officers to do the job. At the James Brown event, the crowd was out of control from the beginning, meaning the police weren't doing their job. When Heidi and I arrived, along with the rest of my family, the crowd had not taken their seats and was becoming rowdy. At one point Heidi was knocked out of her wheelchair by the crowd. In desperation to assist her and make sure it didn't happen again, I called to a police officer standing nearby. He was more intent on watching the show and impressing some young women nearby, so when he failed to respond to my request for assistance, I reached to tap him on the shoulder. Just as I approached him the crowd forward, pushing both Heidi and me into him.

My first reaction was to turn and help my daughter back into her wheelchair before she was trampled by the people around her, who were growing out of control. With my back to him, the police officer grabbed me around the throat and threw me to the ground, ignoring Heidi who, as a quadriplegic, was defenseless against the flood of people around us. Before I could react, the cop had his knee pressed in the small of my back and was handcuffing me, ignoring my shouts that I was producing the show and I only wanted him to help my daughter.

With the help of two other cops, he literally began dragging me out of the arena. On the way, we passed the parks and recreation guy, who I thought would have enough class to explain that I was not some rabble-rousing hoodlum but the producer of the show. I was wrong. Sneering, he jerked his thumb over his shoulder in a gesture that confirmed the police should throw me out. They didn't stop there. They tossed me in a police cruiser and took me to headquarters where they berated and humiliated me with their shouts and threats for an hour before Bridget, Heidi, Kenny and the rest of my family could persuade them to release me.

The incident continues to disturb me. I considered launching a lawsuit against the city but decided against the idea. Whether I had won or lost, it would have tainted me in the eyes of other residents. Some things you just have to put behind you. And that's what I have done.

Besides, more rewarding things were happening. I launched Van Arnem Properties as a commercial real estate brokerage firm, although I had no interest in attending school to earn real estate credentials. Instead, Bridget completed the course. Tammy Springer, who possessed a brokerage license, became a principal in the firm. Now we are trading properties, exploring development possibilities, and generally changing the face of the area for the better. Besides making healthy profits, I'm having fun as well.

What's behind my interest in Florida real estate, something I had found so boring 25 years earlier? Things have changed. More important, I have changed. The opportunities to make major profits dealing in real estate have always been there and will always be there. That was one appeal. Another appeal concerns my lifestyle. I can deal in commercial real estate and not worry about wearing a suit and tie or even shoes. I'm on the ocean with lots of time to work out, practice Yoga, ride A1A to Palm Beach and enjoy life. Yoga serves to open my body, enabling it to reconnect in various locations – in my electrical system, my nervous system, and my circulatory system, which feeds more blood to areas of my body that were starved for years before I began Yoga.

I also have time for our three young sons, who are as active and filled with energy as any boys their age. Right now, my biggest concern is that they involve themselves more in team sports for the lessons they'll learn about working as partners with others towards a common goal. Almost all of us will earn our living from some aspect of business, and the best business people in my experience have also been the best team players at every level. Making the team – being chosen to join a group with similar skills and ambitions, prepared to share success and glory – prepares us all for life in a way few other achievements can match.

I'm especially happy that my brother Kenny plays an important role in the organization. Ken served two tours in Vietnam, much of it under fire, but he still claims that nothing he saw in battle frightened him more than acting as my navigator in a 1984 Cannonball Run. Many people believe the Cannonball Run was fiction, a series of movies in the 1980's starring Burt Reynolds and other characters, but it really does exist.

In a Cannonball Run, the entrants are instructed to get from point A, the starting line, to point B as fast as possible. The two points are separated by several hundred miles, and in an outlaw run there are no other rules – no speed limits and no agreement not to break any laws. The 1984 run was totally outlaw, involving various YPO members who wanted to play Burt Reynolds dodging Smoky for one harrowing day. Everyone drove the fastest car they can get their hands on, including Ferraris, Porsches and Lamborghinis. I chose a jet-black 1984 Chevrolet Corvette to take us from Elgin, Illinois to Duluth, Minnesota, a distance of about 500 miles.

The run was organized by Jim Liautaud, who appropriately made his money designing and manufacturing radar detectors. Out of about 100 YPO members invited, perhaps 50 showed up with their exotic cars at Jim's offices in Elgin, just outside Chicago. We partied that night and the following morning were bussed to our cars, stored in an airport hangar. Kenny and I promised ourselves that nobody was going to come between us and the first-place trophy. We climbed into the car totally prepared for victory – until I asked him to pass me the detailed map from the entrant's kit. "I thought you had it," he said. Ferraris, Porsches and other cars were already roaring out of the hangar and all we knew was the location of five checkpoints somewhere between us and Duluth – wherever that was.

I refused to waste time running back to the hotel for our map and decided to follow one of the other drivers who had boasted, the evening before, about having the best strategy to win the race. I figured he would lead us out of the city and in the right direction – who needed a map? We rode the other guy's tail all the way to the expressway where we became stuck in the slowest, thickest, most maddening morning rush hour traffic I have ever seen. After screaming and thumping the steering wheel in frustration, I swung the Corvette onto the gravel shoulder and took off past the traffic jam, doing about 90 miles an hour with the car's tail wagging back and forth and gravel stones flying from beneath the tires.

Finally, we encountered a turnoff and headed north on two lane roads, leaving Illinois and entering the rolling hills of Wisconsin. Passing through towns and villages I slowed the 'Vette down to 75 or 80; in open country I pushed the 'Vette to 140. At that speed we crested every hill in mid-air, all four wheels off the ground and screaming with excitement.

At one point we encountered a line of traffic behind a slow-moving truck, its speed made even slower in our minds because we had been running at 100+ mph for so long. Without giving it a thought, I pulled into the passing lane and roared by most of the other traffic, planning to make it to the head of the line just before we crested a hill. Bad move. Over the hill, heading straight for us, came a speeding Mack truck. Without enough room to slip the Corvette in behind the truck in my lane, I swung right and touched the brake, putting us into a four-wheel slide and steering the nose of the car in to the small space available in our lane. Now it was a question of which truck would hit us – the one heading our way in the passing lane, or the one we had just cut off. Horns were blasting, tires were screeching, and Kenny was screaming but somehow, I tucked the car into place, the other truck went roaring past, we crested the hill – and we were off again, leaving everyone behind in our dust.

At the first checkpoint I learned we were in eleventh place. Each checkpoint following it we moved up in position until we were sitting in fourth position. Not good enough. I was determined to win this one and pushed the Corvette even harder. Somewhere in the last hundred miles before Duluth I happened to glance to my left and directly into the wide, unbelieving eyes of a Wisconsin highway patrol officer. It took less than a tenth of a second to pass, I'm sure, but I'll never forget his expression and I knew we would be seeing each other again. Soon.

At 140 miles an hour we kept roaring towards Duluth, trailed by perhaps half a dozen state trooper and local law enforcement cars with a helicopter or two tracking us overhead. They followed us all the way to the bar in Duluth that marked the finish line, and only two cars had arrived ahead of me. We spent the next hour or so watching police officers write citations for speeding and reckless driving, greeting the drivers who came in behind us, and celebrating our finish. And our survival.

I still have the plaque declaring us the third-place finishers in that race. It's not very impressive, about the size of a deck of cards – but it sure means a lot to Kenny and me.

My achievements in business have been directed for the most part towards creating a lifestyle, one that I have maintained for the past 35 years. There have been rewards, many of the material I suppose, but I often think that the biggest reward has been my ability to make those I love happy. Making myself happy is fun, of course; making someone I love happy is nothing less than wonderful.

I learned as an athlete that the best preparation and attitude do not guarantee success. Few of us enjoy an undefeated season, and even fewer are blessed with an undefeated life. But none of this means that we shouldn't play the game.

CHAPTER TWENTY-EIGHT

MOTHER THERESA AND DOMINIQUE LAPIERRE

In the early 1990's, at a YPO University weekend in Cannes, France I noticed a Saturday morning presentation by author Domenic Lapierre. His book City of Joy, about lepers in Calcutta, had just been produced as a feature film starring Patrick Swayze, and I grew intrigued by someone who seemed to be focusing so much of his energy and talent on the world's most disadvantaged people.

Eight o'clock in the morning is not the best time slot for any presentation, including YPO sessions in a place like Cannes. Bridget and I entered the hall where Lapierre was to deliver his talk, accompanied by perhaps 60 other YPO members and their spouses. The hall seated about 1000, but none of this deterred Lapierre or lowered his enthusiasm. Looking very natty in blue blazer and gray trousers, he greeted everyone who entered, shaking their hand and thanking them for attending. Then he launched into his presentation.

He told tales of the poor in India and Pakistan, people who lived in deep poverty and enduring unimagined hardships. One of his stories concerned a young girl and her brother, orphaned and abandoned. The boy, who was about six years old, suffered from a debilitating disease. Each morning, at four a.m., the girl rose and walked three miles to a main railroad line where she walked for hours, gathering pieces of coal that had fallen from the steam-driven locomotives. When she had enough coal, she returned to the village and traded it for rice, which she cooked as food for her and her brother, then massaged him to relieve the incessant pain he suffered.

He spoke of Mother Theresa and her work with the poor in Calcutta, and of his plans to produce a motion picture based on her life. The details he provided, and the deep emotion he expressed about the project, won me over. When his presentation was completed, I introduced myself and told him I wanted to assist in any way I could. He welcomed my offer and we created a production company to produce the film, based on his script.

Over the next few years, I sank as much time as I could spare and perhaps half a million dollars into the project. Mother Theresa and I exchanged correspondence, indicating her approval. I produced a video presentation seeking financial support, worked some of the highest officials in the Vatican to ensure approval, and recruited several Catholic business people to lend their assistance. It felt good to finance and work for something that was beyond my day-to-day concerns. I had been born a Catholic and I remained one; now I had an opportunity to express my beliefs and reduce the suffering of others.

And suddenly it ended. Mother Theresa was dying, and the people around her began scrambling for power. She withdrew her approval for the project even as Lapierre was negotiating a deal with Hallmark Entertainment to produce a TV movie to be aired on the Family Channel. Based on the script he had first shown me, it starred Geraldine Chaplin as Mother Theresa. Overnight, my friendship with Lapierre turned adversarial, and my efforts to assist him were quickly dismissed.

I grew more disappointed than angry, and I still am. I take comfort in knowing I had worked unselfishly on behalf of the work of God, and who can regret that? In recent years I have focused my efforts on a more local basis, supporting efforts to help underprivileged children in my area of Florida.

I prayed to the Lord,
*"Take them directly to heaven
and love them as only God loves."*

VAN ARNEM
TECHNOLOGY PIONEER

EPILOGUE

In some areas, I have been more successful, and the success has been heart-warming. Principal among them has been my determination to carry on the work that Heidi began on behalf of people with disabilities.

Shot at age 16 and surviving two years on a respirator, Heidi became a quadriplegic. Living with her survival, she became an amazing entrepreneur, God's child of love, and a rock in our family during the 1980's and 1990's. Heidi didn't act like she was disabled and when with her, you wouldn't have thought that she was completely paralyzed from her neck down. We all came together with Heidi and she brought our family together in a very special way.

Her concept of iCan.com served as a launch for them to access information on products and services to meet their unique needs. Over the years since, things have changed. The issues are different, and the website structure Heidi created is no longer adequate, so I picked up where Heidi left off. The new iCan.net site is designed to build a world-wide community of people with disabilities. In this manner, they can speak with a single strong voice on issues such as stem cell research, which was supported with great passion by Heidi, Christopher Reeve, and others.

Stem cell research remains controversial in some circles, especially where questions of religious values and morality are concerned. The revised website, envisioned by Heidi, will provide an opportunity from many of the people who stand to benefit the most from this work to express their views, shape opinion, and perhaps hasten the day when injuries such as the one sustained by Heidi can be treated successfully.

Among the features of the revised website will be a fully voice-actuated text program, enabling users to have their words converted directly into on-screen text, and have text converted into a natural speaking voice. This represents an important advance, especially when integrated with popular computer sites such as MySpace and YouTube.

Living on the ocean brings its own appeal and satisfaction. The warm waters of the Atlantic have become my back yard in many ways, a blue-green expanse that stretches all the way to Portugal.

At the core of my satisfaction with life, however, is my deepening spirituality. No matter how insane life may become, my spirituality and awareness of God's word enables me to put things into perspective. The fact that God has guaranteed those who believe in him will have everlasting life. Tied to this sense is my deepening respect for truth and honesty, in business and in our dealings with everyone around us. I admit I've played a tough game, in sports as well as in business, but toughness and honesty are not exclusive qualities. Both remain essential to success in almost everything we do.

As a Christian, I suppose my model for this behavior is Christ, who managed to be tough, honest and forgiving. No one can ever measure up to Him, but we must keep trying, He understands and loves us unconditionally.

During the time when I started drafting this book, my 26-year-old son Adam had graduated from The Collective music school in NYC and had just completed his music studies at the Atlanta Institute of Music with honors. Adam was a genius composer, song writer and played quintessentially. Adam was calm peaceful and a loving young man to his family and friends. He was very athletic as a soccer player, free diver, skate boarder and snow boarder.

December 19, 2014 at midnight, my doorbell rang. It was the Ocean Ridge Police. "Do you know Adam Van Arnem?", they inquired. Those words will haunt me until I die. It happened to be my birthday and the whole family was flying to Telluride, Colorado the next day to meet Adam and the rest of the gang. Adam, just twenty-six, was on his way to meet up with the family in Telluride for Christmas, when he was found dead in a Colorado Springs motel from an accidental overdose. I was sick, devastated and lost.

But life goes on and prayers flourish. Soon we were living life again and our family was hurt forever, missing our special Adam. We suffer his loss and he is perpetually in our hearts. The loss of Heidi in 2001 and then Adam in 2014, weighs so heavily and deep in our hearts and overrides our daily thoughts.

In the fall of 2018, Bridget, Heather, her husband Jean and I were returning from a visit to Beirut, Lebanon to see Jean's family during our trip to the South of France. While there I received a phone call from the New York Police department confirming that I was the father of Harold Louis Van Arnem, IV.

"Do you know Harold Van Arnem?"

So familiar...

"Do you know an Adam Van Arnem?"

I knew instantly that HL was gone. I was crushed.

How is this possible?

They reported that he was found deceased in his Greenwich Village apartment. H.L., who was 40, had died in his sleep while sitting on his couch with his life-long companion Pugsly, who had also died in HL's lap. We were all shocked and devastated. I did not even have a chance to say goodbye. I could only remember those great moments together at his last hockey match and his first company Money.net. HL's closest friend was his mom Karen and he had just recently buried her after a long battle with cancer. He had been dead almost a week before anyone discovered his body.

HL founded Money.net a Bloomberg browser functioning terminal replacement for 1/10 the cost. Selected by Investors Digest with a cover story selecting Money.net as the Wall Streets No. 1 disruptor of the year. I invite you to go to Money.net and see for yourself this extremely valuable application he created.

He moved to NYC after a short stay in Paris, where he worked for TOTALe. He returned to the US and was hired on with DOUBLE CLICK a startup and learned much from the software development operations and IPO process. While at University of Miami where he graduated with a degree in International Finance, he bought the domain Money.net.

He initially raised over $15 million primarily from Mitsubishi and began the software development that you see today. We will continue his work and legacy. He was an amazing entrepreneur, very loving and intelligent and a rock in our family as the first-born son. But after he was gone it left a great hole in our family. My two guys who I loved more than I can express were gone.

My son Max was born November of 1990. Max was born and raised in Delray Beach and attended school at St. Vincent and American Heritage.

A gifted athlete, Max played soccer for teams in recreation leagues as well as at his schools. Max's natural abilities of speed, quickness and aggressiveness made him a local premier striker. His brother Adam introduced Max to skateboarding, which became his passion and obsession. Max developed superior skills and quickly became recognized globally. He competed and collaborated with the world's top skateboarders through promotions, marketing and video production. Max's videos continue to be viewed by the world on YouTube. In 2014, after we lost Adam, Max came home to help finish the development of a property design Adam had been working on.

Max developed a clothing line, Swiss Bank, which quickly became a niche brand when he launched it in 2016. Fashion smarts and artistic leanings drove Max to found Swiss Bank, which was an outlet for his vision of clothing and accessories and inspired by his interest in skate wear. Swiss Bank online drew customers from all parts of the world including special interest from Asia.

Early one morning in the fall of 2021 my doorbell rang. I was again greeted with those fateful words.

"Do you know Maxwell Van Arnem?"

I almost fainted because hearing that phrase brought back memories of Adam, and H.L., and now, my Max was the subject. Max was my son, partner, and best friend. And now, at 30, he was gone.

Our youngest and last son Sean was born on June 12, 1996, at Bethesda Hospital in Boynton Beach. From the beginning he was an active baby with blonde hair and blue eyes, a carbon copy of his oldest brother H.L.

Sean was created for water. Born to enjoy and explore the seas, lakes, streams, mountains and Everglades by foot, board, and boat with fishing rods, kayaks, paddle boards, spears, handguns, shotguns and bow and arrow. He was made to experience and preserve God's creations. A born Naturalist, he snowboarded nearly 100 days in a row in Park City Utah one year.

After driving up to the mountains and sleeping in his F-150 overnight, Sean will be up before sunrise, fly fishing native rivers, catching and releasing each day before work.

Sean transferred high schools in his Junior year to Boynton Beach High School, so he could play football and not just be a kicker. He played on the BBHS team that was led by quarterback Lamar Jackson, a Heisman Trophy Winner and future Hall of Famer. Coincidentally, I captained my high school football team that was quarterbacked by Roger Staubach, who also won the Heisman and is a football legend. I doubt any other father and son have shared such an experience.

Sean returned home to build The Maxwell in honor of his brother Max. The Maxwell, which was originally envisioned by Max, is a 23 room, four story luxury condominium across the street from The Adam Hotel, now under the Hampton, built to honor his brother Adam.

After Max passed, I became very ill, depressed and physically in shock. I couldn't walk, talk, or work. I couldn't function. My life was over. I wanted to continue, but was unable to.

After five months of treatment and three separate anti-depression drugs, my therapist and my psychiatrist determined they could not cure my illness and prescribed a three month stay at a Texas mental hospital. At this point, prayer was a constant in my life and I was spiritually inspired to stop the drugs and continue to pray. My daughter Heather returned to Florida from her home to be with me and together we set up an appointment with a naturopathic healer. Someone I had previously met socially and whose treatment vision appealed to me as a possible resource. Thank the Lord I was talking and walking and back to work to finish all of the development projects that Max, Carter, and Jon had started.

Here is where I need to mention Jon Kinsman, my associate and vice president, who has been with me since the very beginning - over twenty years. Jon assisted in all phases of development and property management. He is one of the best land planners in South Florida.

In the beginning, we were anchored by Betty Allen, who was my right hand from 1980 until 2013, when she passes away after a 5-year battle with lung cancer. The other half of that anchor was my brother Ken, the very same Ken I convinced to do the Cannonball Run with me. Ken was a trusted partner in all phases of our companies, starting with ACTS Computing in Detroit in 1968 and continuing until his passing in 2016.

Carter Van Voris joined me in 2013 and is our Chief Operating Officer and oversees all assets, contracts and development. She and Jon make a powerful team that assists in land acquisitions, financing, site planning, design, engineering and all development approvals and complete construction of our developments. They, together with my daughter Heather and my son Sean, will manage and operate our trust into the future.

The End

PHOTO GALLERY

Detroit

DETROIT FREE PRESS/SUNDAY, JANUARY 23, 1983

Sonny Van Arnem: High finance, no net

Billionaire: Mick Flick, Mercedes Heir: Natasha Mussolini, Sonny Van Arnem, Nicaraguan Princess, George Hamilton.

Sonny Van Arnem, Liz Treadwell, George Hamilton.

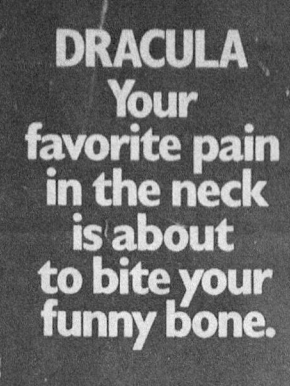

St Tropez- coming off the sail boat from Antilles. Sonny Van Arnem and George Hamilton.

GEORGE HAMILTON
Un Américain à St-Tropez

George Hamilton a fait une apparition l'autre après-midi sur le port de Saint-Tropez. Si l'on reconnaît volontiers que les femmes passent de grands moments pour choisir leurs toilettes, on peut dire de l'acteur américain qu'il ne néglige pas sa tenue vestimentaire...

Dans la boutique « Choses », il a littéralement dévalisé les rayons pendant près de deux heures. Sa meilleure emplette : un ensemble noir qui complète avec beaucoup d'harmonie la silhouette élancée et le visage bronzé de ce comédien d'outre-Atlantique, très remarqué dans « Viva Maria ».

Le lendemain, George Hamilton était la vedette du gala « Atout cœur » qui se déroulait à Cannes.

Au Palm Beach, à l'occasion de cette soirée, ils étaient tous là, ceux dont on parle beaucoup et que l'on ne rencontre que dans les grandes occasions. Mais il y eut une arrivée surprise, qui fit frissonner les dames aux décolletés vertigineux, celle de George Hamilton. En smoking blanc, il fut d'un seul coup l'« Atout cœur » de la soirée, battant de loin tous les princes arabes et européens qui savent pourtant bien jouer du charme et de l'éclat.

Entre le caviar et le homard, dans les pétillements d'un « brut rosé », la vente aux enchères a tenu ses promesses. Une toile de Bellini a atteint 33.000 F, une litho de Chagall 80.000 F, et une eau-forte de Miro 92.000 F. — G.S.

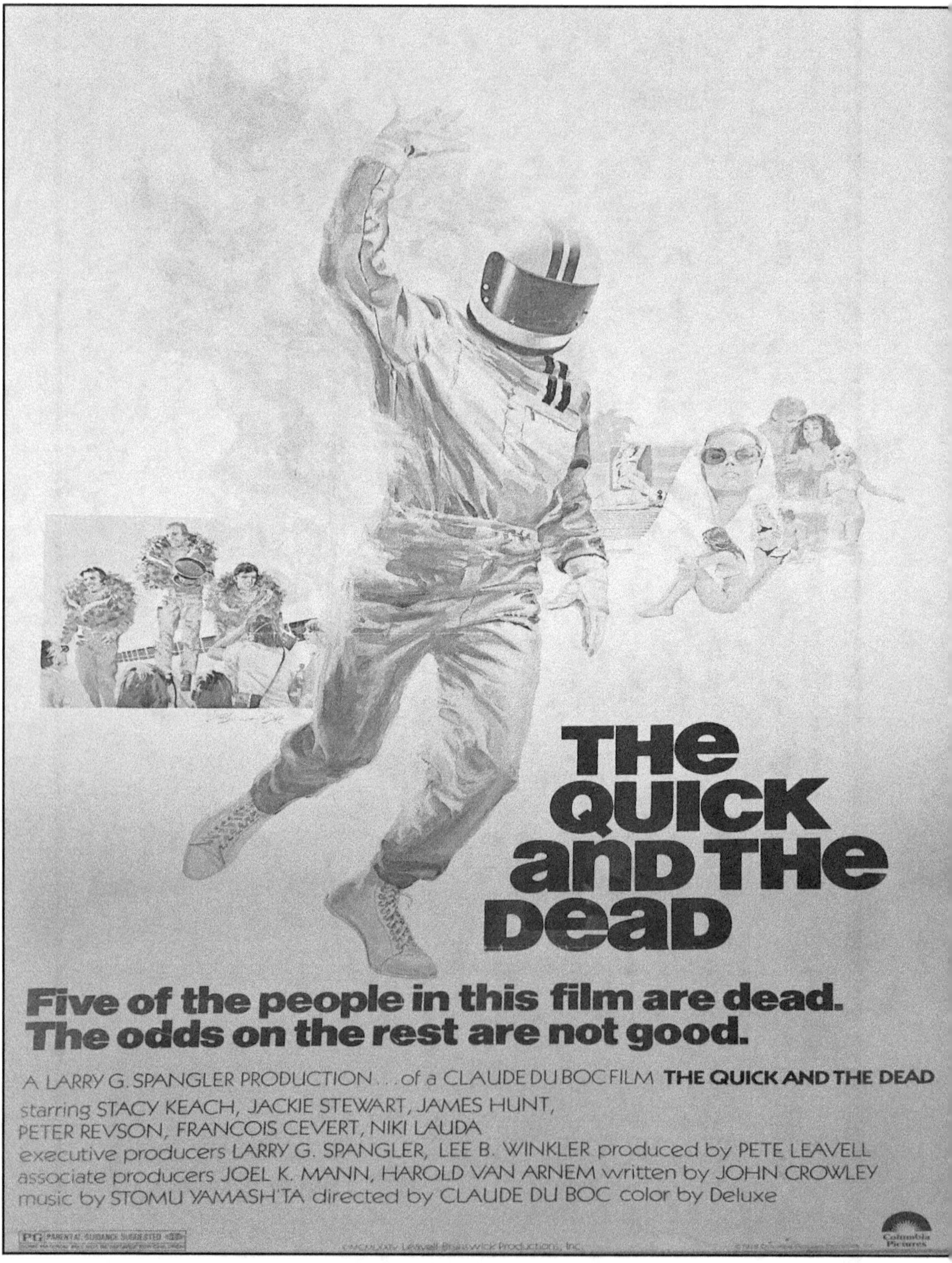
THE QUICK AND THE DEAD
Five of the people in this film are dead.
The odds on the rest are not good.
A LARRY G. SPANGLER PRODUCTION ... of a CLAUDE DU BOC FILM THE QUICK AND THE DEAD
starring STACY KEACH, JACKIE STEWART, JAMES HUNT,
PETER REVSON, FRANCOIS CEVERT, NIKI LAUDA
executive producers LARRY G. SPANGLER, LEE B. WINKLER produced by PETE LEAVELL
associate producers JOEL K. MANN, HAROLD VAN ARNEM written by JOHN CROWLEY
music by STOMU YAMASH'TA directed by CLAUDE DU BOC color by Deluxe
PG PARENTAL GUIDANCE SUGGESTED
Columbia Pictures

IMSA GT- Watkins Glen. Van Arnem Racing.

Robbins-Van Arnem Racing Trans Am Cup. Road America, Wisconsin 24 Hours of Daytona VAR.

Sports Car Club of America
SCCA National Champions
Robbins Van Arnem Racing

Detroit, Michigan — *July*

ABEX SPONSORS JIM ROBBINS CO. CORVETTE

ROBBINS SECOND IN TRANS-AM POINT STANDING

(Troy, Michigan) Ronald L. ...tler, Vice-President of Sales ...nounced today that the Friction ...ducts Division of Abex Corpora... will sponsor a 1973 Corvette, ...ed by the Robbins — Van ...em Racing Team, in the remain... of the Trans-Am events this ... In addition, he pointed out ... the car would also compete in ...cted IMSA races.

...e Jim Robbins Co. Corvette, ... renamed the "Abex-Jim Rob... Co. Special", has run in three ...s-Am events during 1973. At ...ta, Marshall Robbins quali... on the pole and finished third, ...te the fact that the car was ...ed by fuel pressure problems ...ghout the race. At Lime Rock, ...ins and Jerry Thompson co-...e the car to a 5th place finish. In ... races, the Robbins Corvette ...e first American car to finish.

... the 3rd event in the series, ...ins Glen, the Abex-Jim Rob... Co. Special qualified 2nd

MARSHALL ROBBINS

fastest in a field of over 40 cars. The start of the race was run on a wet track and Thompson, who started the race, dropped back to 3rd position. However, by the time the race was one-third over, Thompson had moved the car into the lead and was pulling away from the pack at about 2 seconds a lap. Then, misfortune struck the Robbins' team again, as the carburetor developed a malfunction, causing the car to lose its competitive edge.

With the car having fallen back to 7th place, as the race approached the two-thirds point, Robbins, who took over from Thompson at the midpoint in the race, continued to try to

...nurse the car home, as the cre... unable to repair the carb... during a long pit stop.

Then, on lap 66 of the ...event, it started to rain and R... made a quick pit stop for rai... After 5 laps in the rain, a to... pletely covered the track a... race was red flagged and d... finished. However, during t... rain laps, Robbins moved ... from 7th position to 4th.

Harold Van Arnem, team... er, stated, "Watkins Glen w... disappointment for our team ... the carburetor problem occu... had the race won. However,

VAN ARNEM
CONT.

Silverdome National ASL 1982 Champions.

Pontiac Silverdome: should the city sell it to Van Arnem?

Continued from page one volved in the matter when, a few months ago, he asked Van Arnem whether he knew of anyone who would be interested in buying the stadium. (Van Arnem had been Murphy's campaign manager in 1976.) Van Arnem promised to look into the matter.

Murphy waited while Van Arnem's people put pencils to the problem. Whatever they found must have proven positive because Van Arnem called Murphy back to say that he was interested and could Murphy put him in contact with the right people? Murphy obliged by bringing Pontiac Mayor Holland and Mayor Pro Tem Appleton to Van Arnem's Bloomfield Hills home for a poolside luncheon.

According to Van Arnem, both the Pontiac officials were very receptive to the idea. The snag came when, at a later luncheon, James Clarkson was invited to a similar poolside parley.

"Clarkson seemed cool on the idea," said Van Arnem.

In a phone call after the meeting, Clarkson told Murphy that he was not even interested in dealing with Van Arnem.

Murphy claims his involvement reflects his concern for Pontiac. "I've been a resident for 51 years." He has strong beliefs that are also motivators for his participation. "Things like stadiums should not be owned by the government. That goes for hospitals, too." But now that he has made the initial contacts, he says he is no longer involved. "I have nothing to do with it anymore."

Other people also have strong feelings about the proposed selling of the stadium. Peter V. Tenuta, former city commissioner and now member of the Stadium Authority, feels that Van Arnem's offer "doesn't deserve to be considered." His main concern is that Van Arnem didn't even make the proposal to the commission in person.

Complicating the problem was City Manager Phil Mastin's advice that Van Arnem's proposition would probably be heard around 7 p.m. In fact, at 6:30 p.m. the commission was still not ready to hear new business. Van Arnem and his son left the proposal with the commission and promised to meet them in another session.

Another complaint from members of the Stadium Authority is that the Van Arnem offer is too little. Basically, he wants to pay the city's losses to date ($6 million) and to take over payment of the outstanding bonds ($15.9 million general obligation bonds, $25 million in revenue bonds and the $7 million roof purchase contract).

Tenuta estimates the stadium's value at $125 million and believes that in two or three years the stadium will be making money. Clayton Jones, another member of the Stadium Authority, is in general agreement with Tenuta. His approximate fair market appraisal of the stadium is between $100 and $150 million.

Clarkson said the stadium represents a minimum of $110 million and any serious deal shouldn't be considered for less than $80 million.

McSwigan said, "I'm sure that the Stadium Authority and the city will eventually set a price on it."

Clarkson said that even if offers for the stadium are considered, it would have to be put up for bids. But he went on to say, "If we can put up with a small burden now, I know it can make money from here to eternity."

Jones agreed with Clarkson. "I did not put a lot of blood and tears into this project for the last eight years to not believe that it will make the city money," Jones added. "No other stadium can claim that they built their stadium on time and under budget. But we can."

Despite the authorities, Van Arnem is optimistic about his chances. He has been following recent polls that say the voters of Pontiac want to sell the

AFL/NFL: NFL Pa Strike Game at Kennedy Stadium in Washington D.C. Sonny Co-produced the Strike Game with Ted Turner.

Detroit Express vs. Oklahoma: 33,000 attended and broke attendance record for ASL history.

Stroh Light proudly presents the

1982 American Soccer League Champions

1983 EXPRESS SCHEDULE

DATE	OPPONENT	TIME	DATE	OPPONENT	TIME
SAT MAY 7	PENNSYLVANIA STONERS	7:30 pm	SAT JULY 2	PENNSYLVANIA STONERS	7:30 pm
SAT MAY 14	DALLAS AMERICANS	7:30 pm	Wed July 6	at Pennsylvania Stoners	7:35 pm
Thur May 19	at Oklahoma City Slickers	7:35 pm	SAT JULY 9	OKLAHOMA CITY SLICKERS	7:30 pm
SAT MAY 21	CAROLINA LIGHTNIN'	7:30 pm	Thur July 14	at Dallas Americans	7:35 pm
Wed May 25	at Pennsylvania Stoners	7:35 pm	SAT JULY 16	JACKSONVILLE TEAMEN	7:30 pm
SAT MAY 28	PENNSYLVANIA STONERS	7:30 pm	Tues July 19	at Jacksonville Teamen	8:00 pm
FRI JUNE 3	OKLAHOMA CITY SLICKERS	7:30 pm	SUN JULY 24	DALLAS AMERICANS	7:30 pm
Sat June 4	at Carolina Lightnin'	8:05 pm	Thur July 28	at Oklahoma City Slickers	7:35 pm
THUR JUNE 9	JACKSONVILLE TEAMEN	7:30 pm	FRI JULY 29	CAROLINA LIGHTNIN'	7:30 pm
Sat June 11	at Dallas Americans	7:35 pm	Tues Aug 2	at Carolina Lightnin'	8:05 pm
Sat June 18	at Jacksonville Teamen	8:00 pm	Sun Aug 7	at Pennsylvania Stoners	7:35 pm
SUN JUNE 19	DALLAS AMERICANS	7:30 pm	Sat Aug 13	at Carolina Lightnin'	8:05 pm
Thur June 23	at Oklahoma City Slickers	7:35 pm	Fri Aug 19	at Jacksonville Teamen	8:00 pm
SAT JUNE 25	CAROLINA LIGHTNIN'	7:30 pm	SUN AUG 21	OKLAHOMA CITY SLICKERS	7:30 pm

HOME GAMES IN CAPS
FOR INFO: 335-4170
LISTEN TO ALL DETROIT EXPRESS
SOCCER GAMES ON WNIC AM 13

"Looks like a Stroh Light night."

FOOTBALL BANQUET

'57 grid heroes assemble with Coach McCarthy and Guest Speaker Tebbetts.

Sonny MVP award
Purcell High School
Championship football team Ohio
Dick Anderson Andy
Coach McCarthy

1958 Captains Van Arnem and Schroeder receive congratulations.

Approximately six hundred Cavalier gridiron

Bud Light Tim Mann Triathalon, Oakland County, Michigan.

ACTS Computing signs contract with Lear Corporation for Avionics software development. Lear Jets and Lockheed L1011 wide body passenger jet automatic land system.

IT Staff Lear and Lear President
Grand Rapids, Michigan.

Sonny Van Arnem and Co-CEO Jim Boris of Finalco Inc and CEO of Kempie Securities.

Sonny Van Arnem and Vice President of the United States, Dan Quayle.

DAN QUAYLE
June 4, 1992

Dear Sonny:

Thanks for taking the time to come to the briefing for me on Eight is Enough. Limiting terms of career politicians is the only way to break the log jam caused by special interest politics.

Keep up the good work -- and win in the Fall.

U.S Congressman Mark Foley, Phil McKnight, President of Finalco, Gemini and EU Board Totale, Sonny Van Arnem and House Speaker Newt Gingrich

Russia Dynamo Minsk vs. Detroit Express with Ambassador from Russia to the USA.

Dallas Cowboy Legend Roger Staubach, NFL Hall of Famer, with Sonny, Heather and H.L. Van Arnem at the SanFranciso vs. Cincinnati Superbowl at the Pontiac Silverdome.

William G. Milliken
Governor of the State of Michigan
presents this
Executive Declaration
in Observance of

THE 1982 CHAMPIONSHIP SEASON OF THE DETROIT EXPRESS

The Detroit Express soccer team has brought honor and prestige to Detroit by capturing the American Soccer League's regular season title.

It capped a thrilling season with an exciting finish, overtaking league-leading Oklahoma City in the next-to-the-last game of the regular season.

Detroit and the Express can take further pride in the fact that the league's two leading scorers are members of the team: Brian Tinnion, with 59 points on 22 goals and 15 assists, and Andy Chapman, with 49 points on 22 goals and 5 assists.

The Express now goes on to the league playoffs with the sports fans from Detroit and all of Michigan in their cheering section, and with the best wishes and hopes of all Michigan residents as part of their team equipment.

Therefore, I, William G. Milliken, Governor of the State of Michigan, do hereby issue this Executive Declaration in observance of the 1982 championship season of the Detroit Express, and urge all Michigan residents to cheer on this championship team which has done much for the sports image of Detroit and of Michigan.

Given under my hand on this second day of September in the year of Our Lord one thousand nine hundred eighty-two and of the Commonwealth one hundred forty-sixth.

GOVERNOR

Govenor Milliken Executive Declaration for the Detroit Express.

Inside:
- Problems at FERC — p. 2
- Bank Sees Project Cuts — p. 2
- No Dividend at GPU — p. 3
- CE's $230-M Award — p. 3
- Bonds Join Rally — p. 4
- Utilities in Upturn — p. 4

UTILITY SPOTLIGHT

XXXVIII, No. 51   December 20, 1985   Published Since 1948

VAN ARNHEM SEES COMPUTER LEASING BY UTILITIES SPREADING

NEW YORK—Utilities are getting into computers in a big way these days, according to Harold Van Arnhem, chief executive of Van Arnhem Financial Services.

His firm, which leases computers, numbers among its clients Southern New England Telephone, Pacific Northwest Bell, Ameritech, Mobil Oil, Edison Electric Institute, Detroit Edison and American Natural resources.

"The utility industry represents a very significant opportunity for the leasing industry," he said in an interview here. "Up to this point, they have had their own ways of deferring their taxes, so they're a really good market for us. Not knowing what's going to happen with tax laws in the future, I can't say how long this will last, but the potential is very great."

VAN ARNHEM

Asked why utilities wouldn't do as well if they bought their computers outright instead of leasing, Van Arnhem replied quickly:

"Most of them don't want to be in the used computer business, which is what would happen if they bought their computers."

His company checks out the potential clients' specific needs including the proper computer, buys the necessary equipment for the installation and leases it for anywhere from 24 to 60 months on what is known as a "full payout lease." (The lessee—in this case, the utility—guarantees a certain portion of the cost of the equipment, generally around 89% when the investment tax credit stays with the lessee or 79.9% when the owner keeps the tax credit.)

"What we do is see to it that the client gets his proper return on investment capital," Van Arnhem went on. "We provide the financing for this capital equipment at an impressive rate substantially below their own borrowing rates and substantially below their return on capital needs.

"So it really becomes a question of how inexpensive it is to put this equipment in because the carrying cost is so low. The last thing they want to do is get in that used computer business, and if you buy your equipment, it really means you're in the used computer business. What it amounts to is we now have a new commodity market and they don't have any objections to giving up a 10 or 15% function. Today we give them a present value of 10 to 20% which, 5 years from now is not worth very much. All they're giving up is a potential which they don't believe is going to happen anyway."

He feels that one of the strengths behind this is the fact that this involves an economic decision that is made very simple for computer users.

Firms like Van Arnhem are hooked into a satellite network that keeps tabs on all purchases and sales of computer equipment round the world. He pointed out that "over $30- billion of new computer equipment will be served by third-party leases this year." A year ago it was at the $26-billion level.

Computers that go into this new commodity market are bought and sold by some 200 participants in the satellite network. Some of the leases are also traded.

In most cases, software is not provided, that being the prerogative of the client, although Van Arnhem does finance software.

Firms like Van Arnhem's provide an additional service for clients by being able in some cases to move up the order position for a computer. He noted that at present, because of order backlogs, there is a fairly substantial premium being paid for most computers.

They arrange the specific financing and terms based on a review of the credit position of the client.

"It's up to me to make a residual decision as to what each piece of equipment will be worth 12, 24, 36, 48 and 60 months down the road," Van Arnhem explained. "Then I compute the value of that equipment at a return of somewhere between 10 and 12% to determine my lease rate factor against huge financial institutions.

"Our success comes from the fact that we're competing against companies with huge overhead. I have my own in-house people. We're a small company with under 50 people, but our volume of business is up to about $150-million. We're trying to establish our company as a national competitor. I've been 'cherry picking' for 10 years. It's not hard to make money in our business because we provide so much value.

"At this point, what we're trying to do is build a large portfolio of potential customers."

This is where the utilities fit into his scene. He finds that what utilities want is to have a complete track of every customer, supplier and piece of equipment. The goal appears to be the ability to manage a central flow of information at all times to optimize efficiency.

"The utilities are logical targets since they have over the years been more like a governmental operation with a lot of featherbedding," Van Arnhem said.

Asked about the potential utility market for his services, Van Arnhem replied:

"It's continuing to grow each day. Maybe more so than anyone else, the utilities are going to require automation for consumer reporting and public service demands for reporting. I can't estimate by dollar volume, but it'd be a staggering sum."

He noted that utilities have used a lot of Sperry Univac equipment since that company aimed specifically at the industry. Super-computer mainframes that cost in the range of $5- to $20-million are attracting industry attention at present.

"This will probably last through 1986 at an incredibly fast pace before deliveries are completed as utilities go through a major swap out of old machines," he said.

READ.ME extra

IBM Global Services supplement | November/December 1998

Jeff Ace (left), Business Operations director, IBM Global Services Network Services EMEA, and Harold Van Arnem, CEO Totale.

IBM Global Services signs strategic Business Partner

In one of the most significant strategic channel agreements undertaken by IBM Global Services, it was announced last month that Totale will remarket IBM's network services in 23 countries.

Totale will become IBM Global Services' first EMEA-based International Business Partner, implementing IBM's commitment to significantly increase the amount of business performed through external channels.

The deal, with a $50m revenue commitment, will focus on providing global networking capability to Totale's 20,000 SME customers. It will enhance Totale's strategy of providing e-business solutions on an international basis and of aligning itself with IBM's blueprint for e-business.

Totale — formerly Decision Systems International — already has reseller/remarketing agreements with other IBM divisions, including AS/400, RS/6000, Netfinity and Storage. Augmenting these existing agreements, they will now offer network services in a minimum of 23 countries, focusing chiefly on opportunities in Germany, UK, Belgium, the Netherlands and Spain.

Totale's CEO, Harold Van Arnem, said the new Business Partner agreement with IBM Global Services means customers' e-business needs will be met with an end-to-end capability, covering all aspects of network computing.

Totale will enable increased access to the Small and Medium Enterprise marketplace. In return, they will benefit from IBM Global Services' leading edge technologies and global reach, through its Global Network.

Jeff Ace, Business Operations director, IBM Global Services, Network Services EMEA, says: "This agreement is without question the most strategically important deal that IBM Global Services has signed with a network services Business Partner.

"The European reach of Totale combined with their e-business integrated solutions capability will, I'm sure, create a prosperous relationship for both parties."

It's official: we're No.1

IBM Global Services is the best — no contest.

The official verdict from *Computer Business Review* November '98 — the publication which lists the world's top 50 computer services companies — is that IBM Global Services is the world's premier services company, ranked at number one.

Just getting a place on the list is no mean feat, CBR points out. "Making it on to the top 50 list is getting increasingly difficult. To gain access to the services table, vendors now need revenues in excess of $330 million compared to an entry point of just over $200 million last year.

"More than half the top 50 companies now have revenues measured in billions rather than millions. Power is also being further concentrated at the top. The elite top ten companies now account for nearly two thirds of the total revenue of all 50."

The magazine points out that, in previous years, EDS and IBM have fought for the top place. "There is no contest now. This year IBM Global Services pulled ahead reporting growth of 22 per cent to $19.3 billion."

Much of the revenue is from IBM Global Services' major outsourcing deals and large ERP implementation and systems integration practices, the article adds. It also points to the general health of the services business.

Philip Oliver, IBM Global Services Marketing director, EMEA, is quoted as saying: "We are beating the industry in every category, everywhere in the world."

And with orders in the pipeline valued at more than $50 billion, analysts are confident that IBM Global Services can sustain the 20 per cent plus growth curve.

IBM EU Partnership and most important strategic alliance for IBM.

How to beat bribers
HERBERT ROBINSON, ROBINSON, PERLMAN & KIRSCHNER ☐ 5

Alexandra Armstrong's wealth-building formula
☐ 7

The new world of leasing
HAROLD VAN ARNEM, VAN ARNEM FINANCIAL SERVICES ☐ 9

Better market research
SOLOMON DUTKA, AUDITS & SURVEYS ☐ 11

New cures for old problems
DR. HELEN SINGER KAPLAN, SEX THERAPIST ☐ 13

BOARDROOM REPORTS

August 1, 1986

TAXES TAXES TAXES TAXES TAXES TAX

Harold Van Arnem, Van Arnem Financial Services

THE NEW WORLD OF EQUIPMENT LEASING

One aspect of tax reform that seems *certain* to be adopted is the repeal of the investment tax credit. And with its repeal, many skeptics are predicting *the end* of equipment-leasing deals now used by companies to cut their financing costs and by individuals to cut their personal tax bills.

Surprise: The business reasons for equipment leasing will remain as strong as ever *in spite* of tax reform. And for individual investors, some kinds of leasing will become *even more* attractive.

THE BASICS

In the typical leasing arrangement, a group of individual investors makes a purchase of business equipment and leases it to a company. A leasing company may act as an intermediary by finding the investors, matching them with the right company, physically obtaining the equipment (such as computer peripherals, aircraft or productive machinery) and doing the paperwork.

By leasing instead of buying, a company can obtain:

Boardroom interviewed Harold Van Arnem, chairman, Van Arnem Financial Services, 870 Bowers, Birmingham, MI 48011.

E X E C U T I V E

P R O F I L E

NAME: Harold L. Van Arnem.
HOME: Boca Raton.
AGE: 48.
PROFESSION: Chairman and CEO of the Finalco and Gemini companies.
FAMILY: Wife, Bridget, seven children
HOBBIES: Basketball, aerobics, diving.
GREATEST ACCOMPLISHMENTS: Started first company at age 26; by age 30 owned one of the top ten software companies in the country. Lectured on computers to Soviet Bloc countries. Led an All-Star Professional Soccer team to a national championship victory in 1982. Coproduced the film *Love At First Bite*.
WHY YOU DO WHAT YOU DO: "I enjoy it. I look at business like I look at basketball. I never was good enough or big enough to be a professional basketball player, but I'm big enough and quick enough to be a professional capitalist."
FAVORITE PART OF JOB: Camaraderie, team building, team winning, trust.
IF YOU HAD CHOSEN ANOTHER CAREER: Entertainment—video and film production.
PROFILE: Personable, self-confessed professional capitalist who lives each day by looking at the world as one big adventure.

Boca Magazine.

SIGNATURE

HAROLD VAN ARNEM

WHEN THE PIED PIPER OF ONE of America's leading equipment-leasing-and-income-funds companies announced plans last year to relocate to Boca Raton from McLean, Virginia, 100 or so loyalists followed eagerly. It's not surprising. As chairman and chief executive officer of the Finalco Group and Gemini Equities, Harold Van Arnem has chutzpah. Charisma. And a boyish charm that belies his 48 years. It's easy to liken his unabashed ambition and optimism to that of Donald Trump. Better yet, roll Donald Trump and Tom Sawyer into one and you get a more accurate picture.

Van Arnem, once a collegiate football player at the University of Cincinnati, earned his economics degree and soon after entered General Electric's computer division in Phoenix. As an appointed lecturer at the University of Detroit's College of Engineering, he codeveloped the computer engineering doctoral program and subsequently helped found ACTS Computer Corporation, a software company that was eventually sold to Lear Siegler, Inc. His next major project was The Van Arnem Companies, the forerunner to Van Arnem Financial Services, a computer and capital-equipment leasing firm. Then, in 1988, he purchased Finalco, a 22-year-old company that manages nearly $1.5 billion in equipment, leased primarily to Fortune 500 firms. Along the way, he has coproduced feature films, sponsored an auto-racing team, purchased Sugar Loaf Mountain Resort near Traverse City, Michigan, and owned for a time the Detroit Express soccer team.

For a man who frequently uses sports analogies, it's consistent that he says his management style resembles that of a coach. "For anybody to be enthusiastic about anything, they have to have a reason," he asserts. "It's not just taking a paycheck. It's winning. It's succeeding. It's always better to have more responsibility—to do more, to accomplish more, and to achieve more."

Last July, the Virginia-based flock followed his path to Boca. Today, Finalco and Gemini's corporate headquarters are in a 100,000-square-foot building on Clint Moore Road formerly occupied by IBM. Finalco (a holding company) leases, manages, and finances new and refurbished capital equipment, including computers, aircraft, telecommunication devices, and modular buildings. Gemini specializes in

continued on page 174

BY LAURIE CACACE
PHOTOGRAPHY BY MICHAEL PRICE

Sonny Van Arnem: Nobody can pin him down. Merc[urial,] handsome, super-salesman, maker and breaker of d[eals] with a little-boy name. He wanted to be rich and fa[mous.] But a lot of people got burned playing by his rules. [He] doesn't just want attention,

he wants to be loved

by LAURA BERMAN and TOM HENDERSON

On a bleak Friday in early December, Sonny Van Arnem changed his mind. He would not purchase the Jacksonville Tea Men soccer team, after all. After all the publicity, the statements that the deal was done, "signed, sealed and paid for," after all the assurances, spoken in private, that the deal would go through because, "I mean, it has to go through, it just has to." After all that, there was no deal.

Which was, to some who knew him, not surprising. With similar hoopla and publicity last August, he had announced the purchase of the Edmonton Drillers team in Canada. The checks for $50,000 were in the mail, the deal was wrapped.

The checks didn't go through. Sonny had changed his mind that time, too.

Maybe, though, you don't know Sonny Van Arnem, not personally anyhow, and still have the capacity to be surprised. Sonny Van Arnem? Yes, the millionaire owner of the Express, the producer of "Love at First Bite" (or that was what the gossip columns said, anyhow). The one who lives in a $300,000 architectural wonder of a house that was featured in Life magazine in the '40s, where a Saudi Arabian prince played houseguest last spring. Who has skiied with Olivier Chandon, the Formula I racing driver (heir to the French champagne fortune), toured Europe with George Hamilton, and tasted Cristina Ferrare DeLorean's spaghetti.

He's rich, obviously — and the money, well, it has something to do with computers. You never seem to read about his computer business in the newspapers, although you do read about his $60 million offer to buy the Silverdome and bring the pope in for Mass, and his movie productions. There was a UHF station he was going to buy and an air chartering service and a ski resort — he owns, or maybe manages, Sugar Loaf — and a cable TV deal with Warner-Amex to wire Oakland County that was going to make him the Ted Turner of Detroit.

When you meet him in his Birmingham office — the Van Arnem Building, it's called — his youth is what hits you first. Not only the lean, long build or the chiseled, handsome face that doesn't look 40 (it is) but the easy, boyish way he disarms you. He talks, and while he talks, he's answering the phone and making faces at the callers who can't see him — letting you, a new acquaintance, in on the secret — and when he hangs up the phone, he picks up where he left off.

Or sometimes he doesn't. The thing you notice is how rarely he completes a sentence, or even a thought, because he's on to another sentence, another thought, another concept. Talking with him is like being plunked into a rapidly flowing stream of consciousness, and while he does skip confusingly from one subject to the next, he is so animated standing up and sitting down and spreading his arms, and so enthusiastic about his ideas and his sense of vision that it doesn't really matter where the stream is flowing to.

Someone, a business contact of his, said when you first meet him, he's Mr. Charm, Mr. Wonderful, he's Kirk Douglas. "I wish I were two or three inches taller and like that guy — he reeks of success," said another, former American Soccer League commissioner Mario Marchado. There was a magazine writer so enthralled by Van Arnem's presence, she likened him to Kirk Douglas *and* Paul Newman, then described his near-magical ability to make heads turn from the force of his "magnetic aura . . . his energy, his commanding presence."

He has a cleft in his chin like the actor who played Spartacus but the comparison cuts deeper, to the essence of his style, which is careless, breezy California with the freedom and sense of possibility that California represents. He makes you think of Hollywood — not the solid, circumscribed ways of Detroit, or of Cincinnati, where he grew up and attended college. "I don't have any limits. I play outside people's limits," Van Arnem likes to say. He also likes to say people don't understand that. But they do of course.

How else to explain a businessman becoming his partner after a chance meeting on an airplane? Or a secretary quitting her job in Texas to work for him *in Detroit*? He makes impossi-

Laura Berman is a staff writer in the Free Press

Detroit Free Press.

MICHIGAN TRADESMAN

JULY 1972
VOLUME 89 NUMBER 7

SPECIAL
M.B.A. CONVENTION
REPORT... See Page 9

THE COMPUTERIZED SUCCESS STORY
OF ACTS COMPUTING CORP.
AND HAROLD VAN ARNEM... See Page 4

BANKING AND BUSINESS NEWS

Michigan Banking & Business News

OCTOBER 1975
Vol. 92, No. 10

REPRINT

Van Arnem Co. - -
Specialist in
Asset Financing,
Leveraged Leasing
...See Pgs. 4-6

Principals in the Van Arnem Company (from left): Vice President Thomas Bruce; President Alan Forrester; Board Chairman Harold Van Arnem.

GEMINI GROUP

Corporation
has sold the common stock of
Select Leasing to
GEMINI Financial Holdings, Inc.
Select Leasing is owner/lessor of 6,700
leases of telecommunications, computer and
other capital equipment with an original cost of
$99,000,000

AMERICAN EXPRESS Bank GmbH
has sold 100% of the common stock
of UNIVERSAL COMPUTER LEASING GmbH
and operating subsidiaries: UML, UHG, UBM.
to **GEMINI Equities, Inc.**
assets acquired have an original cost of
over **$500,000,000**

has sold 100% of the common stock of:
CIS LEASING GmbH
CIS COMPUTER LEASING (UK) LIMITED
CIS FRANCE, S.A.
CMI S.A.
to **GEMINI Equities, Inc.**
assets acquired have an original cost of
over **$150,000,000.**

First Interstate Bank Denver, N.A.
has sold its leveraged leases to
GEMINI Financial Holdings, Inc.
The seller was owner/lessor of 3 commercial
aircraft, 54 locomotives, 431 railcars, and
mining equipment with an original cost of
$166,398,774

HOME NATIONAL BANK
of Milford, Massachusetts

has sold its equipment leases to
GEMINI Financial Holdings, Inc.
The seller was owner/lessor of over-the-road,
telecommunications, fixtures, furniture and
capital equipment with an original cost of
$30,000,000

PACIFICORP FINANCIAL SERVICES

has sold its common stock of PCL, Inc. to
GEMINI Financial Holdings, Inc.
PCL is owner/lessor of 679 leases of fixtures,
telecommunications, computers and capital
equipment with an original cost of
$71,402,299
formerly owned by Paccom Leasing

IntelogicTrace

INTELOGIC TRACE TEXCOM GROUP, INC. and THE LOCKWOOD ASSOCIATES, INC.
subsidiaries of Intelogic Trace, Inc.
San Antonio, Texas
has sold substantially all of their assets to
GEMINI Systems Leasing Corp.
assets acquired have an original cost
in excess of **$60,000,000.**

R.J. Leasing, Inc.
a subsidiary of Raymond James Financial, Inc.
St. Petersburg, FL
as General Partner has sold the assets of the
FINALCO INCOME FUNDS to
GEMINI Systems Leasing Corp.
assets comprised of IBM computers
having an original cost
in excess of **$10,000,000**

GEMINI GROUP
HAROLD L. VAN ARNEM, Chief Executive Officer/Chairman • N. PHILIP McKNIGHT, President
1377 Clint Moore Rd., Boca Raton, FL 33487 • (407) 994-9590

John J. Renkes, Jr. - GEMINI SYSTEMS LEASING CORP. • 1377 Clint Moore Rd., Boca Raton, FL 33487 • (407) 994-9590
Beaufort J.B. Clarke - GEMINI FINANCIAL HOLDINGS, INC. • 475 Gate Five Road, Suite 310, Sausalito, CA 94965 • (415) 332-9400
William Larkin - GEMINI SYSTEMS SOFTWARE, INC. • 8415 Datapoint Drive, San Antonio, TX 78229 • (210) 593-5780
John Angus - GEMINI EUROPEAN HOLDINGS LIMITED • Continental House, West End, Woking Surrey, England GU249PJ • 011 44 483 797 157
Horst Gruhlke and Peter Radler - UNIVERSAL COMPUTER LEASING GmbH, AlexandrastraBe 3, 6200 Weisbaden • 011 49 61 188 0951

As appeared in **THE WALL STREET JOURNAL**, *Tuesday, January 8, 1991.*

Bell Atlantic
Computer Products

has been acquired by

Gemini Equities, Inc.

(Formerly Finalco Equities Services, Inc.)

establishing

Computer Product Solutions

Gemini Equities' operating entities include:

- CIS Computer Leasing and Sales—France, Germany, and United Kingdom
- Gemini—Capital, Building Systems, Equipment Management, and Credit Corp.
- Finalco—Equity Services, Fleet Services, Municipal Leasing, and Computer Sciences
- CMI S.A. Switzerland

The undersigned acted as financial advisor to Gemini Equities, Inc. and Bell Atlantic Computer Products, Inc.

Terrence S. Cassidy

FINANCING AT LESS THAN THE PRIME INTEREST RATE

Van Arnem Company...
Specialist in Asset Financing, Leveraged Leasing

By JEROME O'NEIL

BLOOMFIELD HILLS—Propelled by a special expertise in computer sciences, a Michigan corporation has moved to the front ranks of the nation's lease underwriting industry... in the short span of 24 months.

The Van Arnem Company Inc., founded in 1973 with the initial purpose of marketing computers overseas, shifted gears in August, 1974, when it moved into the closely related area of computer and capital equipment lease underwriting.

The move was well planned, well timed and well received.

In the last 12 months, the firm has handled lease projects—most of them involving computer hardware on "leveraged" leases—amounting to more than $35 million in total equipment sales.

During 1976, Van Arnem Company expects to double that figure.

A list of its clients-to-date reads like an abbreviated "Who's Who" in the world of industry and includes such notables as General Motors Corp., several GM divisions, Federal-Mogul and Dow Corning, to name but a few.

And, buoyed by its success, the firm already has accepted contracts and has begun to expand its lease underwriting horizons to encompass various other products, including trucks and heavy manufacturing agricultural and health care equipment, which comprise the backbone of the nation's burgeoning equipment leasing market.

"Our success stems from several things," explains founder and chairman Harold L. Van Arnem from his office at the company's headquarters in Bloomfield Hills. "First, we can speak the data processing manager's language, understand his operational problems, and anticipate his equipment needs.

"Likewise, because of our corporate financial experience and a knowledge of tax accounting procedures, plus an understanding of the need to conserve operating capital as well as such other things as asset depreciation and investment tax credits, we can suggest some very practical alternatives to the corporation's chief financial officer concerning acquisition of new equipment... not just computers but any new machiner or capital equipment.

"And lastly, we've developed—and successfully demonstrated—an ability to structure lease packages that offer maximum tax advantages to both the lessee and the lessor," Van Arnem said.

The Van Arnem Company's shift to lease underwriting didn't happen overnight. It arose out of a basic need to provide early customers with a funding base to facilitate the purchase of computers. The lease concept, with which Van Arnem had prior experience, appeared to offer maximum advantages to the firm's customers—and it also opened the door to further opportunity for Van Arnem Company.

At first, the company worked jointly with an experienced lease underwriting concern. Soon, however, the young firm ventured out on its own. And its initial success was every bit encouraging.

The company's first award was a $2.2 million package involving an IBM com-

COMPUTER ROOM conference at Federal-Mogul brings these four men together. From left: Thomas P. Kelliher, director of management information services for Federal-Mogul; Thomas Bruce, vice president, Van Arnem Company; Patrick A. Dlugokinski, manager of F-M's business administration systems; and Alan Forrester, president, Van Arnem Company. Federal-Mogul is one of Van Arnem Company's clients.

Michigan Banking & Business News

puter system for GM's Packard Electric Div., of Warren Ohio. Next came a $2.1 million computer award from Chrysler Corp., and, early this year, the firm received contracts for computer lease packages from two more clients, one for $4 million and the other for $5 million.

In between that initial award from Packard Electric and the exhilarating $5 million contract, Van Arnem Company also was picking up several smaller awards.

"We got off to a good start and it certainly helped our confidence," says Alan Forrester, president. "But we were confident to begin with . . . we felt we knew the computer business inside and out, and we moved deliberately, making sure we did all of our homework concerning the role of the lease underwriter."

Based on dollar volume, 95 percent of Van Arnems Company's business has involved leveraged leasing, by which both the lessee (equipment user) and the lessor (equipment owner) derive maximum tax benefits. "Capital conservation and long-term financing at an interest rate below prime are the main reasons for a firm to lease equipment," Forrester explains, "but there are other good reasons."

These include:
- 100 percent financing at a fixed rate, thus avoiding the uncertainty of inflation.
- Full tax deductibility of the lease payments.
- The relatively modest nature of those payments compared to alternative financing methods.
- Alternative employment of cash on hand (working capital).
- Preservation of existing credit lines.
- Flexibility in the repayment schedule and in planning and timing further equipment replacement and plant expansion.

"Asset depreciation and investment tax credit are the main factors reducing the overall lease cost," Forrester added. "With the cost of borrowing money currently around nine to 12 percent, leveraged leases can bring about a substantial savings."

Recently, Van Arnem Company structured a long-term leveraged lease package for one customer that worked out to the equivalent of 3½ percent simple interest versus almost nine percent if the money had been borrowed directly by the customer in a convention manner.

"Contrary to current belief, there is a great deal of flexibility in the leveraged lease concept," Forrester says. "For instance, if a lease customer needs to change equipment in mid-lease, Van Arnem Company will arrange a sublease of the original equipment. To this end, we work with over 250 equipment dealers in the U.S. and Europe.

"Similarly, currently installed equipment that is either owned or being rented by the user may easily be placed on a leveraged lease—at substantial savings," Forrester adds.

The role of the lease underwriter, in large part, is to bring two or more parties together to fund capital expansion under the most beneficial tax circumstances. The lessee benefits through lower cost of money and conservation of capital, among several advantages. The lessor gains a substantial tax shelter.

Occasionally, Van Arnem Company participates (as a general partner) in limited partnerships created to act as the lessor, which puts up the necessary equity capital. But often as not, equity capital will be provided by private investors, banks or corporations, all looking for new tax shelters.

Generally, individuals who participate as limited partners are in a 60 percent tax bracket or higher. Corporate investors are in a 50 percent bracket. Each derives similar benefits, including:
- A 10 percent investment tax credit and interest deduction.

HAROLD VAN ARNEM [seated] confers with Lester Schoenfeld, vice president of Merrill Lynch Hubbard Co., a wholly-owned subsidiary of Merrill Lynch Pierce Fenner & Smith, Inc.

- Full asset depreciation, usually at an accelerated rate.
- Residual (resale or re-lease) value of the equipment at conclusion of the lease.
- A steady cash flow and 15 to 20 percent return on investment.

Forrester explained that the amount of equity capital required to set up a leveraged lease is between 20 and 35 percent of total equipment purchase price. The remainder—debt capital—is furnished by financial institutions (banks, insurance companies, pension funds) at an interest rate commensurate with the lessee's established credit rating. And the money thus loaned is fully secured, with the equipment constituting collateral.

The leases are full payout, five to eight year agreements, in most cases.

Van Arnem Company works primarily with the nation's largest brokerage firm, Merrill Lynch Pierce Fenner & Smith, Inc., in raising the required capital. It also deals with other financial institutions on small lease packages, occasionally works with other lease underwriters in the funding end, and does some lease funding entirely on its own.

Depending on the size of the total investment and certain other variables, the

The Oakland Press

BRUCE H. McINTYRE, President & Publisher

RICHARD L. CONNOR, Editor   JOHN E. COOTS, Marketing Director

NEIL J. MUNRO, Associate Editor   ANGELO M. MUNOZ, Business Manager

MICHAEL G. WAGNER, Managing Editor   RICHARD R. LAND, Circulation Director

JOSEPH A. WEILER, Metropolitan Editor   GLENN L. NELSEY, Production Manager

Editorial Page

Silverdome deal should at least be explored

To repeat: The people who own the Pontiac Silverdome Stadium at least ought to have the opportunity to say yes or no to a proposal to sell or rent the structure to a private company.

They are the ones who stand to lose if the Silverdome turns out to be a longterm loser, and winners if it doesn't.

But offers to buy or rent the city-owned Silverdome put forward by Bloomfield Hills financier Harold VanArnem apparently have not been very seriously considered, let alone countered, by Pontiac city commissioners.

In fact on Monday a disgusted VanArnem said that he was withdrawing his offers, but later reconsidered.

"I don't care whether you (the city) like my proposal or not, it's still no reason to ignore both me and it. It's common courtesy to return someone's telephone call," VanArnem told Press reporter Gregory Freeman.

He said only one city official, Pontiac Mayor pro tem John Appleton, returned his phone calls last week.

It is true that VanArnem's purchase offer was almost universally regarded as far too low for the city and far too much of a bargain for him.

On a take it or leave it basis, VanArnem's proposals don't leave much to talk about.

But it is also true that opening offers are traditionally low. Some give-and-take bargaining with VanArnem might eventually produce an attractive offer.

The way things are going, however, the deal will never get that far.

The longterm interests of the Silverdome's owners, the taxpayers of Pontiac, deserve serious consideration.

A rental contract might, for example, be worked out which would serve VanArnem's needs and at the same time still fears that the city would "sell" future Silverdome profits for too little.

The full implications of the sale or rental of the Silverdome in the context of the city's other needs and problems have not been explored; at least not publicly so that the citizens could weigh them, nor have a full range of possible deals.

What sort of package, for example, might the city come up with as an opening bargaining position?

If nothing else, VanArnem's interest should tell the city other investors could be interested, too; ones who might top VanArnem's offer.

Tomorrow The Press is scheduled to publish the results of a scientific public opinion survey it commissioned to discover whether Pontiac voters think the Silverdome should be sold. Of course they had only VanArnem's original rent-or-sell proposal to consider in answering the question.

VanArnem himself suggests that "politics" are preventing serious debate by the city. That may be. Oakland County Executive Dan Murphy, who introduced VanArnem to city officials, and Pontiac City Manager Phil Mastin were rivals for the executive post. Since then it is well known that both have been leery of doing anything that might be construed as helping the other politically.

Both may be looking to a rematch. But it would be ridiculous and shameful to have their personal political problems get in the way of rational government.

For whatever reason, the possibility of selling or renting the Silverdome seems to have been dismissed out of hand. Time may someday prove that was smart.

But it also might not.

Detroit Free Press

DETROIT, MICHIGAN, Sunday, January 23, 1983

50 CENTS

Sonny Van Arnem — Why can't he get any respect? In Detroit magazine

Van Arnem's in big leagues but he strikes out in dome

Harold Van Arnem

By DALE DUNCAN
Of The Oakland Press

BLOOMFIELD HILLS — Since stepping into the big leagues, Harold Van Arnem has yet to get a hit.

"Sonny," as the 34-year-old millionaire financing specialist is called by his friends, has struck out so far in every attempt to arrange a deal to buy or lease the Pontiac Silverdome.

He has yet to bring to the metropolitan area one of the rock concerts he has promised to bring to the 80,000-seat, debt-plagued stadium, although he said he has had "personal contact" with entertainers Boz Scaggs, The Eagles and Rod Stewart.

And Van Arnem is bitter about the way city officials have treated him, refusing to even discuss his dome deal unless he relents and allows a confidential financial and personal investigation.

"If people continue to question our sincerity, I'm not sure we'll decide to make this fight," Van Arnem said.

He said such an investigation is an unfair invasion of his privacy. "They should be concerned only about my ability to live up to any contract we might reach."

"We approached it very idealistically. We were very sincere about wanting to take care of the debt," he said in a recent interview at his home on Long Lake across from the Bloomfield Hills Hunt Club. "I'm tired of traveling from New York to California. I wanted something here I

(Continued on A-2)

SONNY
CONTINUED

figure on campus, always visible, and fond of testing people's limits.

A fraternity brother remembers his "borrowing" people's clothes, without asking. "You'd see him wearing your shirt and ask him about it and he'd say, 'Hey, we're fraternity brothers.' He had no respect for other people's property." The same man says he still considers himself Van Arnem's friend but "wouldn't trust him farther than you could throw a building." "If he saw you with a girl, he'd ask her out the next night, that kind of thing," he says.

But the daring, cut-up side of Van Arnem's personality made him popular. One summer day, he showed up at his job — maintaining a swimming pool — still dressed in a tuxedo, after a long night with his socially prominent friends. In full evening dress, he plunged into the water and began vacuuming the bottom of the pool.

He had the ambition, but not the ability, to become a professional football player, so after graduating in 1964, Van Arnem joined a management training program with General Electric in Phoenix, driving west with his pregnant wife, Karen, and a few possessions. After three years in Phoenix, where his energy and ambition made him look with some disdain at older employes ("all sorts of degenerating minds getting ready to retire," he says), he was assigned to Detroit. But the training program had reinforced his own sense of what he could accomplish. "None of us stayed with GE because they had us convinced we could do anything," he says.

In Detroit, Van Arnem's ability as a salesman and a visionary quickly came together. He was selling computers for GE, selling lots of them, and lecturing at the University of Detroit's engineering school on computers. And in 1968, with a staff of 26 PhDs recruited from U-D, he founded a computer time-sharing company called ACTS Computing Corp., which immediately picked up contracts with Ford Motor Co., Michigan Bell, 50 high schools and three universities. By the end of the year, there were 1,000 teletype machines in the Midwest and New York plugged into ACTS' six computers.

This would be heady stuff for most 26-year-olds, but not for one who envisioned his company becoming a Midwest utility, the next Bell System. "When they start accusing us of being a monopoly, that'll be great," the Free Press quoted him as saying with characteristic bravado in 1969. "I could cash out" (for, he said, a $6 million offer for his ACTS shares), "but it's the last thing in the world I'd do. It's easy to make money. But this is too exciting."

ACTS didn't last much longer as an independent company. The firm's resources were stretched thin by its fast growth and high overhead. Faced with the prospect of an unfriendly takeover by a New York investment firm, Van Arnem sold 65 percent of ACTS to Lear Siegler, a California electronics communication firm. He was still running ACTS, but running it within a disciplined, corporate structure — a

Van Arnem in 1969 as president of ACTS, his first company. "I c time. "It's easy to make money. But this is too exciting." He v

framework that was anathematic to his loose, entrepreneurial style. He liked to do things his way; Lear Siegler had its own way. In 1973, he was forced out.

Like all of Van Arnem's financial dealings, this one was complicated. Forbes magazine reported Lear Siegler paid him $4 million for ACTS, but Van Arnem now won't confirm that figure. Certainly, he made money from ACTS but not from the company's profits, because there weren't any, really. Computer time-sharing then was like owning a soccer team now, he'll tell you. "You can't look at the annual reports for information," he'll say. "You never make money on paper." The evolution of ACTS, his first company, from nowhere to apparent millions to nowhere again is also a scale model of his later ventures. It begins with the creative idea, just a step ahead of its time, and with Van Arnem's salesmanship, his ability to get talented people to clamber aboard, to convince them his enterprise will materialize into great things. And then, when the pieces are finally put together — something happens. There are personality clashes, misunderstandings, arguments over money, a sense of betrayal and disillusionment on all sides.

He landed on his feet. He lectured in Europe for the federal government, a pleasant sojourn won through connections in the Young President's Organization, a group of company presidents under 40 years of age. He started a successful land development in Florida, moving his family there. He founded a new company to sell computers in Europe, but landed only one contract in Yugoslavia. "It was so awful in Yugoslavia, I left."

Back in Detroit in 1974, he launched the Van Arnem Co., the computer leasing firm that is the money-making core of his enterprises. Once again, he was in on the ground floor of a growing field, but this time, no tangib Tax laws make major corporati Arnem, an arrar the lessee. On invest capital. T computer, while in the form of in ciation. At the e commodity tha the open marke get their write-o the end. Van A and usually a pe the computer.

"I don't pe artist who can p of him. I don't b Arnem, who ha "I find people w creatively finan God gave me a n perceive and c important beca

So in 1974, h hiring talent, million worth o overnight. Pro tors. His Cinci biggest corpora leasing comput very rich and w well on his way

Becomin Throu up wi soon h deal, flying an Hollywood roy feel out of his e to make any interest in it, s

ASL PLAYOFF PROGRAM

DETROIT EXPRESS
VS
NEW YORK EAGLES

9-3-81   7:30 P.M.

PONTIAC SILVERDOME

PLAYOFFS AT A GLANCE

...fans are familiar scoring exploits of ...man and Mike ...d might even ...e than four goals ...matches held at ... They have Express' difficult ...ng home positive ...away games and ...ense regain poise ...tion of Ray (how ... Schnettegoecke. ...ow the Express ...as the ASL's best ...aining defensive ...t about the other ...oit begins playoff ...re is a capsule

goalkeeping is solid with George Tarasides. United could be described as an early favorite.

NEW YORK EAGLES—Is it New York Eagles or New York Bolevic? Take a pick. This is virtually a one man team with ASL's leading goal scorer Billy Bolevic (25 goals, nine assists, 59 points). When Bolevic is hot, so are the Eagles. If not, forget it. Most ASL teams have tried everything but shooting Bolevic to stop the burly Yugoslavian. The Eagles' defense is suspect, especially on the road, but lately things have improved on the backline. If Bolevic is allowed to roam unmarked in the penalty area, the Eagles could very well be a darkhorse threat.

CAROLINA LIGHTNIN'—Inconsistant is the word best used to describe the Lightnin' this season. At times, Carolina looks like world beaters, but at others they look confused. With a long break between regular season action and playoffs, the rest could do the team good. The Lightnin' boast a very potent offense, which is led by Tony Suarez who already has four goals against Detroit this season. The defense is tough with goalkeeper Scott Manning guarding the cords. Watch out for a regrouped Carolina squad going into the playoffs.

SONNY VAN ARNEM

"KEEPING ON THE MOVE"

BLOOMFIELD HILLS—Detroit Express Club President, Sonny Van Arnem was recently named Chairman of the Board of the American Soccer League at August meetings in New York, NY today.

Van Arnem, who was a General Partner of the Detroit Express of the North American Soccer League (NASL), previously was on the NASL Board of Directors before joining the ASL this season.

A finance entrepreneur, Van Arnem is the President of the Van Arnem Financial Services, an equipment lease underwriter in Bloomfield Hills, MI. He was a creator of the Doctoral Program of Computer Engineering at the University of Detroit, while founding ACTS Computing Corporation when he was 27 years old. He was also responsible for the development of satellite communications, what is now used for cable television.

Involved extensively in the entertainment and sports field, Van Arnem was the Co-Producer of "Love at First Bite", a movie starring George Hamilton, and he is a partner in Warner Amex Van Arnem Cable T.V.

"Our number one goal is to assist the player development at all levels," Van Arnem pointed out recently. "Americanization is the key and I think we have already a lot of excitement in the Detroit sports community this summer. 1981 is only the beginning."

NIA STONERS
...their division by ...ver New York ...oners have fallen ...es of late. Not ...n offensive threat. ...ly heavily on their ...ch includes ASL ...eeper Tom Rey-...als against. The ...y threat is mid-... Watson (11 goals ...st for 23 points). ...ive goals against ...this season. ...during a recent ...nly won three out ...The Stoners lead ...uickly evaporated ...d themselves in ...in the Liberty. ...Villie Elich revive ...pers and bid for a ...cutive ASL title? ...find out.

UNITED—If some-
...bet his last dollar ...in the playoffs. ...d be a logical ...ress Coach Brian ...s them the best ...league, and for ...Going down their ...rd to find a single ...ould be labeled the ...team. Redmond ...e of the teams' ...ers, but compared ...players in the ...s not saying much. ...ng suit is defense. ...to open its season ...ded Downing Sta-...is hardly accept-...son team, let alone ...onal one. The

ROCHESTER FLASH—One too many teams have gone into Holleder Stadium thinking they could win. Few have. The Flash are tough at home, but since they finished in the sixth playoff position, it won't matter until the second round. The Flash have a good organization with good fan support but play poorly on the road. Rochester, like the Eagles, are a one man team up front and the Flash are now missing their leading goal scorer Mike Laschev, who is out with a separated shoulder. If the Flash can get past the first round, don't count them out.

PRO SOCCER!

Technological advances make computer equipment leasing a sound investment

By HAROLD L. VAN ARNEM

Here's the situation:
- Only 15 percent of the total databases that will exist in 1995 are in use today.
- Advances in speed and density as well as componentry and chip technology have increased the life of computer devices.
- And new generations of mainframes are not replacing existing machines as readily as they once did.

But here's the dilemma: Investors aren't sure that a computer leasing program will guarantee good returns. They fear machines bought for lease today will not be marketable when the lease term runs out.

This fear of obsolescence in the computer industry has stopped many investors from putting their money into a leasing program. Deciding which of the newest computers to buy is hard enough for the individual consumer, but it becomes even more problematic if a large investment is at stake. Who wants to buy a machine that may be outclassed in a matter of years?

As a result of this fear in the marketplace, the real situation — the promise of a wide-open demand for computer devices with improved longevity — gets lost in the shuffle.

Besides improvements in computer technology, another element is acting against the chance that equipment will be considered obsolete. While at one time, the data-processing manager in a company had a free hand in decisions about purchase and upgrading of computer systems, executive management is more sophisticated today.

Managers have had more than 20 years experience with computers; they use the machines themselves and they are informed about the industry. They are concerned with the computer as a management tool, and they are therefore concerned primarily with price performance. Manages want to know if they are getting the most for their money.

Obsolescence

In the computer industry, obsolescence is determined by maintenance costs and their effect on price performance. If a machine breaks down and has frequent repairs, it often becomes more cost effective to replace it. But if a machine is functioning efficiently and serving the needs of the user, it could be more cost effective to hang onto it.

Historically, the rate at which IBM data-processing equipment declines in value over time has depended primarily on the rate of introduction of new, technically advanced equip-

MIDWESTERN PLANNER

ment models and the pricing of such models. The introduction of a newer model of equipment with an improved price performance relationship usually will cause the market price for an older model to decline. As managers decide to keep existing equipment, this will be less of a factor.

Recent events have borne this out. In the past when IBM announced a new generation of mainframes, nearly two-thirds of current users placed orders for the new machines. With the announcement of the new Sierra mainframe, analysts report that fewer than 40 percent of current users decided to replace their existing machines.

Changes in technology also indicate that users may be able to keep their equipment longer. Improvements have been made in densities, the amount of space required to store data, and in speed, how fast data can be read and transferred. Those improvements have been complemented by advances in componentry and chip technology and in peripherals, tape cartridges, tape drives and the like, all of which have given additional reliability and extended life to the devices. Some internal electronics could now last as long as 20 years whereas past technology could render serious problems in five to seven years.

Peripherals

Peripherals compatible with new and existing central processing units have several advantages which protect them from obsolescence. The decline in value of IBM equipment due to technological changes has affected all types of equipment but has been more pronounced with respect to mainframes than with respect to peripheral equipment.

Newer processor models have been introduced which make older models obsolete. Both processor models, however, are compatible with existing peripheral models. For example, the IBM tape drive, 3420, has been able to operate on four generations of mainframe hardware. Peripheral devices also typically require less maintenance than larger mainframes, and they are still in high demand, selling for more than 50 percent of their original value.

In addition, most technical changes affecting their performance are minor. The IBM disk drive 3380, for example, is at a stage where improvements in its density would only be small increments of past improvements. The likelihood of early obsolescence in most devices is reduced because there is less opportunity for significant increases in capacity and speed.

Computer leasing programs have some advantages of their own. Some programs leverage close to 80 percent of the purchase price of the machines. The lease payments go toward paying off the borrowed portion, and at the end of the short lease term, usually 36 to 48 months, the investors own the equipment. They can re-lease it to the user, or sell it at a profit. Even if the price has dropped 50 percent, the investor can more than double the original investment.

The short-term lease has another advantage. Because the equipment purchased for lease is in the first two or three years of its life, by the time the lease is due, the equipment will still be current technology and has potential for long term use.

While many investment programs are income oriented and invest primarily in peripheral devices, in certain situations, investors may buy a mainframe for a tax deferred program. Because the market values mainframes low, the opportunity for leveraging is much greater. Where investors may have to pay 30 percent or more down for peripherals, they may only need 20 percent or less for a mainframe unit.

As computer technology has advanced, the demand for equipment has grown. The capability of smaller computers has increased the trend toward decentralized computing, which in turn increases the demand for the smaller machines and peripherals. There's a "super" market of potential users coming on line and needing equipment. With only 15 percent of databases predicted for 1995 in use today, an eight-fold increase in the market is possible.

And as executive management makes more objective and more knowledgeable decisions about expenditures on computer equipment, the risk of obsolescence is further reduced. With obsolescence proving less a factor, investors in computer leasing programs can be more certain that users will want to lease the equipment for longer periods, thus guaranteeing investors a good return potential.

Harold L. Van Arnem is chairman and chief executive of Van Arnem Financial Services, Inc., of Birmingham, Michigan, specializing in computer equipment leasing.

"Sonny" Van Arnem
President and Owner,
Detroit Express
Soccer Club

Club Information

Harold Van Arnem, Chairman of The Van Arnem Company, Bloomfield Hills-based investment-leasing firm, originally planned to become a professional football player.

He was an honor student and four-letter athlete at Purcell High School in Cincinnati where he captained the 1959 football team that included former Dallas Cowboy Quarterback Roger Staubach. At the University of Cincinnati, Van Arnem plunged into athletics and a five-year co-op program in industrial engineering. But his plans changed. He graduated in 1964 with a bachelor's degree in economics.

He joined General Electric as a management trainee shortly after graduation and in 1967 was assigned to Detroit as a regional administrator.

The following year—he was 27—he resigned from GE and with $1,000 in startup capital formed ACTS Computing Corporation.

Twenty-four months later, in 1970, Van Arnem's success with ACTS attracted Lear Sigler, Inc., which acquired it as a subsidiary with Van Arnem as its operating chief. Van Arnem's introduction of interactive computing throughout the Midwest was a major stimulant in the development of two-way cable television communications. In the six-year span from the time he founded ACTS to 1974 when he resigned, ACTS grew into one of the largest computer service-counselling firms in the midwest with 300 employees, offices and computer centers in 24 cities, and annual sales in excess of $10 million.

As head of the newly established Van Arnem Company, in 1974, he immediately carved out a niche in the rapidly growing leveraged leasing field by leasing used computers overseas.

From this base, Van Arnem has expanded to other types of equipment and now has handled more than $150 million of leased products including manufacturing equipment, transportation and real estate to such blue chip companies as General Motors, Sears, Procter & Gamble, Dow Chemical, Chemical Bank, American Can and AMF.

A sports and boating enthusiast, Van Arnem's other interests are in the areas of communications and entertainment. He is Club President and Owner of the Detroit Express professional soccer team; a partner in the cable television troika, Warner AMEX Van Arnem Cable, Inc., consisting of Warner Communications, American Express and The Van Arnem Company; and is "looking for interesting programming concepts" for cable TV after a successful venture as investor and co-producer with actor George Hamilton in the movie, *Love at First Bite*.

Van Arnem, a member of Oakland Hills Country Club and "The Old Club", resides in the Detroit suburb of Birmingham.

The Detroit Express will begin American Soccer League play this spring, keeping soccer alive and kicking in the greater Detroit area. The man behind the franchise is communications and finance entrepreneur, Sonny Van Arnem.

At one time, a General Partner of the Express when the club belonged to the NASL, Van Arnem switched to the American Soccer League (ASL) because of their philosophy of "Americanization" of the game.

The ASL is the oldest professional soccer league in the United States, starting operations in 1934. Its rules state that there must be at least seven American players on the field at all times. Other franchises include the New England Sharks, Pennsylvania Stoners, Rochester Flash, Carolina Lightnin', Cleveland Cobras, New York United and New York Eagles.

Express Assistant Coach is former English League and NASL player, Brian Tinnion. After a playing career in England, he journeyed across the Atlantic to play for the New York Cosmos in 1976. After playing for the Cosmos, Team Hawaii and Colorado Caribous, he came to the Motor City to play for the Express in 1978 and participated through the 1980 summer season.

General manager of the Express is Denny Gilstad. Gilstad is an executive with the Van Arnem Company. Director of Operations and Assistant General Manager, Steve Unger, is former Express PR Director and has worked with four pro clubs. Public Relations Director for the Express is Donna F. Jarmusz.

On the field, the Express will have a proven goal scorer in the likes of "Randy Andy" Chapman, who won the ASL Rookie-of-the-Year Award in 1979. Chapman has seen action with California and the Cleveland Cobras of the ASL as well as the Wichita Wings of the MISL. Helping him out will be Mike Powers and Steve Westbrook, both of whom hail from the soccer hotbed of St. Louis.

Powers has seen action indoors playing for the Wichita Wings.

In the middle will be collegiate star Steve Westbrook. Westbrook, a product of the fine Indiana University soccer program, comes to the Express with the reputation of being a playmaker.

The midfield will be patrolled by 6'1" Adrian Brooks, an All American number one MISL draft pick (second, NASL draft pick), who is not afraid to rough it up when it is needed. Last season Brooks' tenacious play helped lead the Pennsylvania Stoners to the ASL title.

The imposing 6'5" Dan Mammana will be fending off enemy attackers on defense for the Express. The Argentinian native is a five-time ASL All-Star team member who has played with Utah, Sacramento, Columbus and Cleveland of the ASL before making his way to the Motor City. Lending a helping hand will be University of Rhode Island grad and All American, Kevin Murphy. Murphy, whose brother Ken played with the Express last season, is considered to be one of the best defenders to ever come out of the University of Rhode Island.

Kelvin Norman, a fine indoor player, captained the Denver Avalanche franchise in their inaugural season in the MISL last winter.

A rugged defender, he is considered to be one of the most consistent backliners in the country today.

Diving and stopping the shots dealt by opposing forwards will be 6'4" Tad Delorm. Delorm, who has played with Atlanta and Minnesota of the NASL, is considered to be very agile for his size (6'4", 200 lbs.) by the critics.

Mike Mancini comes to Detroit with both outdoor and indoor experience.

Gus Moffat began his soccer career as an 8-year-old in Scotland. He is an integral part of the Express team. Look for his nonstop effort in the Detroit Express midfield.

Before and after the game...
FOOD & SPIRITS

The Gnome

American & Middle East Specialties
Soft Jazz Entertainment • Wednesday thru Sunday

4124 Woodward Ave., Detroit, MI • 833-0120
3 blocks from Wayne State University

Van Arnem d[...]
offering lease[...]

This letter contains two proposals for the management of the Pontiac Stadium by private enterprise. They are the results of extensive investigation and research into the operating history of the Stadium and the potential market for its facilities.

We have concluded from this investigation and research that the Stadium is a well conceived and well constructed entertainment facility and that is a credit to the vision of the people of Pontiac and their elected and appointed officials. However, we believe that, as long as the Stadium is run by government, it will operate at a loss to the substantial expense of the taxpayers and to the jeopardy of other governmental projects.

Our studies indicate that private enterprise can operate the Stadium at break even or better. We are presenting two proposals which would transfer the operational responsibility to private enterprise. These proposals are tentative and much more time, labor and expense must be incurred prior to entering upon a firm contract. We request, therefore, merely that you indicate to us whether you would be interested in either or both of the following proposals:

Proposal A. Lease-Purchase

A corporation will be formed which will enter upon a lease-purchase contract with the City which will provide:

1. The tenant corporation will pay rent each six months in advance. The amount of the rent for the first five years will be equal to the total obligation of the City and the Authority under the $15,950,000 general obligation bonds, the $25,000,000 revenue bonds and the roof installment purchase contract with respect to the Stadium coming due within the six months after the due date of the rent less the subsidy agreed to by the State of Michigan. After the first five years, the rent will be equal to the total obligations for debt service without regard to the State subsidy.

2. The tenant corporation will contract for, be solely liable for, and pay all operating expenses of the Stadium.

3. The tenant corporation will assume responsibility for the purchase of all necessary capital improvements, both those which you have committed yourselves to acquire and those later deemed necessary.

4. The tenant corporation will have sole control over the operation of the Stadium, subject to such concessions regarding municipal events as may be contained in the lease-purchase agreement and the subject, of course, to all existing leases.

5. The tenant corporation will be entitled to receive and retain revenues from the use of the Stadium.

6. If the tenant corporation shall have paid all rent coming due and fulfilled all its other obligations, after all the bonded indebtedness of the City under the $15,950,000 and the $25,000,000 issues has been paid, the tenant

...ils Silverdome proposals ...urchase and rental plans

...ration will have the obligation to purchase, and the ...will have the obligation to sell, the Stadium for a ... equal to the City's total losses to date, ...imately $6,000,000.

As additonal security for the City, the tenant ...ration will at all times retain unencumbered assets ...ed to the City in an amount equal to the forthcoming ... debt service on the general obligation bonds. If the ... corporation should fail, this will become property ... City.

Proposal B. Rental

...rporation will be formed which will enter upon a ... agreement with either the City or the Authority ... will provide:

During the term of the rental agreement, the ... corporation will have the exclusive control over ...eration of the Stadium subject to such concessions ...ding municipal events as may be contained into the ... agreement and subject to all existing leases.

The tenant corporation will assume responsibility ...e purchase of all necessary capital improvements, ...wn such capital improvements and will lease them ... City at their fair rental value.

The revenues received by the tenant corporation ... be applied in the following order of priority:

a) Payment of operational expenses exclusive of ...gement fee or other compensation to the tenant ...ration;

b) Payment of semiannual rent in an amount equal ... debt sevice on all obligations of the City or the ...ority under the general obligation bonds, the revenue ... and the roof installment contract becoming due ...n the rental period net of the State subsidy;

c) Payment of a management fee to the tenant ...ration in an amount to be determined;

d) Payment to the City of amounts required to ...tain the reserves established under the Lease ...ement between the City and the Authority; and

e) The residue, if any, will be paid to the tenant ...ration and the City according to a formula to be ...mined until the City shall have recovered its losses ...te.

The tenant corporation will be unconditionally ...nsible to meet all debt service requirements coming ...uring the term of the rental agreement.

The term of the rental agreement shall be ten ... The tenant corporation shall have the option of ...ding the term of the rental agreement for two ...cutive terms of five years each. The City will have ...ption, however, of terminating the rental agreement ... terms to be determined at the end of the first five ... of the agreement.

The rental agreement shall accord the City or the ...ority the absolute right to terminate the rental agreement upon default in rent payment or any other substantial default by the tenant.

7. Upon termination of the rental agreement for any reason other than the default of the tenant, the City will purchase the capital improvements made by the tenant according to a predetermined depreciation schedule.

Under either proposal, we would assume full responsibility to pay all debt service under the bond issues other than that provided by the State subsidy. Either proposal would insure the City against budget deficits caused by further losses in the operation of the Stadium. If we cannot make a go of it, you will reacquire full control of the Stadium with all debt service paid in the interim, and, in the case of Proposal A, you will acquire sufficient assets to pay one year's debt service on the general obligation bonds.

We ask that you express by resolution that you are interested in pursuing one or both of the proposals. Upon passage of such a resolution we will work toward presentation of a firm offer in conjunction with the Corporation Counsel and such personnel of the City and the Authority that you direct to work with us.

At the same time, we would expect the City and the Authority to consider resolution of the following matters:

A. Either proposal will require amendment of the Lease-Agreement between the City and the Authority. This Agreement cannot be amended in such a way as to affect adversely the bondholders. The city and the Authority would have to receive a favorable determination from bond counsel, from the Municipal Finance Commission, and possibly from the Oakland County Circuit Court that the proposal has a favorable effect upon the security of the bondholders.

B. Since a portion of the revenues derived by the City from the Agreement with the Detroit Lions, specifically, the stadium service fee, depends upon the revenues needed by the City to meet debt service, an understanding would have to be reached between the City and the Lions that the stadium service fee would continue even though we have assumed the debt service obligation.

C. The Stadium and its facilities would have to continue to be exempt from property taxes or taxes in lieu of property taxes until such time, if any, as the bonds are paid off and title to the Stadium is conveyed to us.

D. It would appear that certain expenses of the operation of the Stadium are now borne by various departments of the City. We would need to know the estimated amount of any additional expenses for water, sewage, trash removal, etc., which would be charged by the City under either of the above proposals.

We hope that this letter initiates a mutually beneficial financial relationship.

Very truly yours,
Harold L. Van Arnem

Ocean front home
Delray Beach 1993 to 2015.

Adios Gold Club.

Our first Florida condo development. Bonita Springs, 309 condo is on the beach and first high rise on Bonita Beach, 1975.

Frank Lloyd Wright Alden Dow Home featured in Life Magazine 1935, Bloomfield Hills, Michigan.

Saber Liner 60 Super Sonic Jet, Boca Hanger.
Sonny Van Arnem, Phil McKnight - President, Finalco, Gemini and Totale.

Meadow Brook Hall, Oakland University, Super Bowl Party.
George and Bobbi Vercamp and Marge Schoth, the owner of the Cincinnati Reds, Major League Baseball.

Stan Dragoti- Directed Love at First Bite and Mr. Mom. Bob Kaufman- Wrote Love at First Bite, Divorce American Style, She's Out of Control.

Sonny Van Arnem, Heidi Van Arnem and H.L. Van Arnem. Pontiac Airport. New Pressurized Navajo just purchased.

A Salute to Super Bowl '82

Pistol Pete Marovich, NBA New Orleans Jazz with Heather, H.L. and Aleise.

Marianne and Roger Staubach with H.L. and Sonny Van Arnem and friends from Dallas, Texas.

Heidi and Bob Segeer at Heidi Foundation Golf Tournament to cure paralysis

US Congressman Vern Buchanan

In Bermuda with golfing friends.
Doctor Bob Johnson
Mark Golden.

Dr. Art Keiser
Greg Wallick
Chairman and CEO Keiser University.

Michael Rose
Chairman and CEO
Holiday Inns
Harrahs Casino
Worlds largest hospitality.

Donna Summer
Delray Beach Tennis Center
Roger King, CEO King World
Concert to cure paralysis
Miami Project.

Adam, Max, and Sean.

My first priority and greatest joy was and is my family.

Sonny and Heather Van Arnem. Express Exhibition, playing goalie.

Sonny, Heather, and H.L. at Aspen, Colorado

Bridget, Max, Sean, Sonny, JJ, Adam, HL, and Heather.

Bridget Telluride

Bridget and Max

Betty Van Arnem and Sonny Van Arnem on the Sonny Express Bertram Yacht.

...ther, Betty, in 1979 aboard the Sonny Express, the $228,000 yacht he wanted to ...his children. Today, there is dispute whether he ever made the down payment.

do things that are more exciting than th
He already had so many other ideas, so projects he was working on. "It's all a gam game," he says of his deals. "I'm not afr compete with anybody when it comes to ca ism."

Most people don't like playing gar someone else's rules, though — cially when the rules change day. Charisma and an entert style attract people and open doors, bu don't cement friendships or win enduring ty. Van Arnem had been in one plac enough that, some people say, he was bec recognized as a user, a manipulator, overwhelming preoccupation was himse threw people away when he no longer h use for them. "Initially, he is fabulous. He across as so sincere, but you have to lo neath that... If you can't do something fo he discards you like a piece of dirt. I have seen anyone treat people as badly as he says Sue McCuish, who worked both fo Arnem and the first Detroit Express North American Soccer League.

Steve Unger, athletic director at Na College in Kalamazoo, describes Van Arr "amoral." "Sonny's got no sense of gratitu people who work for him and do a good mean absolutely none," said Unger, anotl employe fired by Van Arnem.

All around him, his most important rel ships with people were crumbling. Hi Karen filed for divorce in 1978, a mov shattered Van Arnem emotionally. For who he says was his closest friend, left th Arnem Co. in 1980, following six other level employes who had already left the c ny. All except one have sued Van Arnem, ing that he violated profit-sharing compensation agreements he had made.

His $60 million offer to buy the Silve in 1978, though never taken seriously by tl of Pontiac, got his name in the newspaper him the recognition he hungered for. "Doir Silverdome gave me some identity, som that was public," he says today.

(How the offer came about and wha pened afterwards are typical of Van Arne was introduced to Clayton Jones, the dire the Silverdome, by Phil Mastin, a state s who was then Pontiac's city manager. Van Arnem volunteered to help with M fundraising when he ran unsuccessful mayor of Pontiac. "It was just nickel-and stuff, sending out invitations, stuff like says one insider. "But Sonny never through. He didn't do a thing. He left us ing.")

Van Arnem also got ink during the ma ment tiffs (which evolved into a lawsuit) original Detroit Express, which was owne partnership, including Van Arnem, from I 1981. After the Express moved to Washi Van Arnem retained rights to the nam started a new team in the rival American League.

More media mileage resulted from th Van Arnem threw to celebrate the open "Love at First Bite," a $3,400 party at Ben Southfield disco. Kevin Downey, then-ma of Benny's, says Van Arnem refused to $2,200 of the bill, claiming the productio

tiny percentage of the net, not the
many of Van Arnem's deals, learn-m line isn't easy. In his 1980 divorce ified he was never paid any of the ofits and was thinking of suing. But azine, in its September 27, 1982 ssy profile of Van Arnem, noted the ssed $50 million and Van Arnem s keeping only 25 percent of the

d a $325,000 Bloomfield Hills home chauffeur to drive his limousine, ed convenient until his chauffeur horn at some exiting Lions fans in me parking lot, several of whom jumping on the roof and kicking in els. It was a case of becoming a hit

too visible — and Van Arnem sold the car.
After investing in the first Detroit Express team in 1979, he sorted the party invitations by day. That way, if he was free, he could scan the invitations and pick one.

Most of the financial details of the computer leasing business were assigned to his partner, Alan Forrester, an engineer with an MBA and a CPA who was the company's president, and to other top officers of the company. Van Arnem was the salesman, the deal-clincher. In concept, it was an exciting, moneymaking business, but it was an ongoing enterprise, a day-to-day routine.

"I was never really interested in the leasing business," he says now. "It's interesting because you can accumulate equity and make a lot of money (but) making money and accumulating equity isn't all that I want to do in life. I want to

The Quintessence
80 foot Choy Lee fast motor Yacht
1997 to 2012

Lauren Hutton

Deep Impact. Center console fish and dive boat in Bahamas.

Spearing Exumas Snapper
Sean and Dillon

Sean

Heidi Van Arnem

Non-Profit Recipient

The late Heidi Van Arnem, founded the Heidi Van Arnem Foundation in 1992, with a mission to help find a cure for paralysis. Van Arnem, a quadriplegic since age 16 from a gunshot wound to the neck, is an entrepreneur of a successful travel business. She sold her business in 1999 to start iCan.com to harness the power of the Internet and bring information, resources and services to people with disabilities. Van Arnem founded iCan! with a handful of people and the vision to change the world for people with disabilities. In 2½ years, she crafted that vision into what is today iCan! Inc., a solutions and services company for people with disabilities and leaders of business. iCan! has business partnerships with some of the world's largest corporations, including General Motors, America Online, Kmart, Orbitz and PriMedia. Accepting the award on Heidi's behalf is her mother, Karen Zosel.

VAN ARNEM, Adam Sahlin

Adam Sahlin Van Arnem, 26, passed away in Colorado where he loved the outdoors and the mountains. Adam was born on January 13th, 1988, the son of Bridget and Harold Van Arnem of Ocean Ridge. He was the brother of Aleise, Heidi & Heather of Bloomfield Hills, MI, Harold IV of New York City, NY, Maxwell & Sean of Delray Beach, FL and an uncle to John Joseph Chidiac of Bloomfield Hills, MI. Adam graduated from St. Vincent Ferrer in Delray Beach, FL and attended Pope John Paul High School in Boca Raton, FL. He went on to graduate from The Collective Music School of New York and The Atlanta Institute of Music. Music was his passion. Adam played guitar & keyboard and composed & wrote his own music. He loved Jazz and Blues. Adam's close family loves him and looks forward to the day they can be with Adam in Heaven. A funeral mass will be held at 10:30 AM on Friday, December 26, 2014 at St. Vincent Ferrer Catholic Church, 840 George Bush Boulevard, Delray Beach, FL 33483. Entombment will follow at the Boca Raton Mausoleum, 451 SW 4th Avenue Boca Raton, FL 33432. Donations may be made to the Arts Garage (artsgarage.org), 180 Northeast 1st Street, Delray Beach FL 33444. Visit Lorneandsons.com to view and sign Adam's online guestbook.

To express condolences and/or make donations: Visit PalmBeachPost.com/obituaries

Ad shown is not actual print size.

Thank you for reading my book.

While this book speaks about an action-packed life with great successes and failures, my first priority and greatest joy was and is my family.

I always wanted as many children as my wife and the Lord would permit and found great enjoyment witnessing every soccer, basketball, baseball, football, skateboarding, snowboarding, spearfishing, surfing, and boating with my children. Holidays and family gatherings with all seven children were my greatest happiness. I was truly blessed.

A TECHNOLOGICAL EVOLUTION PIONEERED INNOVATIONS THAT CREATED BUSINESS AND PERSONAL ADVENTURES.

VAN ARNEM
TECHNOLOGY PIONEER

Harold "Sonny" Van Arnem was born in Cincinnati, Ohio, the son of a former athlete who, having lost a substantial investment in home building, raised his family by working at General Electric Corporation.

Unfocused at Purcell high school, Sonny found his footing on the football field where future NFL Hall of Fame inductee Roger Staubach was among his teammates. Sonny was elected team captain, and might have enjoyed a professional sports career as successful as Staubach's except for a horrifying accident that left him severely injured.

Van Arnem managed to come back, winning a scholarship and playing for both Xavier University and the University of Cincinnati before accepting a job with GE's Computer Division. After rising to a top position in computer sales, he left GE to launch his own computer timesharing as well as an early software firm in Silicon Valley, where he became a prime contractor for the U.S. Department of Defense.

This marked the first step in a whirlwind of business and personal adventures that included co-developing the doctoral program in computer engineering and software for ILLIAC IV, the world's largest computer at Ames Research Center, located at Moffet Field in California. After meeting and being inspired by the legendary Roger Penske, Sonny participated in auto racing and, along with his partner, won the SCAA Trans A championship.

Other sports seized his imagination and talent. As general partner and owner of the Detroit Express professional soccer team, he watched the Express win the league championship before assuming the position of league commissioner. He also foresaw the growth of sports and entertainment as a pillar of cable TV long before the advent of ESPN. His efforts to purchase the Detroit Red Wings and Pontiac Silverdome, planning to convert it into a unique performance and broadcast facility, epitomized his talent as a sports and broadcast visionary.

His interests extended all the way to Hollywood and beyond. Based on his racing experience, he became co-producer of "The Quick and the Dead", a major motion picture starring Stacey Keach and Jackie Stewart. Partnering with actor George Hamilton, he also co-produced the blockbuster Dracula spoof "Love at First Bite". Van Arnem's involvement with Hamilton and other Tinsel Town personalities serves as a humorous lesson about the ins and the outs of the movie industry.

In other areas, success and tragedy ensued. His fabled vision served him again when he built first, one of the world's largest technology finance and leasing companies, and later created an early Internet Service Provider and web-hosting company.

On a darker front, his beautiful and immensely talented daughter Heidi was shot in the neck, severing her spinal cord and leaving her a quadriplegic. Reflecting her father's spirit and courage, she refused to have the tragedy ruin her life and became a leader in the cause to obtain services and support for handicapped persons, winning recognition and an award from U.S. President Clinton.

Currently active in property development and management in south Florida, Sonny Van Arnem continues to set and achieve goals that amaze those who do not share his energy and determination.

www.ingramcontent.com/pod-product-compliance
Lightning Source LLC
Chambersburg PA
CBHW070046080526
44586CB00013B/938